D1596668

Improving School Discipline:

AN ADMINISTRATOR'S GUIDE

Willis J. Furtwengler

George Peabody College

William Konnert

Kent State University

ALLYN AND BACON, INC.
Boston, London, Sydney, Toronto

Library of Congress Cataloging in Publication Data

Furtwengler, Willis J., 1937–
   Improving school discipline.

   1. School discipline.   I. Konnert, William, 1937–
II. Title.
LB3012.F87   371.5   81-22877
ISBN 0-205-07757-9   AACR2

Series Editor: *Hiram Howard*

Printed in the United States of America.
10 9 8 7 6 5 4 3 2 1   87 86 85 84 83 82

Contents

Preface   vii

PART ONE   1

CHAPTER 1   Discipline Effectiveness   3
Concept of Discipline Effectiveness   4
Dimensions and Components of Discipline Effectiveness   6
Measuring Discipline Effectiveness   16
Summary   33

PART TWO   35

CHAPTER 2   Aims and Climate of School Discipline   37
Discipline Aims   37
Climate Orientations   43
Summary   57

CHAPTER 3   The Reformational Process   59
Background to the Reformational Process   59
Step 1: Student Recognition of the Problem   62
Step 2: Desire to Improve   65
Step 3: Recognition and Commitment to an Acceptable Plan   69
Summary   74

CHAPTER 4   The Penal and Approval Processes   77
The Penal Process   78
The Approval Process   83
Summary   91

PART THREE   95

CHAPTER 5   Conceptual Model of Student Needs and Behaviors   97
Major Categories of Behaviors and Needs   97

iii

Behavior Patterns and Security Needs   102
Behavior Patterns and Caring Needs   105
Behavior Patterns for Belongingness and Impulsive
Needs   108
Summary   110

CHAPTER 6   Specific Student Behavior Patterns and Their
Improvement   113
Onlookers   114
Untouchables   117
Perfectionists   120
Seekers   123
Becomers   126
Performers   129
Leaders   131
Developers   135
Loyalists   138
Operators   140
Teacher Behavior Patterns   143

PART FOUR   153

CHAPTER 7   The Principal and Leadership Assets   155
The Nature of Leadership   156
Penal Leadership Assets   159
Approval Leadership Assets   164
Reformational Leadership Assets   169
Reformational Assets Used for Student Leadership
Development   175
Summary   181

CHAPTER 8   Aspects of the Principal's Use of Leadership Assets   183
Value Orientation   184
The Principal and Effectiveness   188
Errors to Avoid in the Use of Leadership Assets   194
Summary   196

CHAPTER 9   Legal Parameters Affecting Discipline   199
Substantive Due Process   200
Procedural Due Process   209

Appendix A: Discipline Organization Effectiveness Inventory   217

Appendix B: Development of the DOEI Forms I and II   229

Appendix C: Scoring Instructions for the Discipline Organization
Effectiveness Inventory   231

Appendix D: Discipline Position Effectiveness   237

Appendix E: Discipline Unit Effectiveness   243

Appendix F: Creation and Use of a Discipline Data System   251

Index   265

Preface

Principals and other educators need a framework for analyzing and improving discipline. Such a framework must provide options for actions that combine short- and long-range solutions to discipline problems. The concepts and instruments presented in this book suggest methods for assessing and improving discipline that may be better than those now commonly used in our schools. With some adaptation to unique situational factors, the conceptual framework, instruments, and practical suggestions in this book can be applied in nearly any school.

Although the book is directed primarily at school administrators, others may find it beneficial. Chapters 2, 3, 4, and 6 can be used for in-service teacher training. In-service training for administrators may include the chapters for teachers as well as Chapters 1, 5, 7, 8, and 9. Chapters 2, 6, and 8 provide specific methods for on-the-job evaluation and improvement of discipline in the schools. Ideas for further research topics on the subject of school discipline are identified at various points in the book.

The work is organized into four parts, each of which is preceded by introductory comments. Part One defines discipline effectiveness and presents different methods for measuring discipline. Part Two, including Chapters 2, 3, and 4, emphasizes the practical applications of assessing and improving discipline. Why discipline is a problem in most schools is discussed, and techniques are given to alter the aims, processes, and climate factors related to discipline.

Part Three, comprised of Chapters 5 and 6, examines the reasons why students develop specific behavior patterns and the situational nature of discipline problems. Vignettes describe methods for changing inappropriate student behaviors. The last section, Part Four, includes Chapters 7, 8, and 9. These chapters discuss the principal's role in improving discipline. Problems the principal may encounter in attempting to improve discipline are described, with suggestions on how to avoid and/or solve these problems. The legal requirements and guidelines that accompany the handling of discipline situations are also described in this final part.

The book provides a comprehensive discussion of the major elements associated with discipline and discipline effectiveness. It suggests that some analysis of the nature of the problem of discipline in a school should be undertaken before initiating solutions. The link between training students to behave differently and the analysis of organizational factors is stressed throughout the book. It also suggests that few problems of school discipline can be adequately resolved in a short time. This book will help administrators and faculties develop both short- and long-term solutions to school discipline problems.

ACKNOWLEDGMENTS

This book is more than a book about discipline. It is a compilation of the theoretical concepts and practical suggestions relating to schools in a democracy. The book was written in response to the serious social problem of school discipline. It is not possible to recall all of the educators who have contributed to our development of this book over the past seven years. Those people whose contributions were essential to the successful writing of this book are Evelyn Furtwengler and Willis Furtwengler, Sr.; Margaret Konnert and William Konnert, Sr.; Lindsey March; and Orin Graff, whose combined experience as educators exceeds two hundred years, and who provided the first insights into the topic. Many of the practical approaches to discipline which were eventually tested and included in this book were derived from their experiences. Intellectual stimulation and consulting assistance were provided by James M. Kelley, Mary Martin, Leslie Carnes, Don Cheser, and Glenn Bowman. The editorial assistance and personal encouragement of Norman Moore led to the project's successful completion. The comments and contributions our wives made were numerous. Lastly, we would like to thank the many persons whose patience and clerical assistance led to a finished manuscript.

PART
ONE

Part I provides the basic language and conceptual framework for the other three sections of the book. Part I answers the following questions: How is discipline effectiveness defined? When people make judgments about discipline, to what are they really referring? What methods can be employed to measure a person's, group's, or program's discipline effectiveness?

Part I defines terms and provides a basic language for discussing discipline and measures of effectiveness. Numerous examples are presented to help clarify the complex nature of discipline problems. Instruments for measuring discipline effectiveness, developed through six years of research, are explained in this section. The uses of these instruments to isolate the nature and source of discipline problems are also delineated.

For example, one of the instruments can provide data to aid educators in determining the extent to which a person in a particular position is effective in dealing with discipline. A second instrument measures the extent to which a unit, group, or team is perceived by others as being effective in handling discipline. A third instrument makes it possible to determine the effectiveness of the discipline program in a school. The comprehensive nature of this assessment, including the data from the various categories of discipline effectiveness, provides a broad base from which to begin the process of improving school discipline.

CHAPTER

1

Discipline Effectiveness

Several years ago the authors began a search for effective programs designed to improve school discipline. The authors also attempted to determine criteria for measuring the effectiveness of school discipline. From the data collected, judgments were made about discipline effectiveness in individual schools; however, our expectations about the aims and processes used in correcting inappropriate student behaviors varied from school to school. Approaches that appeared to be working well in one school were not necessarily effective in another school. It did not appear that one set of standards could be applied to all schools to determine levels of discipline effectiveness. It was concluded, therefore, that any practical measurement of discipline effectiveness would have to be situational.

Administrators and teachers appear to act before the nature of discipline problems has been clearly defined. For example, most discipline improvement efforts involve training or retraining staff members. But in-service training may not be necessary in some schools: instead, organizational norms may need to be shifted. A school might design an in-service program to help teachers learn how to make students responsible for their own behavior. If those same teachers, however, lack systematic data that can be applied to solving the school's discipline problem, the in-service program may be of little value to that faculty. Diagnosing the areas of discipline effectiveness in a school is essential if appropriate efforts for improvement are to be implemented. Efforts to improve discipline may be extremely helpful in one school but of little value in another school. The present book aims to assist administrators in determining the level of discipline effectiveness in their school. Methods for improving discipline in a school are also described. The diagnosis of discipline effectiveness and the implementation of discipline change processes require time and a commitment to improve the level of discipline effectiveness.

This chapter discusses the concept of discipline effectiveness—its three major dimensions and the methods for assessing those dimensions.

CONCEPT OF DISCIPLINE EFFECTIVENESS

Discipline effectiveness is not an easy matter to define or measure. The level of discipline effectiveness in a school is, in part, a function of how discipline and effectiveness are defined. To be of value to an educator, the definition of discipline effectiveness must encompass various meanings associated with the term discipline and must also be specific enough to lead to a practical diagnosis of the level of effectiveness.

So the first problem in defining discipline effectiveness is the meaning of discipline. Discipline in this context is broad in scope. It includes the roles of principals, teachers, parents, and students in establishing and implementing a discipline program, as well as the program itself—the processes designed to aid students develop social behaviors and attitudes for appropriate participation in an adult democratic culture. The personality or climate of a school is related to the development of appropriate student behaviors and is included in this definition of discipline.

A second definitional problem is determining what is meant by the term "effectiveness." Effectiveness is associated with a variety of terms related to management and education: managerial effectiveness, organizational effectiveness, leadership effectiveness, teacher effectiveness, personal effectiveness, and parent effectiveness.[1] The word effectiveness generally implies the achievement of one or more desired expectations. For example, one school may appear to have effective discipline while another school does not appear to have an effective program. The first school is perceived as achieving expectations while the other is perceived as failing to achieve expectations. Such expectations are defined as those aspirations for discipline that a person believes ought to or should occur. The term "expectations" is used in this way throughout this book. Effectiveness, then, is the extent to which it is perceived that expectations are met.

In Reddin's 3-D theory of management styles, effectiveness is viewed on a continuum that is labeled effective/less effective.[2] Hersey and Blanchard state that effective leadership is "a continuum which can range from very effective to very ineffective."[3] Figure 1.1 depicts the process used in determining the level of effectiveness in a particular situation. An observer first makes a comparison between what is perceived and what is desired or expected. The interaction of perceived and expected behaviors, attitudes, and/or outcomes leads the observer to make a judgment concerning the level of effectiveness. This judgment ranges from effective to less effective along a continuum. This continuum includes both mental and physical measurements of effectiveness and is the basis for our discussion in this book. The concept of discipline effectiveness refers to a concern for the extent to which school-related people and the program in a school are helping the students learn expected social behaviors, attitudes, and personal characteristics.

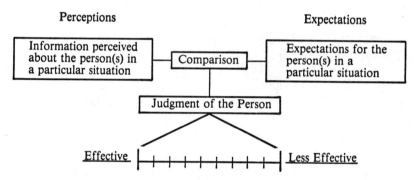

FIGURE 1.1. *Process Used in Determining Effectiveness*

From our research on discipline effectiveness, three categories or dimensions emerged as integral to the concept.[4] The first encompasses the roles of individuals who are involved in some phase of helping students learn social skills. These roles include those of the principal, teacher, student, parents, and any other individual who is involved in attempting to achieve this aim. This dimension of discipline effectiveness is referred to here as *position effectiveness*. The second dimension encompasses the roles of groups within a school community who can have an effect on the development of students' social behaviors and attitudes. Representative groups would be the school administration, the guidance and counseling depart-ment, the academic and nonacademic departments, advisory committees, the school board, and student governance groups. The term *unit effectiveness* is used to denote this dimension: the roles groups play concerning disci-pline. The third dimension encompasses the character of a school (the "discipline organization"). This dimension refers to the current status of elements other than position and unit effectiveness within a school that are designed to accomplish the development of appropriate social behaviors of the young. It is termed the *discipline organization effectiveness* dimension or *discipline program effectiveness*.

Each of these three dimensions provides a separate continuum for determining discipline effectiveness; together, the position, unit, and or-ganization dimensions help to define the concept. *Discipline effectiveness* is the extent to which the desired expectations of individuals, groups, and the discipline organization are perceived as being achieved. When principals, teachers, parents, and students in a school perceive most of these expec-tations as being successfully accomplished, a relatively high level of dis-cipline effectiveness exists in that school.

DIMENSIONS AND COMPONENTS OF DISCIPLINE EFFECTIVENESS

The three dimensions—position, unit, and organization effectiveness—are the significant elements in evaluating and improving discipline effective-ness. Each dimension, moreover, has three important components that help determine the measures of discipline effectiveness within each dimen-sion. The components of each dimension are outlined below; the sections immediately following discuss each dimension and its components in greater detail.

The components within position effectiveness relative to discipline (the role of any individual) that may be assessed are:

1. The way the person acts (individual behavior).
2. The results of the person's behavior (individual outcomes).
3. The person's attitudes, beliefs, values, and needs (individual characteristics).

For unit effectiveness relative to discipline (the role of any group), the following components may be assessed:

1. The functions of the group (group activities).
2. The results of these functions (group outcomes).
3. The norms of the group (group characteristics).

Organization effectiveness (the discipline organization) or program effectiveness may be assessed by measuring the following three components:

1. The discipline processes involved in achieving the aims of the organization (organizational processes).
2. The aims of the organization that relate to discipline (organizational outcomes).
3. The atmosphere of the organization relative to discipline (organizational climate).

There are some obvious similarities among these components, and the degree of similarity will become more evident as each component is discussed.

Components of Position Effectiveness

In the field of administration and management, it was believed for years that people's expectations for a desirable administrative style were constant and that an ideal style for managing existed.[5] In more recent times, it has been proposed that expectations are subject to change and that the situation affects the nature of people's expectations.[6] They change as people assess the conditions in a particular situation. Thus, a principal who is judged to have a high level of effectiveness in one administrative setting may show a low level of effectiveness in a different administrative setting.

The extent to which a person in a position is perceived as fulfilling others' expectations is called position effectiveness. As noted in the preceding section, the expectations and perceptions people use to determine someone's position effectiveness relative to discipline are drawn from: the person's *individual behavior;* the *individual outcomes* of that behavior; or the person's *individual characteristics.*[7] Consider the following example.

A secondary principal in a major metropolitan city succeeded in running a tight ship, and students usually behaved appropriately in the school. This person was viewed as having integrity and other desirable individual characteristics. In July, he was surprised to learn he had been transferred to a smaller school. The reason, he discovered through informal channels, was discipline. For some time he had been criticized for not collecting and using data in dealing with discipline problems. In several situations involving student suspensions he had been unable to produce documented evidence for the suspensions. This principal did not fulfill a superior's specific expectations for handling data.

Students for the most part were behaving appropriately (thus achieving individual outcomes) and the principal was liked and respected (thus meeting expectations regarding individual characteristics). However, his apparent lack of appropriate behavior, not requiring others, or himself, to obtain information—as expected by his superiors—led to his removal from the position. The superintendent in this situation believed the principal was not effective. This illustrates what can happen when role expectations within the individual-behavior component of position effectiveness are not met.

The distinction among the components of position effectiveness is not always precise. The individual characteristics of an administrator, such as dependability and honesty, are not completely separate from the individual behavior of the person. Judgments about individual characteristics follow from people's observations of individual behaviors and/or outcomes. It is often difficult to determine which individual behaviors lead to which conclusions about personal characteristics. For example, it could be argued in the example above that the principal did not achieve the outcome of being able to exclude students from school. The principal may not have achieved this particular outcome, but the determining factor was the principal's failure to meet another major expectation: to demonstrate the ability or desire to organize and use information relating to student behavior.

In another case, an administrator failed to achieve the broad individual outcomes expected for a person in his position. The account goes as follows:

Principal B in a small rural community was known for her contribution to civic organizations. She was fair, dependable, and honest. Her personal qualities were thought to be outstanding. The teachers and community approved of her methods of dealing with discipline problems. But everyone knew that the students were getting away with all kinds of inappropriate behaviors. They increasingly were truant or skipped classes despite the hard-line approach the principal took toward such student behavior. After one extremely frustrating year the principal resigned to accept a position in another school.

This principal's characteristics and behavior seemed appropriate, but her ability to produce specific individual outcomes was not evident. Students acted inappropriately in school, and signs of an overall improvement in discipline were difficult to find. Reddin indicates that achieving the expected outcomes of a position should be the only measure of managerial effectiveness.[8] It may be desirable to measure position effectiveness in terms of outcomes, but it appears that judgments about position effectiveness are affected by expectations and perceptions of the individual behavior and the individual characteristics of the person in a specific position.[9]

The third component of position effectiveness, individual characteristics, is illustrated in the following case.

The middle school principal in a community was commended by a parent group for his outstanding leadership. He had taken a school that was essentially closed to input from the community and had established volunteer groups to work in the school. A variety of advisory groups were formed from the community and the climate became much more open. Two years after the commendation, this principal had to resign due to community pressure. The parents had observed the behavior of the principal in a number of interactions with students and parents. His behavior appeared appropriate, but, nevertheless, something about it bothered the parents. For example, the principal's eye contact with adults and students was extremely poor. Parents concluded that the principal was simply not trustworthy or was hiding something. There was little concrete evidence for this conclusion, but the feelings of the parents were intense and the principal resigned. Although the board of education backed the principal as did the superintendent, the principal chose not to work in the somewhat hostile environment.

The expectation that the principal was to be a person who could be trusted had not been met. The principal may have been trustworthy but the community did not perceive him in that way. His behavior, though not inappropriate by most measures, led to negative judgments about the individual characteristics of the principal.

Incidentally, the principal in this instance commented, "I met my own expectations for my role in that position, hence I was effective." In a sense, the principal did achieve personal effectiveness.[10,11] Although the primary concern in this book is position effectiveness—the extent to which the expectations of others are met—personal effectiveness is a factor that should not be ignored. Conflicts between attempts to achieve position and personal effectiveness often arise, presenting ethical and moral dilemmas for school administrators. Chapter 2 discusses some of the issues in these two concepts of effectiveness.

In summary, the dimension of position effectiveness has three components—individual behaviors, individual outcomes, and individual characteristics. The conclusions people draw about a person's individual characteristics emerge primarily from the individual behaviors the person exhibits and the individual outcomes he or she produces. But all three components of position effectiveness can play a part in the role expectations and perceptions of the principal, teachers, students, and parents involved in the discipline program.

Components of Unit Effectiveness

Unit effectiveness is the extent to which a group in an organization is perceived as achieving others' expectations for that group. The components associated with unit effectiveness are similar to those for position effectiveness. One component is the *group activities* of the unit that relate to discipline. This is similar to the individual-behavior component of position effectiveness. The two other components are the *group outcomes* of the unit, or the results of the group activities, and the *group characteristics* of the unit. These components derive from the views of people outside the group on organizational and group effectiveness. Caplow[12] cites the performance of required functions as one of three measures of unit effectiveness. These functions can be viewed as the activities of the group. Etzioni[13] and Bennis[14] both argue that the criteria for organizational effectiveness should include measures of group outcomes. The particular characteristics attributed to a group through observations of the group's activities and outcomes are a derived indicator of unit effectiveness.

Group activities, it will be recalled, refer to the way in which a unit within a school acts relative to school discipline. More specifically, group activities influence whether a unit is perceived as acting in ways appropriate to the needs of discipline. The following example illustrates the role of group activities in determining unit effectiveness.

A science department in a major city high school decided to approach student discipline differently from other departments in the school. The faculty established a comprehensive merit and demerit system to deal with inappropriate classroom behavior. Reported incidents of inappropriate behavior decreased. The group was viewed by other departments as being a progressive, open, and systematic unit. But the department dropped the merit-demerit system when the amount of teacher time it took to operate the system detracted significantly from the teachers' instructional aims. The unit in this situation was not meeting the expectations of the principal and the teachers' own expectations for the allocation of time to certain group activities. (The principal and the teachers in the unit expected to spend the majority of time on instructional activities.)

Even though there was a significant reduction in the occurrence of inappropriate behaviors (group aims measured by the outcomes achieved), expectations for the amount of teacher time invested in group activities related to discipline were exceeded, and so the activities component of unit effectiveness was not attained.

The second component of unit effectiveness is group outcomes, or the extent to which a unit is perceived as moving in the appropriate direction and is believed to be achieving its group intentions. The importance of group outcomes can be illustrated by the following situation that existed in a rural high school in the northeastern United States.

The vocational education department held classes in a building separate from the main high school building. The vocational teachers had developed over the years a specific set of procedures that students were to follow when their classes met. Observers characterized these teachers as a firm, fair, and consistent group. Their discipline activities included the publishing of a lengthy set of rules and regulations and the severe punishing of students who violated the rules. These group activities were questioned by teachers in other departments and by a few members of the community, although all were pleased with the behavior of the students when they were in the vocational education department. The emphasis was on group outcomes; on how the students behaved. The vocational education department over the years continually received commendations from the principal and privileges not given to other departments. Students acted appropriately when they were in the vocational education building.

Expectations that the students act appropriately in the vocational education building were perceived by the principal, other teachers, and community members as being met. People's expectations for the activities and characteristics of the vocational education unit (or group) were perceived as being met to some extent, but not as well as those for outcomes.

The last unit-effectiveness component is group characteristics, sometimes described as the descriptors of a group. These characteristics resemble the personal-characteristics component of position effectiveness in that they are judgments derived from observation of the activities and outcomes produced by the group. For example:

The nontenured teachers in a school encouraged the entire faculty and the principal to set up a room in the building for in-school suspensions. A school advisory committee became involved in the discussion and made sure the newspapers were informed. The principal straddled the fence between the opinions of the tenured and nontenured faculty. She and members of the school community expected the two groups to be objective in considering the issue. The principal, superintendent, advisory committee, and board of education characterized the nontenured faculty unit as more objective than the tenured group. The in-school suspension program was established. The nontenured group was perceived by everyone except the tenured faculty as achieving a high level of unit effectiveness. The nontenured group was also viewed as having an expected characteristic of a group of professional educators, being objective in decision making. People in the community continued for several years to characterize nontenured teachers as more objective than tenured teachers.

In this instance, judgments were made about the unit effectiveness of tenured and nontenured teachers. These judgments were based on perceptions about group characteristics. The unit effectiveness of the nontenured group based on its characteristics was generally high. The group-characteristics component is an important measure of unit effectiveness.

In summary, all three components—group activities, group outcomes, and group characteristics—contribute to unit effectiveness. A unit can be defined as an entire faculty or divisions within a faculty. People's expectations for the activities in which a group should participate, their expectations for the outcomes of the group's activities, and their expectations for the nature of the group's characteristics are important in determining unit effectiveness, one dimension of discipline effectiveness.

Components of Organization Effectiveness

Components of the position- and unit-effectiveness dimensions focus on specific roles of individuals and groups. The organization-effectiveness dimension focuses on the broad aspects of controlling and changing student behavior. The components of this dimension have been termed *organizational aims/outcomes*, *organizational processes*, and *organizational climate*.

Willower[15] states that there is a pupil-control ideology in schools that follows a humanistic-custodial scale. The humanistic ideology derives from the belief that students are trustworthy and capable of self-discipline. The custodial ideology views students as somewhat irresponsible persons who require strict regulation. The Willower continuum provides a basis for the discussion of the aims for and outcomes of discipline in school organizations. The following example shows how the perception of organizational aims relates to discipline.

The principal and his staff stood for order and control in a suburban school. The number of incidents of inappropriate behavior were few, and those that did occur were with students who were mature and tended to be independent thinkers. The students liked the school because it gave them the security of knowing what they were to do and when. The community became concerned when a school board inquiry indicated that a leader-slave relationship seemed to be developing between the faculty and students. Some people in informal meetings in the small community began to whisper that the students were being programmed to obey without using their own judgment. The community in general expected students to act appropriately, but they also wanted them to learn to become self-reliant and experienced decision makers. The aim of the discipline program as it was being carried out appeared to be to create robots rather than young adults capable of using their own judgment. The school in time did shift its emphasis, but not without a major crisis.

In this example, the school's aim for the discipline program was custodial. In fact, it probably went beyond the limits of Willower's definition of custodial. The community, or a significant group in the community, wanted the discipline program to produce a more humanistic outcome: to provide opportunities for responsible student decision making. The role played by an organization's aim/outcome in its effectiveness is discussed in detail in Chapter 4.

The second component of the organization-effectiveness dimension encompasses the organizational processes relative to school discipline. Three such processes may be assessed. The *reformational process* is the long-range process of helping students learn how to assume personal responsibility for their behaviors. It does not rely heavily on the manipulation of external factors such as rewards and punishments, though some of these may be used as aids in helping students assume control and responsibility for their behavior. Through this process of learning (1) to recognize a problem, (2) to find the desire to improve, and (3) to develop a contract for their future behavior, students begin to exercise self-control.

The *penal process* is the application of corrective measures that are perceived by students as being punitive. It involves the process of learning about the unpleasant consequences of acting inappropriately in a society. The penal process is applied after students have acted inappropriately, not before. The *approval process* includes the application of behavior modification techniques before *or* after the student has acted inappropriately. It can be a preventative as well as rehabilitative process, depending on its use. Both the penal and approval processes in a discipline program involve the manipulation of external variables to effect changes in student behavior.

These three processes constitute the process component of the organization-effectiveness dimension of discipline effectiveness. The use of each is discussed further in subsequent chapters.

The remaining component of the organization-effectiveness dimension is *climate*. The climate component is the nature—open or closed—of the discipline organization of a school. Assessment of this component takes into account (1) the school's degree of openness to objective problem solving, (2) its sense of responsibility for improving discipline, and (3) the extent to which the school is viewed as the source of a problem. For example:

A school in an upper-class suburban neighborhood continually maintained that it did not have significant problems. The teachers and administrators did not feel the need to involve others either in defining or carrying out the mission of the school. Therefore, nothing about the aims of discipline or the processes the school used to change and control student behavior was thought to need attention or could be discussed outside of school. In reality, serious problems existed, particularly with drug use and its related behavioral problems. Many of the parents suspected there might be a problem, but they were not sure. After several student arrests and parent meetings held without school personnel, demands were made on the school to collect data and to discuss the activities of students in school. It took some time and effort, but by the end of the school year, parents and other community members were meeting regularly with school personnel to discuss the facts and issues relating to discipline. The discussions spread to other topics and changes were made in the school in response to the problems.

This incident illustrates at first a closed and then an open climate associated with discipline efforts. The expectations a community has for the climate in which discipline takes place can be a serious problem for school personnel. When the nature of the climate for school discipline falls short of expectations, parents can become extremely concerned.

Summary

The organization-effectiveness dimension considers the specific aims/outcomes, processes, and climate associated with a school discipline program. The position- and unit-effectiveness dimensions consider factors associated with the nature of and roles played by individuals and groups concerning discipline. Table 1.1 charts how each dimension is composed of three distinguishable components. In considering the dimensions of discipline effectiveness, an administrator may want to focus on the similarity of these components. When there appears to be a problem in achieving the level of discipline effectiveness desired, it is sometimes easier to identify the nature

TABLE 1.1.   *Components of the Dimensions of Discipline Effectiveness*

Dimensions	Components		
Position Effectiveness	Individual Behavior	Individual Outcomes	Individual Characteristics
Unit Effectiveness	Group Activities	Group Outcomes	Group Characteristics
Organization Effectiveness	Organizational Processes	Organizational Aims/Outcomes	Organizational Climate

of the component before considering the discipline-effectiveness dimension. For example, it is possible to detect an increase in the number of student offenses (organizational outcome) in a school. Usually when an organizational expectation is not met, an aspect of position or unit effectiveness is also not being met, since discipline efforts are implemented by individuals and groups.

Any component can affect the judgments that are made about the level of discipline effectiveness in a school. The balance that should be maintained in meeting the expectations for the various components in each dimension is an unknown factor. It appears to vary from situation to situation. Research is needed to determine the relative importance of the components of each dimension in a given type of school situation. Measuring the three dimensions of discipline effectiveness and their components, however, is also difficult. Aspects of such assessment are discussed in the next major section of this chapter.

MEASURING DISCIPLINE EFFECTIVENESS

The components of each of three dimensions of discipline effectiveness need to be assessed in order to establish the approximate level of discipline effectiveness for a single school or for an entire school district. Some methods that can be used are introduced in this section. To measure discipline effectiveness, expectations for and perceptions of the dimensions of discipline effectiveness must be identified. The process of assessing these two factors, expectations and perceptions, involves comparing the nature and strength of the expectations with the nature and strength of the perceptions for each of the three dimensions. Our research has primarily focused on methods for measuring program effectiveness rather than position or unit effectiveness. For this reason, the various measurements for program effectiveness or organizational effectiveness are discussed first.

Organization Effectiveness

An account of an actual school experience illustrates methods that can be used to measure the components of the organization effectiveness dimension of school discipline.

A large inner-city secondary school had the reputation of having serious discipline problems. In midyear, a principal with some years of experience was appointed. It took the principal only three months of working with the teachers and parents to discover that their primary concern was discipline. The principal knew that something had to be done. A task force of teachers was formed in May and aspects of the problem were outlined. The plan was to find out what components of discipline were of concern and then take steps to improve the situation. Consultants were hired in August to work with the task force. The consultants held discussions with faculty and students and collected data using the Discipline Organization Effectiveness Inventory.[16] Through these procedures, it was determined that a major concern was to what extent the aims of the discipline efforts were clear and were being achieved. People also had serious questions about the processes used to achieve these aims. The general climate of the program seemed to be another problem area. Eventually, three priorities were established for a discipline improvement program. The faculty and administration would attempt to:

1. Establish a systematic data-collection-and-processing system for discipline.
2. Provide more recognition for appropriate student behavior.
3. Learn how to use punishments with follow-up procedures that place the responsibility for appropriate school behavior on the student, not just the faculty.

Data were collected through interviews with the faculty and by administering the discipline inventory a second and third time during the year. Both the inventory data and the comments from the faculty led to the following conclusions about accomplishments for the year. Major steps had been taken toward full implementation of a systematic data-collection-and-processing system. Vice-principals, instead of reacting to one crisis after another, were beginning to get ahead of potential problems, and they found that it was possible to take preventative steps. A variety of individual and group procedures were established to provide recognition to students and faculty for appropriate behavior. The third priority was delayed for a year, but some people began to find ways of helping students learn to be responsible for their own behavior after being punished.

Two methods of assessing the extent of organization effectiveness are demonstrated in the preceding example. The first method of measurement involved a faculty orientation period during which time the faculty began to think about and discuss the elements of the discipline effort at their school. Once the faculty had a common language to describe the components of the discipline organization, they were able to make some estimates about the extent to which these components were being achieved in their school. A second method used for measuring the components of organization effectiveness was a questionnaire designed to determine expectations and perceptions about each of the components. The Discipline Organization Effectiveness Inventories (I and II) are excellent instruments for collecting data on the organizational components of school discipline. These two inventories were specifically developed to measure expectations for and perceptions about a discipline organization. In fact, the components of the organization-effectiveness dimension emerged from research designed to assess the effectiveness of discipline efforts made in schools.

Using the above two methods, data were collected on the specific concerns individuals had about various aspects of their school's discipline organization. From these data, seven major components of a discipline organization were finally identified. When an individual expresses dissatisfaction about discipline in the schools, the person's specific concerns usually lie within one or more of seven major components. The components include an aims/outcome scale, three processes scales, and three climate scales. They are assessed in two stages. In the first stage, Discipline Organization Effectiveness Inventory I is administered to elicit the expectations for discipline in a particular school. The respondent is asked to circle the letter that best represents his or her expectations for each item on the instrument. Each item represents a plausible discipline practice within a school (or school district). The letters represent the following choices:

A–Very much like the item on the left

B–More like the item on the left than the one on the right

C–A little more like the item on the left than the one on the right

D–A balance between the items

E–A little more like the item on the right than the one on the left

F–More like the item on the right than the one on the left

G–Very much like the item on the right

An example of an inventory item and the interpretation of a response to it is shown below.

Item: The discipline organization in (my school) should:

| Avoid penalizing students for their constant misbehavior | A Ⓑ C D E F G | Penalize students who constantly misbehave |

Interpretation: Response B means that the respondent believes that students who constantly misbehave should seldom be penalized.

The second stage of assessment includes administering Discipline Organization Effectiveness Inventory II. This instrument is designed to elicit perceptions of the extent to which each organization-effectiveness component is being achieved. Inventory II asks the respondent to select an item from a set of responses identical to those on Inventory I. An example follows:

Item: The discipline organization in (my school) is:

| Not penalizing students for their constant misbehavior | A B C D E Ⓕ G | Penalizing students who constantly misbehave |

Interpretation: Response F means the respondent believes students who constantly misbehave are frequently penalized

The scoring of Inventories I and II generates data that can be plotted on seven discipline organization-effectiveness profiles. Procedures for scoring are detailed in Appendix C for the interested reader. These profiles indicate the degree of effectiveness for each organizational component. The seven profiles and indications of how they might be plotted appear in a facsimile following this paragraph. Some prior explanation is in order. A bar graph for each profile summarizes the hypothetical response data. The

"E" represents the individual or mean score for the expectations regarding that scale. The "P" represents the individual or mean score for the perceptions regarding that scale. The bar graph presents visually the approximate gap between the mean scores for expectations and perceptions. A large gap between scores on one scale is not comparable to a gap on any other scale. Large differences between expectation and perception scores does indicate a need for further investigation through discussions or more detailed questioning.

Specimen Profiles Resulting from the Discipline Organization Effectiveness Inventory

---

Profile No. 1:   HUMANISTIC PHILOSOPHY

This profile reflects the extent to which a discipline organization provides or should provide students with the desire and ability to resolve personal problems, needs, or conflicts without inconveniencing or burdening others. A high expectation score on this index indicates a strong belief that students should not annoy or significantly inconvenience others when fulfilling personal needs or resolving day-to-day problems. A high perception score indicates that students in that school resolve their personal problems or needs without inconveniencing or disturbing others. Students who exhibit this desire and ability derive intrinsic rewards from acting appropriately and showing consideration for the aims and needs of others.

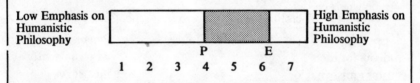

| Low Emphasis on Humanistic Philosophy | | | | | | | High Emphasis on Humanistic Philosophy |

P   E

1   2   3   4   5   6   7

Profile No. 2:   REFORMATIONAL PROCESS

This profile reflects the extent to which a discipline organization emphasizes or should emphasize the importance of placing the responsibility for a person's behavior on that person. A high expectation score on this index indicates a strong belief that students should assume responsibility for their behavior and decisions. A high perception score indicates a belief that students are assuming responsibility for their behavior. Student control of some school activities and minimal external constraints are signs of an organization that emphasizes individual self-governance.

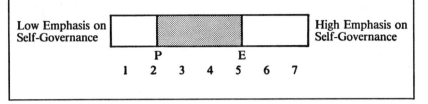

Profile No. 3:   PENAL PROCESS

This profile reflects the extent to which a discipline organization emphasizes or should emphasize the relationship between inappropriate behavior and penalties. A high expectation score on this index reflects a strong belief that students should experience penalties as a result of acting inappropriately. A high perception score indicates that students are being penalized as a result of inappropriate behavior. Loss of privilege, isolation, and suspension are examples of penalties that may be used in the penal process.

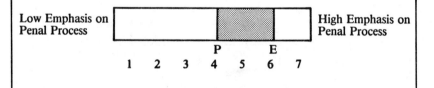

Profile No. 4:   APPROVAL PROCESS

This profile reflects the extent to which a discipline organization emphasizes or should emphasize the relationship between appropriate behavior and extrinsic rewards. A high expectation score in this index indicates a strong belief that people should reward students for appropriate behavior. A high perception score indicates a belief that the students do receive rewards from others for appropriate behavior. Recognition, additional responsibility, and greater decision-making autonomy are examples of extrinsic rewards that may be used in the approval process.

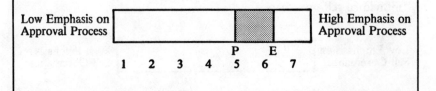

Profile No. 5:   PROBLEM-SOLVING ORIENTATION

This profile reflects the extent to which a discipline organization emphasizes or should emphasize the orderly collection and utilization of data about discipline as a means of solving discipline problems. A high expectation score on this index indicates a strong belief that data are being collected and used as a basis for decision making. Forms for reporting incidents, forms to summarize student offenses, a centralized discipline data-processing center, and an open communication link with the public are examples of an openness to objective problem solving as it relates to discipline.

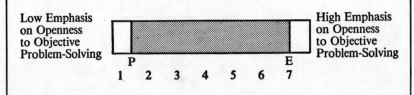

Profile No. 6:   DISCIPLINARY RESPONSIBILITY ORIENTATION

This profile reflects the extent to which discipline is viewed or should be viewed as being the responsibility of the school. A high expectation score on this index indicates a strong belief that a school should assume the major responsibility for improving school discipline. A high perception score indicates that a school is assuming the major responsibility for the resolution of discipline problems; evidence includes commitments by educators of time and money and concentrated team and individual efforts to improve the discipline process in schools.

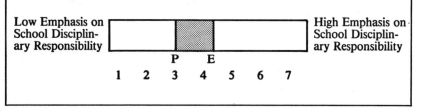

Profile No. 7:   SOURCE-OF-DISCIPLINE-PROBLEMS ORIENTATION

This profile reflects the extent to which causes of discipline problems are viewed or should be viewed as associated with schools or with the community. A high expectation score on this index indicates a strong belief that a school would be the major cause of discipline problems that might occur there. A high perception score indicates that a school environment is viewed as the primary cause of current discipline problems. Evidence for this view can range from a scarcity of opportunities to help individual students become responsible for their behavior to a low degree of supervision of students in situations where they are easily tempted to act inappropriately.

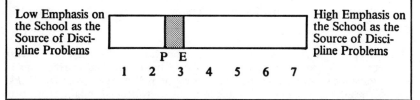

Position Effectiveness

A person's position effectiveness can be assessed by determining the difference between other people's expectations and perceptions regarding the three components of position effectiveness. (These components are the behaviors, outcomes, and individual characteristics associated with a person in a particular position.) In general, the larger the gap between the expectations of a group of people and the reality of these components (*as perceived by the group*), the lower the level of position effectiveness. For example, if the faculty of a school expect the principal to maintain a highly organized system to control students and the principal is perceived as having a loosely organized, decentralized system for monitoring student behavior, the principal may be viewed as having limited position effectiveness.

This section describes some methods to assess position effectiveness. If a person wants or is expected to improve position effectiveness, the person can attempt to change the expectations of others, the perceptions of others, or both. But change depends on an accurate assessment of position effectiveness.

Obtaining measurements, however, can be difficult. An administrator's estimate of his or her own position effectiveness is likely to be quite different from the estimates of those with whom one works. Halpin's[17] research has led to the conclusion that an administrator's description of his or her own position effectiveness may have little relationship to others' perceptions of the same administrator's position effectiveness. Katz and Kahn[18] describe some of the factors that affect the process of trying to communicate about position effectiveness. For example, the similarity between sent and received messages is influenced by the properties of the sender(s), the focal person, the substantive content of the expectations conveyed, the clarity of the communicator, the interpersonal relationship between sender and receiver, the structure of the school organization, and the position that the person receiving the information holds in the organization.

In considering a method for assessing position effectiveness, Huckaby writes:

> If a principal chooses to assess his own position effectiveness, he could ask the faculty to indicate, in written or verbal form, their expectations of someone in the position and their perceptions of this person and the work. The effectiveness of such a method, however, depends on the answers to several questions. Will the person ask the right questions? Will the teachers answer honestly? If they do answer honestly, will they express themselves accurately? If they do, will the words used have the same meaning to teachers as they do to the principal? Will the person ask members of his faculty or only a sample? If the person asks a sample of the faculty, will they be representative of the entire faculty?[19]

Huckaby adds that if an administrator can get feedback from those with whom he or she works in a manner that avoids some of these problems, the probability is increased that the feedback will be reliable. However,

Huckaby states that it must be assumed that totally accurate feedback is not possible. Regardless of the format used, moreover, information that the administrator receives will be shaped to some extent by the perceptions of that administrator.

At least two methods are available to begin to assess position effectiveness as it relates to discipline effectiveness: discussions with others and the use of feedback from survey instruments. Discussing with other people their expectations for and perceptions of position effectiveness is a rather quick and direct method for assessing position effectiveness. But given the concerns Huckaby enumerates, it may not be possible to obtain accurate data via such discussions.

Instead, we suggest that a data base of information be accumulated. Two effective kinds of survey instruments have been found: the first is a structured opinionaire that generates anonymous expectation and perception data about each of the three position-effectiveness components; a second type, similar to the first, provides anonymous expectation and perception data about the patterns of behavior associated with the person who holds the position. These patterns combine the behavioral and the personal-characteristics components of position effectiveness. Both types include a separate measure of the outcomes that are expected and perceived of a person in the position being assessed. Determining position effectiveness by assessing behavior patterns of students, teachers, and administrators is described in Chapters 5 and 6.

A tool that measures the three components of position effectiveness (behavior, individual characteristics, and outcomes) will be discussed here. The Discipline Position Effectiveness Survey[20] is one format that can be used; it provides data on all three components. However, this survey instrument should be adapted to fit the needs of a particular situation.

To use the Discipline Position Effectiveness Survey, have selected participants complete Form 1 and Form 2. Form 1 asks respondents to record their *expectations* for a person in a particular position. Form 2 asks them to determine their *perceptions* of the person now holding that position. On Form 2 respondents are asked to check the extent to which each outcome described in Form 1 is achieved. It is important to avoid trying to summarize the data from each item on the completed surveys. Differences between expectations and perceptions of the same item should be discussed, since they may reveal a problem.

The position effectiveness profile for the individual characteristics of a secondary principal appears in Figure 1.2. In this instance, an entire faculty of thirty-seven teachers and a vice-principal responded to the Discipline Position Effectiveness Survey. The E's in the boxes represent the

	A	B	C	D	E	
1) Secure	E		P			Insecure
2) Firm		E			P	Flexible
3) Objective			EP			Sensitive
4) Aware of important information		E		P		Unaware of important information
5) Closed to suggestions			P		E	Open to suggestions
6) Bold, innovative			P	E		Cautious, careful
7) Withdrawn			P		E	Assertive
8) Pessimistic			P		E	Optimistic
9) Unaware of needs of others				P	E	Sensitive to needs of others
10) Lenient		E	P			Demanding
11) Warm, caring	E			P		Impersonal, distant
12) Suspicious of others		P		E		Trusting of others
13) Inconsistent					EP	Consistent
14) Work-oriented			EP			People-oriented
15) Systematic				E	P	Spontaneous

FIGURE 1.2. *Discipline Position Effectivness Profile, Individual Characteristics Section*

average location along the continuum of respondents' expectations for each of the individual characteristics items in Form 1. Similarly, the P's represent the average location of respondents' perceptions for these same items as recorded in Form 2. The letter codes above the boxes represent the following types of responses:

A. Very much like the item on the left

B. Like the item on the left

C. Balance between the item on the left and the item on the right

D. Like the item on the right

E. Very much like the item on the right

(The expectations survey and the perceptions survey also employed this set of response choices.)

In Figure 1.2, some items exhibit fairly large gaps between expectations and perceptions. The items with the largest gaps should be reviewed with people in the school organization to determine to what extent the information is consistent with the views people express orally. For example, the second item of the profile in Figure 1.2 may suggest a major problem area. It appears as though this principal is viewed as loose and flexible when people expect the person in that position to be firm. The principal needs to check out this information with other people who will be candid in their observations and judgments.

The principal's position effectiveness profile for the behavior component is shown in Figure 1.3. This profile was arrived at in the same

	A	B	C	D	E	
1) Covers up own errors			P	E		Admits own mistakes
2) Closely supervises others		E	P			Allows others freedom
3) Listens to others	E		P			Ignores others
4) Puts things off		EP				Follows through
5) Organizes, plans ahead		E		P		Reacts to things as they happen
6) Treats others fairly	E		P			Gives some special privileges
7) Shares information	E		P			Keeps others "in the dark"
8) Discourages people			P	E		Encourages and supports people
9) Makes people responsible for their own behaviors		E		P		Assumes responsibility for the behavior of others
10) Makes decisions alone			P		E	Shares decisions with others
11) Provides recognition to others for accomplishments	E		P			Ignores the accomplishments of others
12) Punishes people for mistakes they make		P			E	Ignores or helps people learn from the mistakes they make
13) Avoids, ignores problems				P	E	Identifies, solves problems
14) Acts promptly	EP					Hesitates and delays action

FIGURE 1.3. *Discipline Position Effectivness Profile, Behavior Section*

manner as the profile for the individual characteristics component. Information in this profile shows many behaviors that are viewed as appropriate by the respondents. The principal needs to examine those items that show gaps. Although the larger gaps on some items would suggest a more serious problem, do not conclude that this is the case. The scales are not comparable to each other. That is, a small gap on an item may be viewed as a serious problem whereas a large gap on another item may not be perceived as a problem area.

A position effectiveness profile for the outcomes component is derived in a slightly different fashion. Discipline-related outcomes are those things a principal, for example, should produce outright or should cause to be produced through influencing others. On Form 1 Survey participants state what they believe should be the outcomes for one who occupies the position in question. These outcome statements are then compiled on Form 2. Outcome statements necessarily differ from position to position. The respondent to Form 2 is asked to indicate the expected level of accomplishment for each statement and to determine the extent to which the person achieves this. For example, an outcome statement for the position of school principal might be "Punish students immediately when they are sent to the principal's office by school personnel." A respondent's expectation for and perception of the principal's performance regarding this outcome would be indicated on Form 2. The response choices would be as follows:

The person in this position (should/does):

A. Never achieves this outcome

B. Seldom achieves this outcome

C. Sometimes achieves this outcome

D. Usually achieves this outcome

E. Always achieves this outcome

The profile produced by responses to these two instruments is illustrated in Figure 1.4.

These data provide some specific clues as to what is expected and how much of it is not being accomplished. In this case, for example, the faculty wanted to develop a plan for improving discipline but thought that the principal, for whatever reason, was not working toward such a plan or process involving the faculty. The principal who received this data on planning was astounded. He thought he had made an honest attempt to obtain faculty involvement in decision making. The principal realized that

Outcome Statement	Response

	A	B	C	D	E
1) Students respect the person			P		E
2) Develop a systematic approach to dealing with discipline				P	E
3) Punish students immediately when they are sent to the office			P	E	
4) Help the faculty develop a plan to improve discipline		P			E
5) Support the faculty when they act without thinking			E	P	
6) Involve the community in volunteer groups to help with discipline in the school			P		E

FIGURE 1.4.   *Position Effectiveness Profile, Outcomes Section*

the faculty still believed they were not involved in planning. A lengthy faculty meeting developed around this issue once it was clearly identified.

Some administrators ask that the data from Form 1 of the Discipline Position Effectiveness Survey be assembled by a neutral third party who would also state the outcomes for Form 2. This third party may also assemble the information that is returned on Form 2. It is important that respondents feel free to answer the opinionaires honestly if their information is to be of any value in assessing the position-effectiveness dimension of discipline effectiveness.

This method provides an opportunity to review a person's individual characteristics, behaviors, and outcomes, beginning the process of diagnosing to what extent discipline position effectiveness is being achieved.

The second method for assessing position effectiveness considers personal characteristics and behavior together, as they appear in behavior patterns or styles. As previously stated, this assessment method (an analysis of the situation and the appropriateness of behavior patterns) is discussed in detail in Chapters 5 and 6.

The discussion method may have value when used as a follow-up to the collection of written survey data. The example given of the Discipline Position Effectiveness Survey relates to administrators, but the survey can be modified to determine the position effectiveness of teachers, students, and others who are involved in the discipline effort. The survey instruments, though in need of further development, provide a point of departure in assessing position effectiveness in relation to discipline practices.

Unit Effectiveness

Unit effectiveness relative to school discipline can be assessed by some of the same methods just described for measuring position effectiveness. The components of unit effectiveness—the activities, outcomes, and character-istics of a group—need to be determined. Again, desired expectations for the group and other people's perceptions of the group must be measured in order to ascertain the differences between expectations and perceptions. Where possible, it is useful to discuss these expectations and perception with the school staff. In situations where it is difficult to do so, it may be useful to develop an instrument similar to the Discipline Unit Effectivenes Survey.[21] This two-part survey instrument (Forms 1 and 2) should not be viewed as containing all the variables that may describe unit effectiveness The items on the survey instrument are only suggestions—a guide to be ginning the task of assessing discipline unit effectiveness.

A unit effectiveness profile for the group characteristics of a faculty might appear as shown in Figure 1.5. The E's in the boxes represent the average location along the continuum of respondents' expectations for each characteristic (Form 1 responses). Similarly, the P's represent the average location of respondents' perceptions for these same items (Form 2 re sponses). The letter codes above the boxes represent the following type of responses:

A. Very much like the item on the left
B. Like the item on the left
C. Balance between the item on the left and item on the right
D. Like the item on the right
E. Very much like the item on the right

In Figure 1.5, some of the items show gaps between expectations an perceptions. These items should be discussed within the group. If it ap pears that some items accurately reflect the present state of affairs in th group, then decisions must be made about the extent to which improve ment is necessary. For example, a gap between expectations and percep

	A	B	C	D	E	
1) Supportive of members		E	P			Lacking support for members
2) Open		E		P		Closed
3) Interested only in members of the group			P		E	Interested in others
4) Independent			EP			Dependent
5) Firm		P	E			Flexible
6) Planned		P	E			Spontaneous
7) Concerned		E		P		Unconcerned
8) Negative			P		E	Positive
9) Nonintellectual			P	E		Intellectual
10) Power oriented		EP				Unconcerned with power
11) Emotional			P	E		Objective
12) Assumes responsibility for its actions	E		P			Avoids being responsible for its actions
13) Initiating		E			P	Passive
14) High Morale	E	P				Low Morale
15) Unproductive		P			E	Productive
16) Change-oriented		E			P	Status quo-oriented

FIGURE 1.5.   *Discipline Unit Effectiveness Profile, Group Characteristics Section*

tions about the productiveness of the group (item 15) may be important to review.

The unit effectiveness profile for the group's activities is shown in Figure 1.6. This profile was arrived at through the same process used for the group's characteristics. The profile indicates that several of the group's actual activities are viewed as being different from activities that respondents expect from the group.

A sample of a profile for unit effectiveness outcomes, those things that people think a group should produce or cause to happen, is shown in

	A	B	C	D	E	
1) Help other groups		E	P			Hinder others
2) Make all decisions	P		E			Share decisions with other groups
3) Closely observes the activities of others			P		E	Allow other groups freedom to choose
4) Reject authority			PE			Follow orders
5) Communicate with other groups	E	P				Fail to communicate with other groups
6) Plan their activities		E	P			Lack a coordinated effort
7) Recognize the accomplishments of their group			E	P		Ignore the accomplishments of their group
8) Work slowly			P		E	Work rapidly
9) Avoid conflict with other groups	E		P			Challenges the activities of other groups
10) Creates alternatives			E	P		Set responses to problems
11) Set reasonable goals			E	P		Set unreachable or easy goals
12) Prepared	E			P		Unprepared
13) Evaluate own progress	E				P	Ignore evaluation process
14) Avoids leading			P	E		Provides leadership

FIGURE 1.6. *Discipline Unit Effectiveness Profile, Activities Section*

Figure 1.7. On Form 1 of the Discipline Unit Effectiveness Survey, respondents list what they believe should be the discipline outcomes for a group (unit) in question. These outcome statements from Form 1 are compiled on Form 2. On Form 2, respondents are asked to indicate the desired level of accomplishment for the unit and the extent to which the unit actually achieves each outcome. For instance, one outcome statement in this example was "Students in the halls between classes are supervised by teachers." Each respondent's expectation for and perception about this statement were indicated by one of the following choices:

The group:

A. Never achieves this outcome

B. Seldom achieves this outcome

Outcome Statement	Response				
	A	B	C	D	E
1. Students in the halls between classes are supervised by teachers			P		E
2. The number of discipline problems is being reduced				P	E
3. Student discipline problems are documented			P	E	
4. Incidents of inappropriate behavior in the halls are given attention.		P		E	
5. The faculty is aware of potential discipline problems			P	E	

FIGURE 1.7.   *Discipline Unit Effectiveness Profile, Outcomes Section*

C. Sometimes achieves this outcome

D. Usually achieves this outcome

E. Always achieves this outcome

Figure 1.7 gives a sample of outcome perceptions and expectations for a faculty. The teachers as a group are perceived to be providing less than the expected amount of supervision in the halls between classes. The teachers are also viewed as not meeting some of the other outcome expectations. The responses on this inventory came from the department chairman and administrative staff at the school.

SUMMARY

Some methods for measuring the broad dimensions of discipline effectiveness have been presented. Both discussion and data generated by survey instruments should be helpful in assessing strengths and weaknesses related to discipline effectiveness. Caution should be exercised when using the instruments to avoid drawing unwarranted conclusions from the data. However, the data can provide a point of departure for discussion of discipline effectiveness.

NOTES

1. William J. Reddin, *Managerial Effectiveness* (New York: McGraw-Hill Co., 1970); Fred E. Fiedler, *A Theory of Leadership Effectiveness* (New York: McGraw-Hill Book Co., 1967); and Thomas Gordon, *P.E.T. (Parent Effectiveness Training)* (New York: Peter H. Wyden, 1970).

2. Reddin, p. 45.

3. Paul Hersey and Kenneth H. Blanchard, *Management of Organizational Behavior: Utilizing Human Resources* (Englewood Cliffs, N. J.: Prentice-Hall, 1977), pp. 115–16.

4. See Appendix B for a description of the development of the Discipline Organization Effectiveness Inventory and of the previous work conducted under the writers' auspices that led to these conclusions.

5. Robert R. Blake et al., "Breakthrough in Organization Development," *Harvard Business Review* 42 (1964):135.

6. Reddin, pp. 15–17.

7. William O. Huckaby, "Changes in the Effectiveness and Awareness of Public School Principals Following Their Participation in the Monitoring Effectiveness Process" (Ph.D. dissertation, George Peabody College for Teachers, 1977), pp. 22–23.

8. Reddin, p. 3.

9. Jacob W. Getzels and Egon G. Guba, "Social Behavior and the Administrative Process," *School Review* 65 (1957):423–41.

10. Huckaby, p. 24.

11. Reddin, pp. 7–8.

12. Theodore Caplow, "The Criteria of Organizational Success," in Keith Davis and William G. Scott (eds.), *Human Relations and Organizational Behavior: Readings and Comments* (New York: McGraw-Hill Book Co., 1969), p. 96–98.

13. Amitai Etzioni, *Modern Organizations* (Englewood Cliffs, N. J.: Prentice-Hall, 1964), ch. 2.

14. Warren G. Bennis, *Changing Organizations* (New York: McGraw-Hill Book Co., 1966), pp. 52–53.

15. Donald J. Willower, Terry L. Eidell, and Wayne K. Hoy, *The School and Pupil Control Ideology*, Penn State Studies No. 24, 2nd ed. (University Park, Pa.: Penn State University, 1973), pp. 4–6.

16. A copy of this instrument appears in Appendix A. For a description of the development of the instrument and survey procedures, see Appendix B.

17. Andrew W. Halpin, *The Leadership Behavior of School Superintendents* (Chicago: Midwest Administration Center, the University of Chicago, 1959), p. 85.

18. Daniel Katz and Robert L. Kahn, *The Social Psychology of Organization* (New York: John Wiley and Sons, 1966), pp. 182–98.

19. Huckaby, p. 31.

20. A copy of this instrument appears in Appendix D.

21. A copy of this instrument appears in Appendix E.

PART TWO

In Part II (Chapters 2, 3, and 4) seven components of school discipline effectiveness are discussed. Part II deals with the following questions: What is the purpose for discipline—is it to teach students to be respectful, obedient adults, or is it to teach students to be self-governing individuals? How are these purposes achieved? Should punishments and penalties be used in schools? Should educators reward students for their appropriate behaviors? What must occur when handling a discipline problem to increase the probability that the student involved will not repeat that behavior?

Chapter 2 discusses the various purposes for discipline and describes the "climate" factors that have an impact on peoples' perceptions of discipline. These factors are the perceived causes of discipline problems; the person(s) who are responsible for solving the problems; and the nature of the decision-making processes. This chapter presents different methods for arranging data to enhance effective decision-making about discipline.

Chapter 3 discusses the steps that must be taken with a student to increase the chances that the student's inappropriate behavior will not recur. Practical methods for achieving these steps are presented. Chapter 4 describes the uses of punishments and rewards as measures to control student behavior. Advantages and disadvantages of each of these measures are explained.

CHAPTER

2

Aims and Climate
of School Discipline

Chapter 1 described the three dimensions of discipline effectiveness and
ways to measure the components of these dimensions. One dimension,
organization effectiveness, involves an examination of the organization's
aims for discipline, its processes for achieving those aims, and the climate
of the organization. This chapter considers the aims of discipline in schools
and the aspects of the environment (the climate) that affect discipline improvement. Discipline processes are discussed in Chapters 3 and 4.

DISCIPLINE AIMS

In a speech at the 1976 National Conference on Citizenship Education,
Ewald B. Nyquist, former commissioner of education in the state of New
York, made the following comments (as published in *Phi Delta Kappan*).

> Our schools and colleges do many things to enhance the quality of life of
> each individual who attends them. This is an appropriate purpose. All
> people are not alike in their needs, abilities, and aspirations, and this

equality consists in treating unequal talents unequally. Each person should be helped to become all that he or she is capable of being. However, it is incumbent upon all educational institutions to transcend particularist purposes. Whatever else they do, nothing is so important over the long haul as to draw out our common humanity and thus create a better community, a community that will be tolerant, compassionate, just and humane.

What we need in our society is nicer people; people who are richer on the inside than they are on the outside, people with more trust and tenderness, people who care for and share with one another, who have the capacity to discover and appreciate the worth of others and who are not disturbed by difference in background, behavior, and life-styles; people who, when they knock on themselves, find someone at home whom they like; in short, people who want to be better human beings in a more humane community.[1]

Reflecting on the kind of education that provides for these aims, Nyquist continued: "The student must learn how to make choices freely and to comprehend and evaluate the consequences of his or her choices. Implicit in the concept of freedom is responsible action, which cannot be equated with license. Individuality does not diminish responsibility or accountability for one's acts."[2] Finally, Nyquist declared that "no student should be turned out of our high schools without ever having come to grips with what it means to be a part of a larger community."[3]

Nyquist's statements contain the elements of the aims of discipline. Implicitly, he suggests that tension exists between learning to make one's own choices and learning to be responsible for being part of a community. Historically, the aim of school discipline was the control of the behavior of students through the use of force. In recent decades, this aim, both in the imposition of restraints on individual students and in the use of force as a means of perpetuating the interests of society, has been changed somewhat by the concept of self-direction. The tension between the two aims of obedience to external authority and the development of self-control is evident in Willower's[4] work describing the schools' differential emphases on controlling the behavior of students. Willower argues that there will always be a conflict between custodial aims that focus on learning to respond to another's authority and the humanistic aim of learning to direct one's own behavior. Willower concludes that schools aim primarily for pupil control and that preoccupation with this aim can be seen in the organizational and social structures of the school. The two sets of aims appear to exist on a continuum, from humanistic to custodial goals. The custodial approach includes emphasis on the content to be taught, teacher direction, rigid classroom procedures, and social disengagement from pupils; the custodial type of school organization places greater emphasis on external order, primitive sanctions and inflexibility in teaching strategies and views student behavior in stereotyped moralistic terms.[5]

But the emphasis on teaching students to obey an external authority can become extreme.

A secondary school principal was "charismatic"—extremely popular with the students. This principal had a reputation for demanding obedience to his authority, and the school was characterized as having many rules and regulations. One day a student defied the principal's authority. Both the principal and the student found themselves in the schoolyard; the principal physically put the student on the ground, sat on the student, and bounced up and down several times. Much of the student body observed this action from their classrooms. The student who had disobeyed was led back into the building and returned to classes. Students defended the principal by saying that nothing happens to a student who obeys. The students believed they attended an excellent school because they were secure knowing exactly what behavior was expected and when. However, it appeared to some members of the board of education that the students were expected to leave their minds at the entrance to the building when they came to school. After several more incidents, the principal was fired, but not without strong student protest.

This example, although unusual, is an actual case. It shows the danger of an overemphasis on teaching students to follow a person with legitimized authority. This principal believed that the authority of the school was his own personal authority. The principal emphasized custodial aims and had a leadership style that encouraged slave-like behavior from students.

Milgram's experimental research testing the limits of obedience to authority in adults revealed a shocking result. His study showed that many ordinary people would perform harsh acts on other human beings in response to requests by an experimenter (to increase the intensity of electric shock to subjects; unknown to the first group, the shocks were not actually administered). Milgram wrote:

The results, as seen and felt in the laboratory, are to the author disturbing. They raise the possibility that human nature, or more specifically the kind of character produced in the American society, cannot be counted on to insulate its citizens from brutality and inhumane treatment at the direction of malevolent authority. A substantial proportion of people do what they are told to do, irrespective of the content of the act and without limitations of conscience, so long as they perceive that the command comes from a legitimate authority.[6]

Acceptance of authority is necessary for the functioning of a society, for it is difficult, if not impossible, for any individual to comprehend all the goals and behaviors necessary to maintain a democracy. One cannot argue with those who want to live in a society in which a person's actions are based on "principles, ideals and feelings for others."[7] As a practical reality, however, time never permits the reaching of a consensus for each decision made and implemented in society. People must learn to moderate some of their personal wishes to the desires of a group and its goals. But an over-emphasis on teaching students to submit to authority can lead to a lack of individual self-governance and conscience.

Other authors have stressed the humanistic aim of discipline, which encourages self-governance or self-direction. Tanner, in her book *Classroom Discipline for Effective Teaching and Learning*, states the following as the primary goal of discipline:

> Self-direction in children is our overriding educational goal. Socialization is inherent in self-direction. Random, unsocialized behavior is the very antithesis of self-direction. Developing self-direction in children means helping them to become responsible individuals who know how to act and how not to act and to care for themselves and others.[8]

She continues, in another context, saying that "submission to authority is incompatible with the discipline that we want—self-direction."[9]

Willower suggests that the humanistic approach includes an emphasis on student-directed activities, flexible classroom procedures, and a more permissive attitude toward students. The humanistic school organization stresses self-discipline, democratic processes in the classroom, and flexibility in approach to the curriculum and its objectives; it views students without moralistic overtones.[10]

Humanism is defined as the desire to put human welfare above all other concerns. Essentially this means that whatever decisions are made and implemented, the projected outcomes must be in the interest of those most likely to be affected. The aim of humanism is to develop students with the desire to act in ways that will not only be personally satisfying but will also be in the interests of others. The outcome will be behavior that is beneficial to the person and to those with whom the person associates. The development of individuals with a humanistic outlook is a goal that can be achieved, just as students can learn to submit to external authority. Tanner argues that:

> Children do not automatically become self-directing as they grow older. Nor do they necessarily develop the abilities to cooperate with others. . . . Cooperation and inner direction must be consciously taught the same as any other educational objective.[11]

Yet the question persists: which should schools try to accomplish through discipline, the custodial goals or the humanistic goals? People agree that students should learn to act appropriately in and out of schools, but they may disagree on who should be responsible for controlling behavior. Some people argue that teachers should directly control students' behavior. Others maintain that students should control their own behavior. The former group stresses obedience to authority and the latter emphasizes self-control. Are these two aims mutually exclusive, as some educators have suggested? Research provides some ways to consider this question.

Piaget,[12] Kohlberg,[13] and Glasser,[14] respectively discussing the stages of growth, moral development, and appropriate mental health, stress the importance of students' learning to respond to situational factors. These authors argue that students should react to situational factors by assuming personal responsibility. Students should make judgments and decisions based on their own feelings of justice. Piaget, Kohlberg, and Glasser urge educators to design educational opportunities that help students learn to do things not because obedience is demanded or because others will approve, but because they have their own standards of what is appropriate and inappropriate. Hunt suggests that a student's conceptual level is the key factor to consider in determining the instructional stance toward discipline.[15] Some students need a structured and directed approach, while others can best learn appropriate behaviors through a little direction and guidance. For example:

> Students in a school were accustomed to submitting to the rather arbitrary authority of the teachers and the school system; the dominant attitude among the educators was custodial. A new principal attempted to implement humanistic aims. The students and teachers, believing the principal was soft and unorganized, a pushover, almost caused the principal to lose his job.

In this case, the change from a strong custodial aim to a humanistic one was attempted in too brief a time. The principal appeared to be unaware of this situational factor and encouraged students to make their own decisions through participation in decision making. The long-range goal in this situation may be to emphasize humanistic aims, but the immediate goal should be custodial aims. Obedience to authority outside of oneself may serve as a short-range solution to a long-range problem.

Hersey and Blanchard provide a framework for determining how much autonomy and structure people may need in different situations. Hersey and Blanchard suggest that the more immature a group is in its abilities to accomplish things as a group, the more structured or custodial the discipline needs to be. They argue that as group members learn to act appropriately, their needs for a more humanistic and mature approach to discipline will emerge.[16] In some situations, as described above, it may be extremely important to emphasize custodial rather than humanistic control factors. Likewise, in other situations it is appropriate to stress humanistic rather than custodial factors. Estimated measures of the maturity (intellectual and moral) of the individuals in a group are possible. Research findings involving levels of maturity and other situation elements provide one basis for determining whether to emphasize humanistic or custodial aims.

In a democracy, the individual is considered primary, and the population attempts to govern itself through representation. One of the purposes for schools is the perpetuation of this form of government. A self-governance system relies heavily on an educated population where individuals are capable of making their own decisions and are asked only occasionally to obey an external authority in achieving the aims of the society. Adults must act appropriately without extensive external constraints if the glue that holds a democracy together is to stick effectively. The long-range aim for discipline in a democracy must reflect a major concern for humanistic control. At times, custodial aims take precedence, to keep students from being harmed or from hurting each other. But submission to a single authority or leader who demands slave-like behavior should not be taught. Instead, respect for the needs of the group (which expects reasonably appropriate individual behavior) should be emphasized. Acceding to group needs, however, does not eliminate the responsibility each person has for evaluating the appropriateness of a group's desire.

Humanistic discipline should include ways for students to experience making decisions that affect others and for students to assume responsibility for the welfare of others. A school system offers ample opportunities for such learning experiences, if school personnel desire to take advantage of them. This does not mean giving the school over to the students. Rather, it means developing structures whereby students can take on significant responsibilities within well-defined parameters. The "leadership corps" discussed in Chapter 7 is one example of such an opportunity.

If the ultimate aim of discipline is humanistic—to produce young adults who will act appropriately with a minimum of external constraints in a variety of situations—then learning to satisfy one's individual needs without inconveniencing and disturbing others is extremely important. This statement should not be interpreted as suggesting that cooperative ventures are not desirable. Rather, students should be viewed as acting inappropriately when their needs for approval, security, control, and recognition can only be satisfied by behaviors that inconvenience or disturb others. A person's desire to act appropriately must be accompanied by an awareness of the needs and desires of other people in the situation. This awareness can be dulled if a person is constantly seeking satisfaction of personal needs through others. For example, some people feel good about themselves only when others praise them. The person(s) who are constantly giving the praise may not find this activity satisfying, but the person who requires the praise may not be sensitive to the cost of giving it. Such situational sensitivity may occur if students become aware of their own needs and develop methods for satisfying those needs without assistance from people who may find little satisfaction in responding to the needs of others.

In summary, the ultimate aim of discipline to develop humanistic individuals is a worthy goal, but the need, when appropriate, to consider short-range custodial aims is also important. The processes for achieving the aims of external and internal behavior control are complex, as will be seen in the next two chapters.

CLIMATE ORIENTATIONS

The climate component of discipline organization effectiveness includes three major orientations: (1) the orientation of the faculty toward the school as a source of the discipline problem; (2) the orientation of the staff and others toward the school's responsibility for improving discipline; and (3) the orientation of those involved in discipline problem solving. These three elements reflect the atmosphere of the discipline organization. The first concerns the causes of discipline problems. Many other causes exist, but it seems essential that the school minimize its own contribution to the problem. A few causes other than those attributable to schools are reviewed in this section. The second orientation involves developing and maintaining a commitment to improve discipline. Suggested ways for administrators to do this are provided in this section. The final orientation we discuss is objective problem solving, including the use of concrete information relative to discipline problems.

Attempts to identify the reasons for an apparent increase in the severity and frequency of inappropriate acts in schools have been frustrating. Some of the clues in recent research findings are discussed here.

Both societal variables and schools appear to cause school discipline problems. The societal variables include the communications media, especially television, and the home environment. Leifer, Gordon, and Graves[17] found that the greater the similarity between events acted out on television and a student's own situation, the more likely the student is to imitate any violence or aggression shown. Leibert,[18] after reviewing the research on the relationship between television viewing and aggressive behavior, concluded that "There is a reliable and socially significant relationship between the amount of violence which a child sees on entertainment television and the degree to which he is aggressive in his attitudes and behavior." It is becoming apparent that when students are exposed to hours of violence on television, the result may well be antisocial, aggressive, and sometimes violent behavior. This cause of school discipline problems continues to be ignored by large segments of the population.

The influence of the home is also a significant cause of discipline problems in the schools. Thurston, Feldhusen, and Benning[19] conducted an extensive study of students in grades three, six, and nine and found substantial differences between the discipline problem student and the student who acted appropriately. The homes of the discipline problem students typically included the following elements:

1. Discipline by the father was either lax, overly strict, or erratic.
2. Discipline by the mother was also irregular or otherwise inadequate.
3. The parents were indifferent or even hostile toward the children.
4. The family seldom operated as a unit.
5. Parents had difficulty involving the children in talking things over.
6. The husband-wife relationship lacked closeness and equality of partnership.
7. The parents found fault with their children.

8. Mothers were not happy with the community in which they lived.

9. The parents' response to a child's inappropriate behavior was anger and physical punishment for the child.

10. Parents believed that they had little influence on the development of their children.

11. The parents believed other children were exerting bad influences upon the parents' children.

12. The parents' leisure time included few cultural or intellectual activities.

The schools themselves do sometimes cause discipline problems. Polk and Schafer argue strongly in *Schools and Delinquency* that serious cases of inappropriate behavior result from negative school experiences[20] (e.g., some students experience repeated failures or never receive the rewards that other students of different ability and status receive). Other writers, such as McPartland and McDill, suggest that schools cause behavior problems because they fail to involve students in any of the decisions affecting their lives in school.[21] Finally, the National Institute for Education's report, *Violent Schools—Safe Schools*, maintained that large city schools facilitated discipline problems through their large, impersonal, overcrowded, difficult-to-manage school organizations.[22] Of course, some of the school-related causes of discipline problems are not the educator's fault, but come out of a societal breakdown in the financial and attitudinal support systems that schools must have to provide for the needs of different students.

Regardless of the combination of causes or the specific sources of discipline problems, it is important for a school trying to teach appropriate behavior to avoid focusing on its own contribution to inappropriate acts among students. School personnel may come to believe that they are contributing to discipline problems, and a sense of self-blame may result. Some introspection and the belief that the faculty is causing some instances of inappropriate behavior is healthy, because this attitude can stimulate a belief that the problem can be shared. On the other hand, if self-blame becomes excessive among the faculty, it may cause frustration and produce little improvement in discipline. Kelley found that relationships exist between levels of perceived self-blame and levels of anxiety among individual educators in metropolitan schools.[23] If such anxiety includes an overconcern about the school's being a source of discipline problems, discipline problems may actually increase. In summary, although a school can perhaps do very little to reduce the societal causes of misconduct, such as the impact of television and the home environment, the school also has a responsibility to minimize the extent to which its personnel are contributing to the problem.

Regardless of the source of the problem, school personnel need to determine how responsible they feel for improving discipline. The extent to which faculty and administrators believe they are bringing about an improvement in school discipline is the key indicator of staff effort toward improving discipline. A high sense of responsibility for improving discipline is usually associated with a commitment to action. If a school staff believes it has this responsibility, the incidents of inappropriate behavior may decrease. When the staff does *not* feel responsible the following can occur:

> In a large, inner-city school the teachers turned their heads away from incidents of inappropriate behavior in the corridors and sometimes in the classrooms. A sense of hopelessness prevailed among the educators. Correcting inappropriate behavior was not something that was considered one of their responsibilities, and an attitude of cooperation did not prevail in the school. One teacher said, "You are on your own in this school, so you learn not to feel a sense of responsibility for any of the actions of students beyond those in the classrooms. The behavior of students in the classroom may be something you have to contend with, but outside the classroom it is someone else's responsibility."

This faculty member felt little responsibility for the improvement of discipline in the school. McClelland suggests that those individuals who want to be responsible for improving a situation, and who do not fear failure, will tend to set reasonable aims for improving the situation.[24] Those who want to avoid responsibility and are also fearful will sometimes set unreasonable goals which they cannot achieve or set modest aims, too easy to attain.

The level of felt responsibility can be increased through the faculty's participation in goal setting. It is important that faculty members work through a process that can help them establish reasonable aims for improving discipline. It is not uncommon for faculties to try to solve the entire problem of school discipline in a very brief period of time. In so doing, they set impossible goals. When their aims are not accomplished, they blame consultants, the principal, or other people. The failure, in fact, was caused by the establishment of an impossible task.

Along with having a feeling of responsibility, the faculty should believe they can make a difference in the situation. Ultimate responsibility for improving discipline usually belongs to a person in a position of authority in the school organization. But administrators who aid the faculty in developing strong feelings of internal control are more apt to find the faculty is ready to assume responsibility for improving school discipline than administrators who emphasize external control in the school. A centralized decision-making process, in which the administration makes the decisions with a minimum of participation, can lead to a low general sense of responsibility for improving school discipline. The problem of school discipline is a shared problem: participants must achieve a sense of personal responsibility for improving the situation before there will be any real change in a school. A climate in which faculty, students, administrators, and parents believe that they all can produce positive change and exert some control over external events is a climate conducive to improving school discipline.

Associated with a strong sense of responsibility for improving school discipline must be an appropriate attitude toward solving the problem. A faculty may believe that it is the source of some problems, but it may not be open to using data in a way that can improve the situation. However, sound decisions about what is needed to improve school discipline cannot be made in a closed environment in which decision making is subjective rather than objective. Too many people (participants and observers) are involved in the discipline process to warrant excluding them from decision making activities. An attitude of openness toward problem solving in a school can be demonstrated by: (1) a systematic process of collecting information about discipline; (2) evidence that decisions are based on the information collected; and (3) a sharing of the problems of and solutions to school discipline with all participants. Students, faculty, principals, and parents need to see that these factors exist. Sharing of information should occur when it is appropriate to bring all a school's resources together to prevent potential problems and to solve those that have developed.

Data Support System

Objective problem-solving requires a data support system that is both useful and takes a minimal amount of time to operate. The need for a data support system, the categories of data, and policies for using the data are discussed in this section.

Teachers and administrators occasionally try to change a student without the benefit of information on the previous actions of the student.

Administrators may be unaware of the number of times they have used the same penalty on a student, with little success. Administrators also find it difficult to support teachers who have sent students from the classroom to the office for minor offenses, if those teachers have failed to report previous classroom incidents involving the same students. School officials are sometimes caught unprepared to deal with inappropriate behavior, which might possibly have been predicted from data about the mood of the students. Consistency and fairness in dealing with discipline problems are hard to maintain without the knowledge of what happened prior to an incident. Duke outlines a set of six basic components that must be included if a discipline program is to be effective;[25] the first component is the collection of accurate data on discipline. Objective decision making and problem solving depend on a broad data support system.

The creation of a data system for objective problem solving requires standardized information and policies for the use of such information. Information related to discipline permeates the school organization. The selection of the useful information from among the available data and the classification of that information are extremely important. The following categories for the collection of discipline information are suggested:

1. Information about students, such as:
   A. Demographic
   B. Psychological
   C. Achievement
   D. Behavioral (Student Inappropriate Behavior Incident Reports).
2. Teacher-administrator responses to incidents.
3. Position effectiveness information.
4. Unit effectiveness information.
5. Discipline organization effectiveness information.
6. Categorized offenses.
7. Corrective measures.

A person or persons in the school should be assigned to the continuing collection and processing of this information. A central location in the building seems to be the most effective physical arrangement for this task.

The discipline data support system should include readily available information about the students. Most student records contain demographic, psychological, and achievement information. Clues about the nature of a student's discipline problem may be available from such information and may help the staff to aid the student in correcting inappropriate behavior. However, classroom behavior information is frequently not available in student files. This sort of information will be discussed in more detail in Chapter 6. Behavioral information should be primarily collected in the classroom by the teachers who work with a student throughout the day. The data may be in the form of incident reports on behavior. An incident report includes five categories of information relative to classroom discipline:

1. The name of the student.
2. The specific description of the offense.
3. The specific corrective measure.
4. The date the offense occurred.
5. The signature of the person making the report.

All too frequently, the information that gets recorded by teachers about an offense is of a generalized nature, leaving much about what occurred to the imagination of the reader. For example, at a hearing about a student's actions, written evidence was entered into the teacher's testimony that stated, "This student is disruptive, rude, and inconsiderate. His behavior is that of a person much younger than himself." The hearing officer pressed the teacher to clarify and support the conclusions drawn. Unfortunately, the teacher was unable to describe the inappropriate behavior with any degree of accuracy. If tapping a pencil on the desk is inappropriate, then the teacher should write, "The student was tapping his pencil on the desk." This seems very obvious, but in the heat of this kind of situation, recording the facts about what happened is frequently omitted. The exact nature of the teacher's corrective action should also be recorded, even though this is not considered to be student behavioral information. For example, if a teacher decided just to talk with the student about his or her behavior, then the record should reflect such action; of course, the date, time, and place should also be included in the record. Students tend to repeat many of their school behaviors. These behaviors can be categorized in behavior patterns, and such patterns can be recorded as part of the student file. Sample categories of student behavior patterns are described in Chapter 6.

One fundamental problem in public-school discipline is the extreme variance in the disciplinary expectations and perceptions held by different individuals and groups. Added to this is a variance in expectations within a group. Sometimes the same teachers who have worked together for years have different disciplinary expectations and perceptions of which they are not aware. One teacher may punish a student rather severely for sitting on a windowsill, while another may see little, if anything, wrong with this behavior. A citizen may believe that the students are running the school, while administrators may believe that they (the administrators) are exercising too much control.

Usually little formal attention is given to identifying what is expected by the faculty, students, and parents about discipline in a school. Likewise, information about what people believe is true about the discipline in a school is seldom available.

Other kinds of information concern the relationship between student offenses and faculty corrective measures. Faculty, students, and parents appear to have varying opinions of which inappropriate student behaviors should be considered serious and which should be taken lightly. They also may have different ideas about which corrective measures, including penalties, should be used for serious offenses.

Categories can be established for what are considered serious and nonserious offenses and what are appropriate corrective measures. The Pennsylvania State Department of Education produced a chart that offers implicit direction as to which inappropriate behaviors should be considered serious, who is presumably responsible for handling the problem, and what are the range of corrective measures that could be used to deal with the problem.[26] The Pennsylvania chart is reproduced in Table 2.1. The information collected in the Pennsylvania system is more extensive than may be necessary, but data on what is expected and perceived about offenses and corrective measures need to be collected. Specimens of the Pennsylvania data collection instruments appear in Figures 2.1 and 2.2. These levels and measures will vary from one school to another, just as principals and teachers sometimes vary in their perceptions and expectations concerning offenses and corrective measures. Specific information on the expected and perceived levels of offenses and penalties will help to achieve objective problem solving. The categories of information just outlined provide a framework for determining what information is to be collected. Appendix F provides an in-depth discussion of the creation and use of a discipline data system.

Policies for Information Use

Before data in the support system can be used in problem solving, the question of who has access to what information needs to be settled in the form of general policies. Administrators who deal directly with discipline or are responsible for it must be included in policies establishing access to the information, and other school personnel with a valid reason for access must also be included. Policies need to indicate the persons who are to participate in the flow of information. An example of one school's policy for the flow of information in behavior incidents is as follows:

Classroom	(a) Classroom incident is recorded on a form.
Processing Center	(b) The form goes to a processing center (Vice-principal's office or special data processing center) where data are broken down and compared with other data according to policies.
Classroom	(c) Summary reports sent back to teacher.

The classroom incident forms are forwarded to the central processing area as soon as possible, and summary data are returned to the teacher.

Another policy should establish a monthly review disciplinary council. The purpose of such a council is to review the summary data on discipline with a view to identifying improvements in discipline effectiveness. A review committee composed of faculty and administrative personnel can identify problems and make recommendations for changes in discipline procedures. This group should be viewed as one of the vital committees in a school; appropriate release time needs to be provided for those serving on this committee.

Policies need to be established on how long data are kept—which data are retained after students graduate or are transferred to another school if a student transfers. All discipline data on students, except any record of criminal offenses and expulsion, should be removed from the files after a student graduates. In the case of transferring information from school to school, it is best not to provide a written record of specific offenses and corrective measures because the situational factors of a different school may prove to be a positive influence on a student's behavior. Unless policies are developed and agreed on to guide faculty and administrator use of information and to guard against misuse, the value of the data support system for objective problem-solving will be constantly threatened.

TABLE 2.1. *"Guidelines for School Discipline" (Pennsylvania State Department of Education)*

Student Misconduct/ Response	
Levels	*Examples*
I. *Minor* misbehavior on the part of the student that impedes orderly classroom procedures or interferes with the orderly operation of the school. These misbehaviors can usually be handled by an individual staff member but sometimes require the intervention of other school support personnel.	Classroom disturbance Classroom tardiness Cheating and lying Abusive language Nondefiant failure to complete assignments or carry out directions
II. Misbehavior whose *frequency* or *seriousness* tends to disrupt the learning climate of the school. These infractions, which usually result from the continuation of LEVEL I misbehaviors, require the intervention of personnel on the administrative level because the execution of LEVEL I disciplinary options has failed to correct the situation. Also included in this level are misbehaviors that do not represent a direct threat to the health and safety of others but whose educational consequences are serious enough to require corrective action on the part of administrative personnel.	Continuation of unmodified LEVEL I misbehavior School tardiness Truancy Smoking in unauthorized areas Using forged notes or excuses Disruptive classroom behavior Cutting class
III. Acts directed against persons or property whose consequences *do not seriously endanger* the health or safety of others in the school. These acts might be considered criminal but most frequently can be handled by the disciplinary mechanism in the school. Corrective measures that the school should undertake, however, depend on the extent of the school's resources for mediating the situation in the best interests of all students.	Fighting (simple) Vandalism (minor) Possession/use of unauthorized substances Stealing Threats to others
IV. Acts that result *in violence* to another's person or property or which *pose a direct threat* to the safety of others in the school. These acts are clearly criminal and are so serious that they always require administrative actions that result in the immediate removal of the student from school, the intervention of law enforcement authorities and action by the board of school directors.	Unmodified LEVEL III misconducts Extortion Bomb threat Possession/use/transfer of dangerous weapons Assault/battery Vandalism Theft/possession/sale of stolen property Arson Furnishing/selling/possession of unauthorized substances

TABLE 2.1. *(continued)*

Disciplinary Structure	
Procedures	*Disciplinary Options/Responses*
· There is immediate intervention by the staff member who is supervising the student or who observes the misbehavior. · Repeated misbehavior requires a parent/teacher conference and a conference with the school counselor and/or administrator. · A proper and accurate record of the offenses and disciplinary action is maintained by the staff member.	Verbal reprimand Special assignment Behavioral contract Counseling Withdrawal of privileges Time-out room Strict supervised study Demerits Detention
· The student is referred to an administrator for appropriate disciplinary action. · The administrator meets with the student and/or teacher and makes the most appropriate response. · The teacher is informed of the administrator's action. · A proper and accurate record of the offense and the disciplinary action is maintained by the administrator. · A parental conference is held.	Teacher/schedule change Modified day Behavior modification Time-release program Social probation Peer counseling Referral to outside agency Paddling In-house suspension Transfer
· An administrator initiates disciplinary action by investigating the infraction and conferring with staff on the extent of the consequences. · The administrator meets with the student and confers with the parent about the student's misconduct and the resulting disciplinary action. · A proper and accurate record of offenses and disciplinary actions is maintained by the administrator. · There is restitution of property and damages.	Temporary removal from class Social-adjustment classes Homebound instruction Alternative program Temporary out-of-school suspension Full out-of-school suspension
· An administrator verifies the offense, confers with the staff involved and meets with the student. · The student is immediately removed from the school environment. Parents are notified. · School officials contact law enforcement agency and assist in prosecuting offender. · A complete and accurate report is submitted to the superintendent for board action. · The student is given a full due process hearing before the board.	Expulsion Alternative schools Other board action that results in appropriate placement (see discussion of expulsion issue)

FIGURE 2.1.   *Instrument Used for Collecting Data on Student Offenses*

Personal Ranking of Offenses

Directions

Rank the following student offenses from 1 to 38 according to the seriousness with which you believe each offense should be viewed. This should be a personal ranking of the way you feel. The feelings of others or existing rules and regulations within the school should not be factors in this ranking. Place a 38 next to the offense you believe should be viewed as the most serious.

_____   Making undue classroom noise

_____   Using profanity

_____   Tardy to class

_____   Major destruction of school property

_____   Rape

_____   Drug possession

_____   Defiance of teacher or other school official

_____   Lying to teacher

_____   Smoking on school property

_____   Refusing to do an assignment

_____   Truancy

_____   Assaulting a teacher

_____   Fighting with another student

_____   Extortion

_____   Kicking the chair of another student

_____   Indecent exposure

_____   Stealing from students

_____   Homosexual acts

_____   Unexcused absence from class

_____   Talking without permission

_____   Classroom harassment activities

_____   Stealing from teachers

_____ Major destruction of student property
_____ Possession of weapons
_____ Drug use
_____ Cheating
_____ Gum chewing
_____ Minor destruction of school property
_____ Writing obscene notes
_____ Sexual activity in the halls
_____ Bullying other students
_____ Whispering in class
_____ Leaving school grounds without permission
_____ Throwing eraser in classroom
_____ Lying to another student
_____ Passing notes in class
_____ Using obscene gestures in the halls
_____ Wearing clothes with obscene pictures

FIGURE 2.2. *Instrument Used for Collecting Data on Corrective Measures*

Personal Ranking of Corrective Measures

Directions

Rank the following corrective measures from 1 to 35 according to the seriousness of the occasion when they should be used. Place a 35 next to the corrective measure that in your opinion should be used for the most serious offense. This should be a personal ranking of the way you feel. The feelings of others or existing rules and regulations within the school should not be factors in this ranking. (If you would never use a particular corrective measure here, place an "N" beside this item. Please do not use an "N" beside more than four items.)

_____ Student pays for damage to property
_____ Student repairs or maintains school property
_____ Teacher counsels student after class

_____ Suspend student from school

_____ Give additional classwork assignments

_____ Call police

_____ Shout at student

_____ Isolate student from the group

_____ Withdraw a classroom privilege

_____ Detain student after school

_____ Hold parent conference with teacher

_____ Teacher sends letter to parents

_____ Expel student

_____ Student attends group counseling sessions

_____ Ignore student's behavior

_____ Student makes public apology to class

_____ Refer student to juvenile court

_____ Send student to the principal

_____ Take away recess or free time

_____ Assign repeated writing of sentences

_____ Change student's seat in classroom

_____ Suspend student from class but let him or her remain in school

_____ Hold parent conference with teacher and principal

_____ Principal sends letter to parents

_____ Have student stand in hall during class time

_____ Request help from counseling service

_____ Belittle student in private

_____ Belittle student in front of class

_____ Give verbal reprimand in private

_____ Give verbal reprimand in front of class

_____ Lower student's grade

_____ Slap

_____ Paddle

_____ Penalize entire class for actions of a few

_____ Have student(s) write essays on an assigned topic

SUMMARY

The aims of a school discipline organization extend from short-range custodial goals to long-range humanistic aims. Each school has to determine its unique situational factors and find the appropriate balance between these two sets of aims. The research on human development can help in establishing these aims. The right kind of organizational climate can foster their attainment.

The climate of a discipline organization includes the extent to which a school is viewed as contributing to the problem, the degree of responsibility school personnel feel for improving the situation, and the extent to which there is an openness to objective problem solving.

Causes of discipline problems include both societal and school factors. A school can exercise some control over its contribution to discipline problems but cannot influence societal causes as extensively. However, the responsibility for improving discipline needs to rest with those who participate in the process of helping the students learn appropriate social behaviors. A climate conducive to objective problem solving depends on a sound data base and a willingness to use data in decision making. Methods for collecting such information and using it to improve discipline are discussed in Chapter 7. First, however, the next two chapters will complete the discussion of the processes used to influence student behavior.

NOTES

1. Ewald B. Nyquist "The American 'No-Fault' Morality," *Phi Delta Kappan* 58, no. 3 (1976):275.

2. Ibid.

3. Ibid., p. 277.

4. D. J. Willower, 'Some Comments on Inquiries on Schools and Student Control," *Teachers College Record* 77 (1975):32–59.

5. Donald J. Willower, Terry L. Eidell, and Wayne K. Hoy, *The School and Pupil Control Ideology*, Penn State Studies 24, 2nd ed. (University Park, Pa.: Penn State University, 1973): pp. 4–6.

6. S. Milgram, "Some Conditions of Obedience and Disobedience to Authority," in E. D. Steiner and M. Fishbein (eds.), *Current Studies in Social Psychology* (New York: Holt, Rinehart & Winston, 1965), pp. 261–62.

7. Laurel N. Tanner, *Classroom Discipline for Effective Teaching and Learning* (New York: Holt, Rinehart & Winston, 1978), p. 4.

8. Ibid., p. 140.

9. Ibid., p. 4.

10. Willower, *The School and Pupil Control Ideology*.

58   CHAPTER 2

11. Tanner, p. 27.

12. Jean Piaget, *The Moral Judgment of the Child* (London: Routledge and Kegan Paul, 1932).

13. Lawrence Kohlberg, *Education for Justice in Moral Education* (Cambridge, Mass.: Harvard University Press, 1970), pp. 57–65.

14. William Glasser, *Schools Without Failure* (New York: Harper and Row, 1969), pp. 12–24.

15. David E. Hunt, "Conceptual Level Theory and Research as Guides to Educational Practice," *Interchange* 18, no. 4 (1977–78):82.

16. Paul Hersey and Kenneth H. Blanchard, *Management of Organizational Behavior* (Englewood Cliffs, N. J.: Prentice-Hall, 1977), pp. 217–23.

17. A. D. Leifer, N. J. Gordon, and S. B. Graves, "Children's Television: More Than More Entertainment," *Harvard Educational Review* 44 (1974):213–45.

18. R. M. Leibert, "Television and Children's Aggressive Behavior: Another Look," *American Journal of Psychoanalysis* 34 (1974):99–107.

19. John Thurston, John Feldhusen, and James J. Benning, "A Longitudinal Study of Delinquency and Other Aspects of Children's Behavior," *International Journal of Criminology and Penology* 1 (1973):341–51.

20. K. Polk and W. E. Schafer, *Schools and Delinquency* (Englewood Cliffs, N. J.: Prentice-Hall, 1972).

21. J. M. McPartland and E. L. McDill, *Violence in Schools* (Lexington, Mass.: Lexington Books, 1977).

22. National Institute of Education, *Violent Schools—Safe Schools* (Washington, D. C.: U. S. Department of Health, Education, and Welfare, 1977).

23. James M. Kelley, "The Relationship Between Teacher Anxiety Levels and Teacher Perceptions and Expectations of the Disciplinary Process" (Ph.D. dissertation, George Peabody College for Teachers, 1979), p. 49.

24. David C. McClelland and David G. Winter, *Motivating Economic Achievement* (New York: The Free Press, 1971).

25. D. L. Duke, "A Systematic Management Plan for School Discipline," *NASSP Bulletin* 61 (1977):1–10.

26. Pennsylvania State Department of Education, *Guidelines for School Discipline* (Bethesda, Md.: ERIC Document Reproduction Service, ED 144 207, 1977), pp. 13–14.

CHAPTER
3

The Reformational
Process

School officials are seldom concerned about students who act appropriately in school situations. These students (usually the majority) not only know how to act and when to act in certain ways, but they do so with a sense of personal responsibility. The "reformational process" is a systematic way to help students achieve this level of personal responsibility. It is a process that leads to internalized control rather than external control. As such, it is a long-range solution to discipline problems. Its purpose is to help students establish their own sets of principles.

BACKGROUND TO THE REFORMATIONAL
PROCESS

The process of changing inappropriate behavior is complex. Kindsvatter[1] suggests that the techniques used to help students change their behavior must be designed to fit each student's problem and help the student adjust and cope—not just to control that individual. Deibert and Harmon,[2] in *New Tools for Changing Behavior*, list the first step in the process of changing behavior as the "careful and controlled observation of the behavior as it is presently occurring." Unfortunately, at the secondary level of education it is difficult to take time for such carefully controlled observations. Accurate assessments of inappropriate situations and behaviors are important if time permits. Deibert and Harmon recommend several actions parents should take in trying to help students change their behaviors. They advise parents to:

1. Analyze the situation.
2. Determine consequences of the behavior to the student.
3. Indicate the desired behavior students should exhibit.
4. Determine conflicts with peer activities. Are the desired behaviors in conflict with what the student's friends will be doing?
5. Compromise. Establish a compromise between their (parents') expectations for the adolescent and what his or her friends are doing.
6. Involve the adolescent. Seek opinions from the student on what he or she understands to be acceptable rewards for performing appropriate behaviors.
7. Arrange expectations and payoff. Parents and adolescent set up a list of responses they expect from each other, where specific appropriate behaviors lead to appropriate payoffs.

These steps, though not complete, suggest some of the items that should be included in the reformational process.

Three general issues for the process of changing behavior emerge from the research. Madsen and Madsen identify one major issue: they state that problem identification is a logical point of contact when attempting to change behavior.

> Assessing who has the problem requires a teacher to decide if the problem really belongs to the student or to the teacher. Often both have a problem; the child, an inappropriate behavior that needs to be changed; the teacher, the responsibility to do something about changing it.[4]

Madsen and Madsen have suggested that a problem should receive direct attention and analysis, including how a student perceives the payoff for his or her behavior. After the problem has been identified, students should want to exhibit the behavior that meets the expectations of the teacher. According to Madsen and Madsen,

> Experimentation in learning demonstrates that: (a) if a student knows specifically what is expected of him and (b) he wants to do it, then (c) he

probably will. The necessity for specific measurable goals (expectations for students) have already been mentioned. The crux of the problem rests with (b), arranging the contingencies of reinforcement so that a student will want to do what the teacher expects.[5]

Creating within students the desire to change is a second major issue. Developing this desire appears to be important in the process of changing behavior. Regarding this desire, Madsen and Madsen state that:

> Behavioral change must be based on reason: people work for things that bring pleasure, people work for approval of loved ones, people change behaviors to satisfy desires they have been taught. . . .[6]

A third major issue that emerges from the various books and articles on the topic of behavior change is the concept of establishing responsibility for behavior through a plan or contract. Glasser,[7] in *Schools Without Failure*, suggests the establishment of a behavior contract with students that clearly identifies joint areas of responsibility and the structural contingencies, such as rewards. Other writers also point to the need to help students establish the capacity to stay with a task by using contracts with structural contingencies such as rewards and punishments. These three issues—problem analysis, the creation of a desire to improve, and the establishment of a contract for appropriate behavior—are the basis for steps in the reformational process.

It can be concluded from the research and from personal experience that there are three basic steps involved in helping a student reach the point where he or she has the desire and knowledge to act appropriately. These steps are:

1. Student recognition of the problem.
2. Student desire to deal with the problem or change behavior.
3. The existence of a plan of action that the student is committed to follow.

These three steps are the keys to the reformational process. There are two phases in each step. The first phase is assessment. Assessment is necessary to determine the degree to which students who have the problem are aware of it, want to improve, and have a plan of action. At the conclusion of the assessment phase, school personnel must determine if the student is ready to proceed to the next step. If it is determined that the student is not ready for the next step, appropriate work needs to commence with the student to bring about the proper level of readiness. Specific activities may be used;

methods for achieving each phase in the three steps are numerous. This chapter examines several of the more appropriate possibilities for each step.

STEP 1: STUDENT RECOGNITION
OF THE PROBLEM

Teachers and administrators should assess the degree to which the student considers his or her behavior to be inappropriate. It is assumed that the teacher is constantly monitoring the behavior of the student and determining the extent to which the behavior is causing a problem. Students have no reason to change behavior if they do not know they are doing anything wrong. The nature of this assessment can take many forms. For example, a teacher or faculty member may question the student, may seek to discover reactions by watching the student's nonverbal behavior, or may even simulate the situation to reveal the degree to which the student recognizes the problem. The purpose of each method is to determine the extent to which the student recognizes the problem. The teacher or administrator attempts to assess the degree to which the student (1) is aware of his or her past actions and feels a sense of responsibility for these actions, (2) is aware of the expectations of others, and (3) recognizes discrepancies between his or her actions and the expectations of others. Knowing the student's expectations and desires is obviously important in helping a student recognize the gaps between his or her own expectations and those of others. This knowledge will help identify the problem.

After the assessment, the teacher and/or principal may conclude that the student does not recognize the problem. The educator must initiate some plan to bring about student awareness of the problem. While we would like to be able to prescribe a set method for helping teachers assist students in identifying a discipline problem, no one method seems to be the best for the variety of situations that teachers encounter. Some teachers may decide to tell students about the expectations of others and to ask them if they understand. Other teachers may want to establish more rules and regulations or may change a student's situation to one that punishes the student or denies privileges. A penalty may attract the attention of the student so that he or she begins to ask questions as to why such treatment is necessary. Sometimes it is necessary to try a variety of techniques to help a student recognize the problem in terms of others' expectations.

Palmatier[8] suggests several approaches to completing this recognition phase—talking to students in private, listening to their view of the situation, and then informing the student of the problem. One procedure for handling counseling sessions is as follows. First, the administrator should make sure that the student is aware of the present environment. Second, the administrator should state the problem and help the student recall the incident. Third, the administrator should help the student become familiar with the expectations of others and see why the student's behavior was viewed as inappropriate. Fourth, the professional staff member should aid the student in learning to recognize the discrepancies between what was done and what is expected in a situation. Lastly, the staff member should help the student recognize the responsibility each student has for his or her own actions. Step 1 in the reformational process is completed when it has been determined by the administrator that the student recognizes the problem.

An example follows of leading a student through Step 1: the experience of Joe (a student who recently moved into the school district) in the first week at his new high school.

The school Joe had previously attended was rather lenient on smoking. Little was said when some of the students ducked outside for a cigarette or two before classes. Joe has started this practice at his new school, which is less tolerant of smoking on the school grounds. He has seen some of the other students sneaking cigarettes between classes. In addition, Joe, like many students, has not taken the time to read the student handbook that explains the smoking policy. On Thursday, Joe is found smoking by a teacher outside of the building between classes. He is taken to the office where the opportunity to move about the building during his lunch hour is denied him for a week. Joe accepts the loss of his privilege (part of the penal process) but expresses unhappiness over the entire situation.

Instead of stopping at this point, the assistant principal, Mr. Goodhines, takes the time to talk briefly with Joe. In taking Joe through Step 1 of the reformational process, Mr. Goodhines reminds Joe that he is attending a new school and that schools have different rules and regulations. In this particular school, a stringent policy is in effect with respect to smoking. Goodhines then states the problem again as he sees it and has Joe explain when it occurred. Who was responsible for Joe's smoking the cigarettes? There is no doubt that Joe is aware of what he has done.

Next, Goodhines asks Joe to review the policy on smoking in

the student handbook. After Joe has examined the policy, Mr. Good-hines has Joe explain to him what he believes the policy says. The interpretation Joe gives of the policy is accurate. During the school day smoking is permitted for twenty minutes after lunch in an area near the athletic field if the student has a signed consent statement on file from his or her parent or guardian. Goodhines follows up with a brief explanation of why the school sees the need for such a rule. Following a brief discussion, it is evident that Joe realizes that his actions were not in keeping with the expectations of the school.

Joe is now ready to go on to Step 2 of the reformational process (to be described later on). Leading the student through Step 1 was relatively easy. The severity of the problem was acknowledged by the student and the principal. The student displayed some reluctance to admit that his was a serious problem, as is often the case. At times, of course, the process will be much more difficult and time-consuming than illustrated in the fore-going example.

Two major factors in the attempt to help students view a behavioral problem are the students' mental development and their moral develop-ment. The mental stages of development are described by Piaget.[9] Ac-cording to Piaget's theory, the mental stages of growth include a stage three, concrete operations (ages 7–11), and a stage four, formal operations (ages 12–20).[10] In stage three, while students can recognize other points of view and can exchange ideas, they are unable to think conceptually and determine the scope of a problem. Generalizing about the problems of human relationships is difficult for students whose mental capacity has not yet developed beyond the concrete operations of stage three. Some students appear to be slow in their mental development, arriving at stage four as older adolescents. Consequently, until that time they are unable to partic-ipate in analytical thinking and cannot generalize about their problem. Conversely, students in stage four of mental development are usually quick to detect a problem and to project their behaviors into the future in terms of their ideals and principles.

Other students have difficulty in viewing a problem as adults view it because their moral judgment is at a different stage than that of an educator. Kohlberg's[11] stages of moral development suggest the difficulty that a principal, counselor, or teacher may encounter when trying to help students become aware of a behavioral problem. Behavior that teachers and principals expect may not be viewed by students as morally appropriate; hence, students are in a difficult situation: they may want to meet a teacher's expectations but believe that by doing so they would go against their own standards. Students may deny that a problem exists as long as they can morally justify their actions to themselves. For example, Bill is threatened by Ralph's use of power through peer penalties and rewards. Bill determines what is right and wrong by weighing the anticipated consequences from Ralph. This kind of moral code is at Kohlberg's preconventional level (stage 1). A teacher who judges right and wrong according to fixed rules and the maintenance of the social order has difficulty understanding why students do not simply do their duty to the school—e.g., by showing teachers respect—for the sake of the social order. Such a belief is at Kohlberg's conventional level (stage 4). The teacher says, "Don't you know what is right and wrong?" and the student replies facetiously, "Using whose moral value system? Mine or yours?" Unfortunately, students may see the difference between their own expectations and those of the teachers, but may believe it is not a problem—students will do the "right" things according to their own stage of moral development.

Both mental and moral development can have an impact on students' perceptions of what is a problem and what is not a problem. Slower mental development does not mean that mental recognition of a problem is less important than moral recognition. On the contrary, administrators must design methods for helping students develop both mental and moral capabilities. School personnel may sometimes be satisfied by a quick mental review that Step 1 has been fulfilled. That is, a teacher may simply observe the behavior of a student and know that the student is aware of a problem. The key point is that school personnel must be satisfied that Step 1 has been fulfilled before moving on. It is very easy for school personnel to make invalid assumptions about student readiness for Step 2. Sometimes a teacher knows perfectly well that the student has a problem and cannot believe that the student or anyone else would think otherwise.

STEP 2: DESIRE TO IMPROVE

It is not uncommon to find students who understand the behavioral problem but who do not care to meet others' expectations or to change their behavior. Such students may discover that they would rather meet their own needs and expectations, often at the expense of others. It is evident that a student must want to change or reach outside himself if he or she is to exhibit appropriate long-lasting self-controlled behavior. On occasion, students who are aware of their past actions will fail to admit that they were responsible for these actions. Their desire to improve is not under control. Such a situation can occur when students believe that they have no control over their future—i.e., that what happens to them is controlled by external forces.

Rotter[12] has described this feeling of internal versus external control in discussing the behavior of students. When students feel that their behavior is influenced by authority figures, luck, fate, or social change, they believe they are externally controlled. Students who are controlled internally have a feeling of responsibility and believe they are able to manipulate and control the environment. Furthermore, students who feel internally controlled perceive a cause-effect relationship between their behavior and what happens to them. In some students, the feeling of external control is so strong that they do not feel any personal responsibility for a behavior problem or for a discrepancy that may exist between the expectations of others and the behavior the students exhibit. To such students, the situation is out of control; their behavior is not something they can manage. Hence, a personal desire to improve is not a choice that these students can make.

It is possible to change a student's behavior through controlling environmental rewards and punishments. But after the school ceases to be a controlling influence, the student must be able to assume personal responsibility for acting appropriately. Training toward self-control, therefore, must be started while the student is still in school. One of the key indicators of whether a student wants to improve is the degree to which that student seems to regret what has taken place and the intent behind the action. If a student expresses concern for a wrongdoing (i.e., believes his or her actions were morally wrong and inappropriate) and an administrator senses that the student really regrets the action, then a desire to change may be presumed. In many instances, this element cannot be assessed without examining the student's present attitude toward past offenses. The important issue is the degree to which the student wants to improve. If a student has not repeatedly caused problems, it is likely that this student does not need as strong a commitment to improve as the student who has a record of repeated offenses. Techniques for making this assessment include observing the student's nonverbal reactions to an incident, talking with the student about personal feelings, and determining the degree to which the student is able to relate the most recent incident to past offenses.

If it is determined that a student does not have a sufficient desire to improve even though he or she may recognize the problem, then the faculty, staff, and principal must all work to help the student develop a positive attitude toward changing his or her behavior. This is easier said than done. Most student behavior reflects student needs and desires for certain rewards. According to Deibert and Harmon, to be consistent with the law of reinforcement:

> We therefore have to assume that any behavior which is repeated again and again must be producing a reward (desired outcome). Otherwise, according to the law of reinforcement, it would not reoccur. Only behaviors that produce rewards (desired outcomes) tend to be repeated. Therefore, if we observe a behavior occurring repeatedly, we have to assume that there is present in the situation some reward or desired outcome which supports it.[13]

If the student and teacher can identify the reward the student is receiving, then it would seem appropriate to try any technique or procedure that might help the student receive a similar or replacement reward. Alternative methods of achieving rewards can include helping the student recognize the contributions the student may make to the group, to individuals in the organization, and to him- or herself. In most instances, when a student recognizes the contribution that can be made to oneself by satisfying personal needs or desires through appropriate behavior, the student's attitude will improve.

Some students do not find it easy to imagine themselves making positive contributions to themselves or others. Techniques to help a student develop the desire to improve include appealing to the student's desire to be trusted and awakening the student's desire for some immediate reward that would not normally be received. Another technique involves penalties that students will experience if they fail to act appropriately. It is best to keep the focus on the desired behavior, because thoughts about inappropriate behavior, regardless of the penalties, may in fact prompt the very behavior one wishes discontinued.

A danger exists in using rewards and penalties to help a student develop the desire to behave appropriately. The student may feel that the only reason for acting appropriately is to receive a personal "payoff" from such behavior or to avoid specific penalties. If students are to develop self-control on a long-range basis, it is important that they learn to act appropriately in situations where there may be little or no penalty or immediate personal payoff. People are not machines, and this fact needs to be considered in working with students to develop a desire for appropriate behavior. The fewer rewards and penalties that have to be used in bringing about the desire to behave appropriately, the better—particularly if the rewards are external.

The preceding case of Joe and his smoking problem can now be continued to illustrate Step 2 in the reformational process. At the conclusion of Step 1, Joe had realized his actions were not meeting the expectations of the new school. However, it is possible that Joe saw that his actions really antagonized the school personnel and caused quite a stir. He may enjoy controlling the behavior of school officials. Thus, even though Joe may realize that his actions do not meet school expectations, he may have no desire to change because of his feeling of being in control of things. Leading Joe through Step 2 is an attempt to create in him a desire to correct his problem behavior.

Since Joe is new to this school, the assistant principal, Mr. Goodhines, decides to talk with Joe about how the students are integrally involved in helping to manage the school. He explains the school's Leadership Corps and how it works with the principal in establishing and monitoring school rules. He further explains that the smoking regulation is one that the Leadership Corps helped develop and one that the student body generally supports. He tells Joe about other kinds of authority the students exercise, such as approving all student awards and monitoring all financial accounts within the school. As he talks, Goodhines detects a noticeable increase in interest on Joe's part. Joe further displays his interest by beginning to ask questions about the school. This may be an attempt to manipulate the principal's behavior, but is likely to result from a sincere interest. Before long, Joe is asking how one goes about becoming a member of the Leadership Corps. He likes the concept of student involvement and sees how obeying the smoking policy has possible payoffs to him as well as to the other students. Joe now sees a need to follow the smoking regulations of the school. He is now ready to go on to Step 3.

This illustration of a student progressing through Step 2 of the reformational process may appear somewhat like a television serial. In reality, such happy endings are not always possible, but whatever the motivation the student must have an internal desire to act appropriately before it is possible to go on to Step 3. School personnel should be cautious about deciding when a student is ready to move to acceptance of a corrective action plan.

The school official must be convinced that the student is sincere in his or her desire to act appropriately. Sometimes a student will say, "Yeah, I want to act better," but it is quite evident that real desire is missing. More than a verbal commitment is needed. The desire to improve is closely related to the student's commitment to an acceptable plan. And unless the student recognizes the problem and has some desire to improve inappropriate behavior, the behavior is likely to be repeated, even with the best of plans and contracts made through Step 3 of the reformational process.

STEP 3: RECOGNITION AND COMMITMENT TO AN ACCEPTABLE PLAN

The third step in the reformational process is concerned primarily with the student's plans. The student and educator must both agree to an acceptable plan or contract and the student must have a strong commitment to the plan. Stuart, Jayaratne, and Tripodi[14] worked with teachers and parents to develop behavioral contracts with a group of secondary students. Significant improvements in behavior were found for the students with contracts, compared to those who received a different form of attention. It is a necessity that a student mentally develop a plan and, in some cases, physically produce the plan for changing behavior in certain situations. Administrators should assess whether the student has a clear and acceptable purpose and a workable strategy for achieving that purpose. In making this assessment, it is important to determine the clarity of the student's aims and the appropriateness of those aims. It is not infrequent to find a student who has a purpose that is not in keeping with the aims of the institution. Assessment must include not only the appropriateness of the student's goals and desires, but the clarity of the goals and the student's commitment to them.

It is important also for a principal to assess the degree to which a student knows how he or she plans to achieve the established aims and whether the student will accept responsibility for carrying out the plan. A student who cannot assume the full responsibility for it needs assistance. Frequently, a student needs to build support and assistance into the plan to be successful in changing the behavior. If the student is unwilling to share with someone else a portion of the responsibility for his or her plan, it is unlikely that the plan will be successful. The principal, moreover, needs to assess the degree to which the student has included in the plan an opportunity for periodic evaluations or feedback. Without feedback the student has no way to assess the degree to which progress is being made toward the desired behavior. Positive movement must be able to be assessed if the student is to change behavior. In sum, an assessment must be made of the degree to which the student is committed to fulfilling the entire contract. Without this commitment the planned appropriate behavior may not occur.

Of the three steps of the reformational process, Step 3 generally requires the most time. It is often best accomplished by working individually with a student to develop aims and strategies for achieving specific goals. Several works in the literature indicate a process for obtaining this result. Laurel Tanner, in writing about models for discipline, discusses a personal, social growth model as follows:

> A third emergent model of discipline is the personal social growth model. Unlike other models, the goal is to enable individuals to manage their own behavior. This ability comes from experience. To develop self-direction in pupils is to provide them with opportunities to choose appropriate behavior for meeting a goal or solving a problem.[15]

Tanner goes on to say that:

> The ability to manage one's own behavior requires the feeling that one is internally controlled rather than externally controlled. Teachers can help pupils develop this feeling by pointing out when they have successfully completed a task by their own efforts, they can foster internal locus of control in unsocialized pupils by redirecting negative behavior into socially useful behavior.[16]

Homme[17] has developed ten basic rules to describe the characteristics of proper contingency contracting. Polsgrove and Mosley[18] suggest a four-phase program, including student contracting, to gradually develop student self-control. The requirements for an effective behavioral contract emerge from such works as these. Three important criteria are suggested for helping the student develop a plan: (1) Aims must be clarified, (2) strategies must be developed, and (3) evaluation (feedback) must occur.

The first criterion for a successful plan is that it should reflect a clear and reasonable aim. For example:

A student who had been suspended from English class was establishing a plan for improving classroom behavior. Applying some of the steps in the need-for-achievement model described by Aschuler, the student discussed with a teacher the environmental or school factors that would prevent success, the fears of failure, the hopes for success, the feelings of failing and succeeding, and the help the student might seek in attempting to avoid a recurrence of the problem.[19] A day later, the student was again sent to the office from the same English class.

What went wrong? From the information provided it appears that a major ingredient in the plan was missing. Seemingly, the student did not clearly define the aim or the way he or she would act in English class. The student did focus on some elements that should be considered in establishing plans, but the goals were never explicit.

Avoiding inappropriate behavior is not the same as a clearly defined aim describing what the student will be doing in place of the inappropriate behavior. A properly defined aim specifies the precise positive activities in which the student imagines him- or herself participating. For example:

One student wrote three specific aims to achieve in math class after having had a number of minor problems in that class. These aims were: (1) complete outside assignments for the next five days, (2) answer at least three of the teacher's questions, and (3) select a front seat in the room to avoid talking with others during the period. The math teacher and this student, after reaching agreement and implementing the plan for five days, extended the same contract to ten days, then to one month. The student went six months before having another minor disciplinary incident.

One of the difficult aspects of helping a student set goals or aims is determining the level of difficulty of the tasks. The aims should not be considered too easy or too difficult by the student. Some students may try to set such aims to avoid assuming responsibility for the success or failure of the task. Aims that a person considers reasonable tend to make the person more responsible for the outcome of the plan.[20]

The second criterion for a student's plan is the development of a strategy for achieving the desired aims. For example:

A student who had been caught smoking in the restroom decided to go to the toilet areas of the school twice during the day, around 10:00 A.M. and 2:00 P.M., to take care of personal needs without stopping for a smoke, staying in those areas no more than four minutes. The student was asked if a permit to the school's lunch-time smoking area was needed. The student indicated that the desire to smoke could be handled without a permit. Two days later the student was again caught smoking in the restroom.

This student probably had good intentions and was committed to achieving the aim. In developing the strategy, there was an underestimation of the amount of external control the student would need to accomplish the aim. As the situation worked out, the student did need a permit to the school's smoking area during the lunch period. With the built-in support of the smoking area permit, the student was able to follow the original plan. In this case, the strategy for achieving the student's aim should have included an alternative way to satisfy his need to smoke.

As a final example of the application of Step 3, the illustration of Joe and his smoking problem is extended below.

Initially, Joe needs to get to the point where his aim is to smoke only after lunch and in the designated area. (Perhaps his ultimate aim should be to stop smoking altogether.) In developing a strategy to achieve this aim, Joe first will need to obtain a permission slip from his parents. Secondly, Joe may decide not to carry cigarettes with him during the day. Provision might be made for him to obtain his cigarettes from his locker after lunch and return them to the locker before his next class. Thirdly, Joe might decide that he does not need to go near an exit between classes, thus reducing the temptation to borrow a cigarette and slip out. A time might be set aside as part of the evaluation phase for Joe to check with the assistant principal each week to report on his progress and level of satisfaction with the plan.

In developing the methods students will employ in their plans, the following issues should be considered:

1. The degree to which the students can be responsible for the strategies themselves (internal control).
2. The availability of and need for outside assistance, external controls, and structured contingencies.
3. Obstacles that could prohibit the implementation of the plan.

Changes in behavior are likely when the student receives help in detailing a reasonable step-by-step process toward the aims.

The last criterion for the development of a successful plan is the opportunity for the student to get feedback on the student's progress. Checkpoints and feedback reports can provide appropriate reinforcement or show the need for adjustments in the plan. For example:

> One student requested feedback at the end of each class period for a week. A 3" x 5" card for recording was devised. Figure 3.1 shows the type of card the student used. Notes were entered on the card by each of the student's teachers after each class. The student knew almost immediately how he was being perceived and received reinforcement for appropriate behavior. At the end of a week, the student took the card to the vice-principal to discuss the progress made in correcting his behavior.

Helping the student plan for continuous feedback is a necessary step in the formation of a successful plan.

Teachers' Initials	M General Perfor-mance	M Social Effect-iveness	T General Perfor-mance	T Social Effect	W General Perfor-mance	W Social Effect	T General Perfor-mance	T Social Effect	F General Perfor-mance	F Social Effect	Comments (over)
1											
2											
3											
4											
5											
6											
7											

Performance Key

A - Excellent   D - Fair

B - Very Good   E - Poor

C - Good

Social Effectiveness Key

1. Appropriate attitudes and behavior
2. Could use slight improvement
3. Needs improvement

FIGURE 3.1.   *Weekly Student Performance and Social Effectiveness Report*

If the three requirements for reformational planning are met—clear aims, strategies for achieving them, and designed feedback episodes—the plan is likely to be carried out successfully. It is necessary that the plan be acceptable to the student and be one to which he or she is committed. However, the plan must also be acceptable to school officials. Both parties must agree on the plan and believe it will work. Since the goal of a comprehensive disciplinary process is to develop individuals who are capable of exhibiting self-control, investing energy in helping students plan their own behavioral goals and strategies is a worthwhile use of professional time.

What should be done if a student breaks the contract or does not follow the plan? This is a legitimate question that has frequently arisen in seminars conducted by the authors. It may be necessary to invoke an immediate penalty in response to a breach of contract, but the steps in the reformational process must again be followed with the student, unless this violation of the plan was the "last straw" that results in expulsion. A staff administrator and the student should conduct a detailed analysis of the steps that led to an unsuccessful contract. Did the student recognize the problem? Does he or she really want to change? Was the plan sound? A new or revised plan must be developed, perhaps with more external controls and with the extension of less trust to the student. A person learns that trust is earned and that it will be extended as an ability to fulfill certain responsibilities is demonstrated.

SUMMARY

This chapter has presented a reformational process that is designed to help young adults develop the desire and knowledge to act appropriately with minimal need for external constraints or rewards. The three basic steps of the process are: (1) student recognition of the problem, (2) student desire to change behavior positively, and (3) establishment of an appropriate plan of action to which the student is committed. Each step has an assessment phase to determine the student's status. If appropriate readiness on the part of the student is not apparent, a second phase follows to raise that readiness to an acceptable level.

NOTES

1. R. Kindsvatter, "A New View of the Dynamics of Discipline," *Phi Delta Kappan* 59 (1978):322–25.

2. Alvin N. Deibert and Alice J. Harmon, *New Tools for Changing Behavior*, rev. ed. (Champaign, Ill.: Research Press, 1973), p. 37.

3. Ibid., pp. 97–99.

4. Charles H. Madsen, Jr. and Clifford K. Madsen, *Teaching/Discipline* (Boston: Allyn and Bacon, 1974), p. 33.

5. Ibid., p. 42.

6. Ibid., p. 23.

7. William Glasser, *Schools Without Failure* (New York: Harper & Row, 1969), pp. 22–24.

8. Larry L. Palmatier, *De-Pupiling the Defiant Student: The Guidance Clinic* (West Nyack, N.Y.: Parker Publishing Co., 1976), p. 3.

9. Jean Piaget, *The Psychology of Intelligence* (New York: Harcourt, 1956), pp. 87–158.

10. Ibid.

11. Lawrence Kohlberg, *Education for Justice in Moral Education* (Cambridge, Mass.: Harvard University Press, 1970), pp. 57–65.

12. Julian B. Rotter, "Generalized Expectancies for Internal Versus External Control of Reinforcement," *Psychological Monographs on Congenitive Processes* 80 (1966): p. 1.

13. Deibert and Harmon, p. 15.

14. R. B. Stuart, S. Jayaratne, and T. Tripodi, "Changing Adolescent Deviant Behaviour Through Reprogramming the Behaviour of Parents and Teachers: An Experimental Evaluation," *Canadian Journal of Behavioural Science* 8 (1976):132–44.

15. Laurel N. Tanner, *Classroom Discipline for Effective Teaching and Learning* (New York: Holt, Rinehart & Winston, 1978), p. 15.

16. Ibid.

17. L. Homme, *How to Use Contingency Contracting in the Classroom* (Champaign, Ill.: Research Press, 1970), pp. 14–21.

18. Lewis Polsgrove and William Mosley, "Management for Inner City Classrooms," paper presented at the 54th annual International Convention of the Council for Exceptional Children, Chicago, Ill., April 4–9, 1976, p. 17.

19. Alfred S. Aschuler, Diane Tabor, and James McIntyre, *Teaching Achievement Motivation* (Middletown, Conn.: Education Ventures, 1971), p. 43–47.

20. David C. McClelland and David G. Winter, *Motivating Economic Achievement* (New York: The Free Press, 1971).

4

The Penal
and Approval Processes

The reformational process, as we have seen, seeks an internal change in the student so that he or she will have the knowledge and desire to act appropriately in the future. The approval process and the penal process use external variables as a means of controlling a student's behavior for his or her benefit as well as for the benefit of other individuals and groups. Redd and Sleater state that "All living organisms—animals as well as people—will continue to do things that bring them rewards and will stop doing things that result in punishment (the law of effect)."[1] The approval process uses positive cause-effect relationships with the environment while the penal process uses cause-effect relationships in a negative, fear-inducing manner. The penal process fulfills a group expectation that certain actions will be penalized, whereas the approval process fulfills a group expectation that particular behaviors will be rewarded. The reformational process is often a long and time-consuming process, as opposed to the penal process which is a short-range answer to the discipline problem. Penalties may be selected and applied so that they also contribute to the reformational process, but the primary use is to satisfy the group expectation that some behaviors will be punished.

THE PENAL PROCESS

A basic assumption of our society is that there is a need to control an individual's actions so that the person will benefit, or at least not be detrimental to, other individuals, groups, and organizations with whom the individual is associated. For instance, it has been determined by lawmakers that driving on the right-hand side of the road at a speed less than the stated limit makes driving safer for all of us. If a person is apprehended by a law enforcement officer for driving on the wrong side of the road at an excessive speed, he or she may expect to receive an appropriate penalty as determined by our legal and judicial systems.

Authors, educators, and psychologists hold differing opinions about the types of actions the penal process represents. Glasser, in discussing meetings called to solve social problems, points out that faultfinding and punishment should be avoided during these meetings. He writes that:

> The pseudo-solution of problems through faultfinding is one of the most worthless pursuits continually to occupy all segments of our society. Its constant companion, punishment, is equally ineffective. Punishment usually works only the first time, if at all. After the first time it works only with successful people, who ordinarily don't need it. Much more often, punishment serves as an excuse for not solving a problem rather than leading toward a solution.[2]

Redd and Sleater add that:

> Many behaviorists feel that punishment is a bad thing. B. F. Skinner warns that it can have disastrous side effects and that it fosters subservience. Others claim that punishment just does not work. Perhaps it is because the idea of inflicting pain and suffering is repugnant and psychologists have intended, by and large, to oppose the use of punishment. . . . The behaviorists' recommendations appear to be based on emotion and conjecture rather than on clear scientific evidence, for little research within psychology has been directed toward the possible harmful effects of punishment. It is not surprising that psychologists really know very little about the adverse consequences that affect our behavior. But, research with animals fully shows that . . . specifically, effects of punishment seem to depend on the circumstances in which it is experienced.[3]

Redd and Sleater also point out that behaviorists in general do not recommend punishment.

The penal process is an important component of the discipline process, and the cause-effect relationships that the penal process represents are a necessary and effective means for enforcing rules and regulations. In fact, Solomon[4] indicates that the suppressive power of punishment has been understated. Effective enforcement through the use of punishment contributes to the welfare of all individuals within the school setting. The penal process illustrates cause-effect relationships in their purest form. Students learn that specific inappropriate behaviors on their part will elicit certain unpleasant responses on the part of school personnel. Dreikurs and Cassel[5] point out the difference between logical consequences that express the reality of the social order and punishment that has no real connection to the inappropriate behavior. The penal process includes those unpleasant responses reflecting the rules of living which must be learned to function effectively in society. There is a fine line between logical consequences, defined in this way, and punishments.

Our society is based on cause-effect relationships. In the earlier example of inappropriate driving habits, society demands payment for infractions of the law. It is conceivable that a careless driver realizes at the moment he or she is stopped by an officer than an error has occurred and determines not to repeat such actions. However, even though in this instance the person has been rehabilitated in an extremely short time (even before a penalty has been received), society still demands that he or she pay for the inappropriate action. There may be debate over how severe the "payment" should be, but few would advocate doing away with the payment. Thus, if one accepts the premise that one of the functions of school is to prepare the student to take his or her place in society, it certainly would be unrealistic to place a student in a school environment that did not reflect cause-effect relationships, both positive and negative.

Knowing that certain negative consequences will follow certain behaviors serves as an external control over students and members of other groups in preventing some discipline problems. A student who has a fear of going to the principal's office may act appropriately to avoid this penalty. Likewise, if members of a group know that they will receive a penalty commensurate with their offense, they must weigh their possible actions against the probable consequences. Often this is enough to deter inappropriate actions by group members. The distinct possibility also exists that the student will come to value and enjoy appropriate behavior while avoiding unpleasant consequences. In other words, even though initially the appropriate behavior was brought about through the knowledge of specific penalties that would be forthcoming if inappropriate behavior was exhibited, the desire to act appropriately can later become internalized, and thus a true long-range change in behavior can occur. For example, it is very possible that by behaving appropriately in order to avoid a penalty, a student may experience significant personal satisfaction in working toward the goals of a group.

Some writers contend that nothing more negative than ignoring a student's behavior should be used in school discipline. They contend that ignoring inappropriate behavior or not reinforcing will make it disappear. For instance, Deibert and Harmon write:

> So it is that research into behavioral laws not only points out the value of attention in encouraging appropriate behaviors, but the equal importance of withholding attention from, or ignoring, inappropriate behaviors in order to eliminate them.[6]

Problems with this approach may develop. One is that anything that reinforces inappropriate behavior must be identified and removed, but identifying the reinforcement(s) may be difficult. A second problem is that simply ignoring behavior that is injurious to others and to oneself has neither party's best interests at heart. If a teacher is intent on controlling behavior, it may be necessary to ignore it while several variables possibly affecting the behavior are manipulated to find the reinforcing variables. Thirdly, the students' cognitive processes could very easily lead them to assume that certain behavior is appropriate because it is ignored. Students could assume that the teacher has no adverse feelings toward the behavior.

Inappropriate behavior should seldom be ignored. It might be appropriate to do so when a student is seeking adult recognition in the teacher's reactions to inappropriate behavior. In some instances, a logical penalty is needed. Few teachers can do without this tool in their attempts to maintain a good learning environment in the classroom.

Implementing the Penal Process

Much of the research on the effects of penalties in the school setting has involved younger children and exceptional children. Little research has been done in the effects of penalties on adolescents and young adults in school-related situations. However, through analysis of past research and personal experiences, some guidelines emerge for an effective application of the penal process. One guideline recognizes the importance of timing in administering a penalty. An inverse relationship exists between the suppression of inappropriate behavior because of a penalty and the time lapse between the behavior and the penalty.[7] The inappropriate behavior will be minimally affected by the penalty if a considerable amount of time has elapsed. This fact suggests that as often as possible the penalty should be administered within the classroom setting, where the time lapse will be shortest and the cause-effect relationship greatest. Sending a student to the principal's office for the administration of a penalty increases the time span between the commitment of the offense and the receipt of the penalty. However, sitting in the principal's office for a period of time reflecting on the inappropriate behavior and the possible penalty affects some students to begin to change their behavior. (Sitting in the office becomes part of the penalty.)

A second guideline involves the effect of penalties when no behavior alternatives are presented.[8] The need for a student to know what accepted modes of behavior he or she might use in similar circumstances in the future is emphasized in Step 3 of the reformational process. Any penalty must be combined with an explanation of alternative forms of behavior if it is to be effective.

The third guideline suggests that extended periods of penalties should usually be avoided. Penalties have a tendency to lose their effect when intensity is gradually increased over a series of penalizing situations. For instance, a firmly stated "no" seems to be more effective than a shake of the head followed by increasingly stronger "no's."[9] Perhaps firmness and decisiveness are the order of the day. Again, teacher discretion is encouraged. One must guard against "penalty overkill."

A fourth guideline states that consistency in administering penalties is a necessity. Redd and Sleater write:

> The negative consequences which are fairly mild or are presented occasionally are less likely to change behavior than if they are intense and experienced frequently.[10]

The penal process must be used in conjunction with the reformational and approval processes. A principal who uses one or two of the processes to the exclusion of the third is probably lowering position effectiveness relative to discipline. Penalties must be administered or disapproval expressed in some manner every time a particular misbehavior occurs. A misbehavior must not be punished one day and ignored the next. In addition, some consistency should exist throughout a school as to what constitutes a misbehavior. A range of alternatives should be established for punishing some of the more common misbehaviors. Frequency of occurrence is another factor in determining penalties and is dealt with elsewhere in this book.

A final guideline for the penal process is that the student should know why he or she is being penalized. Such awareness strengthens the cause-effect relationship between the behavior and the penalty. It is quite easy for misunderstandings to arise between student and teacher as to why a particular penalty was administered. A student, for example, may feel that being isolated from others for two hours is a rather severe consequence for being two minutes late to class. This student was not made aware of the true reason for his isolation; it was assigned not because the student was two minutes late for class but because the student was untruthful as to why he had been late. This guideline suggests that the use of reason in lieu of emotion in establishing and administering penalties is indispensable. It seems obvious that a staff member should be thinking clearly when considering penalties for students, but all too often the heat of a confrontation leads to emotionally laden decisions.

Limitations on the Penal Process

It would be inappropriate to leave this discussion of the penal process without a word of caution concerning the possible negative consequences of inappropriately administered penalties. One limitation is that a student may choose to generalize the penalty to situations for which it was not established. For instance, the student may become moody, cease to respond to the teacher, or stop learning. Another limitation is that the use of extreme penalties can also produce increased aggression, particularly if a student feels the penalty was arbitrary or unreasonable (a punishment). An individual who perceives himself or herself as being treated unfairly tends to strike back in some manner. Our society and, hopefully, our schools provide acceptable ways to strike back. Processes are available to address alleged grievances. However, through frustration and/or lack of knowledge, the student likely will strike back in ways quite unacceptable.[11]

A third limitation is that to a student who is in need of attention, a penalty can be viewed as a reward—the attention desired by the student. That is, every time the student receives a penalty he or she may, in fact, feel rewarded through the recognition thus received. The effectiveness of a penalty thus is related to the student's view of the penalty—it may serve as a means of satisfying the student's need for recognition or control. In some instances when the penalty is viewed as a payoff or recognition, the inappropriate behavior increases when the penalty is reduced. Deibert and Harmon suggest this outcome may occur. In these situations, a student is trying desperately to get the payoff (punishment or control over others), which worked before.[12] Deibert and Harmon call this "limit testing." But ignoring or stopping the penalty will produce a reduction in the amount of attention the student receives. It may be necessary to increase attention and praise for other behaviors (appropriate ones) that have not been rewarded.[13]

Improper administration of penalties may lower the student's self-esteem but this effect may not be long lasting. Few people go through life without some humbling experiences. In some situations, embarrassment is an appropriate penalty. However, we must hasten to add that in other situations the use of embarrassment is most inappropriate and detrimental.

The past decade seems to have brought about a lessening of emphasis in society and in schools on helping students learn about their responsiblity to others and to the groups with whom they associate. Penalties when used as the logical consequences for inappropriate behavior can help change students' behavior as it relates to other people.

THE APPROVAL PROCESS

This section examines how school administrators can prevent inappropriate student behavior in the first place or, conversely, how they can maintain or increase desirable student behavior. The approval process differs from the penal and reformational processes. The penal process uses penalties to reflect a teacher's disapproval and to punish a student for inappropriate behavior after it occurs. This process teaches the student about the cause-effect relationship between socially unacceptable behavior and the needs of the school as an organization. The penal process, in part, is a response to other people's expectations and is used to induce fear. It is also a means of providing immediate feedback to the student and others about inappropriate behavior. In the reformational process, the three steps (an individual student's awareness of the problem, his or her desire to act appropriately, and a plan to learn to do so) suggest that there is an internal state that a student must reach before the student can exhibit appropriate behavior in the same set of circumstances. The approval process, by contrast, can be implemented by a teacher with all students, prior to the observation of any inappropriate student behavior. The approval process is never punitive; in this way it differs from other forms of behavior modification. It is designed to create good feelings rather than unpleasant ones and is similar to the penal process in that it provides immediate feedback to students and can fulfill others' expectations. The approval process is one alternative for achieving Step 2 in the reformational process.

Although the approval process is external to the student rather than internal, it can help to bring about an internal change. It creates an environment that accentuates and rewards positive, appropriate behavior. When a student is unaware of the teacher's plan to encourage appropriate behavior, the approval process can bring about a desire to act appropriately. Many teachers use the approval process without realizing it. For example, a teacher may be pleased with a student's social behavior, so the teacher verbally commends the student for his or her actions. The teacher's physical posture and facial expressions reflect approval; the teacher approaches the student with an attitude of warmth. To show the extent of the approval, the teacher may provide the student with additional privileges.

The approval process of rewards and incentives has some limitations for modifying behavior. The process assumes that student behavior is influenced by external environmental factors, primarily the behavior of others. But Davidson and Seidman,[14] in their review of studies using behavior modification techniques, conclude that these approaches have generally had positive effects on social behaviors and have led to a reduction in aggressive behavior, violence, and delinquency. According to Deibert and Harmon, the law of reinforcement states that "any behavior that is followed by a reward is likely to increase in frequency and any behavior that is not followed by a reward will tend to decrease in frequency."[15]

Steps in the Approval Process

The first step in the approval process is to identify the social behavior that students are to learn. It is not uncommon for teachers to approve student behavior that they later discover they do not want the student to repeat. For example:

> One teacher thought he would reward a ninth-grade girl who had a tendency to make sarcastic and often challenging remarks. The teacher approved of this behavior by picking up on sarcastic statements and frequently debating with the student, thus giving her recognition. (The teacher used the debate to provide a break in serious classroom discussion.) As would be expected, the student began to exhibit the behavior more frequently, and exchanges between the

student and the teacher got completely out of hand. After several weeks of reinforcing this student's behavior, it was difficult to decrease the frequency of her remarks.

The teacher may have mistakenly identified the behavior as one that should be reinforced. It is essential that teachers, with student involvement where possible, identify the socially acceptable behaviors that students are to learn.

The second step in the approval process involves determining which method(s) of approval will reinforce the appropriate behavior. Madsen and Madsen list the following potential reinforcers:[16]

1. Words (spoken and written rules).
2. Facial expressions.
3. Physical proximity.
4. Activities and privileges (group or individual).
5. Things (tokens, materials, food, playthings, money).

Each of the above can be used to reward appropriate student behavior. The first three are personal methods of approval. For example, a teacher may talk to a student, provide visual approval, or give the student special privileges such as additional freedom and responsibility. For some students, a word of approval is enough. Others need a smile and an approving word or two, while still others need social rewards—recognition, and autonomy. O'Leary and O'Leary[17] report that there appears to be an increase in the use of these natural reinforcers rather than tangible rewards. The use of nontangible reinforcers may help the teacher who abhors the use of extrinsic rewards to accept the approval process as one tool for improving student behavior.

Several factors influence the effect of rewards or reinforcers. Deibert and Harmon state that there are four principles of the law of reinforcement: timing, pairing, scheduling, and shaping.[18] Deibert and Harmon argue that the time lapsed between an appropriate act and the giving of the reward is important: "For rewards to be most effective they must be given immediately after the behavior occurs that we want the children to learn."[19] The second principle, pairing, is the use of two types of rewards simultaneously. According to Deibert and Harmon, this "makes it even more certain that the person will want to repeat the behavior which produces them."[20] Deibert and Harmon believe physical and verbal rewards used together can provide more reinforcement than each when given separately.

The principle of scheduling is associated with how frequently rewards are given. Deibert and Harmon distinguish the timing principle from the frequency principle by stating that the former governs the speed with which a reward is given and the latter governs intervals with which it is given. They further break down the scheduling principle into two phases: the continuous phase and the partial phase. In the continuous phase, a student is rewarded every time he or she exhibits an appropriate behavior. In partial scheduling, the frequency of rewards is decreased as the student repeats the behavior. Deibert and Harmon believe that rewards given to students half the time they show appropriate behavior should not be scheduled. For example, rather than providing a reward for every third instance of appropriate behavior, it would be better to reward students without a planned schedule. Redd and Sleater state that "a reward given out more rarely can often have a far more powerful effect on behavior than a reward that comes every time a behavior occurs."[21] An intermittent reward may be a more effective reinforcer. Deibert and Harmon's fourth principle, shaping, holds that appropriate complex behavior can be learned most easily by breaking it into steps or single responses. Shaping involves analyzing a task, breaking it into small pieces, and rewarding the student for accomplishing each individual stage of the task. Ribes-Inesta and Bandura[22] describe methods for shaping the attendance behavior of students who exhibit violent behavior.

The second task in the approval process, selecting the method of reward and considering what factors will influence its effect, was considered earlier. The third step in the approval process is the close monitoring of the student's behavior after the reward or reinforcement has been arranged. The evaluation of a reward's effectiveness is essential. For example, if a teacher smiles in response to appropriate behavior, the smile may be in part responsible for the behavior.

A fourth step in the approval process involves determining when the external approving agent can be terminated. At some point, a student should find within himself or herself the rewards and reinforcement necessary to continue appropriate behavior. As soon as a teacher has determined that the student has achieved the second step in the reformational process without the help of external approval, the reward should be discontinued—if it is a structured, unnatural, environmental response (e.g., giving tokens).

An example of the application of the four steps in the approval process is shown below.

Step 1

The teacher wants a particular student, Ann, to listen to other students when they speak in class. She decides that Ann is listening when she is not interrupting others with her own talking.

Step 2

The teacher decides to provide verbal approval coupled with a privilege. After Ann has listened to another student talk, she will say, "Ann, I am certain you heard————; what might you add in response to the statements just made?" In effect, the teacher praises Ann and gives her the privilege of responding or talking. This is something Ann apparently likes to do.

Step 3

The teacher watches Ann's behavior to see if she jumps at this opportunity to speak. If she does, then her previous behavior of being quiet has been properly reinforced. But if the verbal recognition and privilege are viewed as punishments, the reverse effect has occurred, and Ann has been punished as a result of listening to others.

Step 4

After several days of rewarding Ann for listening, the teacher skips the reinforcement to see if the habit of listening has been formed. Can Ann go without the reward without slipping back into her old style of interrupting others? The teacher reduces the reinforcement until none is needed.

Learning to apply the four steps of the approval process is essential to the long-range prevention of discipline problems. With appropriate training, teachers can learn to apply the process effectively.

The law of reinforcement or the approval process is a necessary factor in the entire discipline process, but its application in the educational system needs to be considered very carefully. Redd and Sleater discuss the potential hazards of reinforcement. They assert that by deceptively simple changes in responding to what people do, long-standing habits and patterns in behavior can be radically altered. They note that, "Classic examples are the practice of slavery and the regimes of totalitarian governments. With behavior modification at its disposal, there is practically no limit to the control that one group of people could extend or exert over another."[23] In brief, reinforcement is effective, "but danger ensues when control is not balanced. . . .";[24] that is, when the process of manipulating other people's behavior is carried to extremes. The approval process, though effective in many instances, has some limitations to which we turn in the subsequent section.

Limitations on the Approval Process

One of the limitations of the approval process is assessing the effectiveness of different rewards or tokens. The use of a smile to induce different appropriate behaviors by the same student provides one method for ascertaining effectiveness. If the reward (a smile) is working, it should become an incentive for different kinds of appropriate behavior. An example follows of another less effective method that teachers sometimes use to determine the influence of a particular reward on student behavior.

A teacher is concerned with the number of times a student is late for class. The teacher first counts frequency of events (tardiness) to use as a baseline. It is extremely important to establish this baseline data when attempting to determine to what extent a reward has caused a change in behavior.[25,26] During this phase the teacher does nothing to try to change the behavior of the student. Once the baseline information is available, the teacher tries a technique such as giving recognition to the student when he is on time. While the teacher is providing this reinforcement, the teacher records the number of times the student is late for class. If the technique works, the number of times the student is prompt will increase and the tardiness decrease. But suppose the principal has intervened by standing in the hall. Is it the teacher's or the principal's efforts that cause the behavior to change? To be sure, the teacher may stop providing recognition when the student is prompt. Suppose the student's tardiness now goes back to the level it had before the teacher provided recognition (even though the principal is still in the hall). It becomes evident that the teacher is probably controlling the behavior of the student. Now, the teacher re-institutes the recognition for being on time, and prompt arrivals again increase. The teacher has discovered a technique that controls the behavior of this particular student.

There are several obvious problems with this approach to determining the effects of the reward technique. It may be critical to the student's future that he not be late. Should the teacher stop the recognition just to prove control and increase the potential risk to the student? Should the teacher ignore the behavior in order to find a baseline frequency of offenses? Suppose the student encounters a serious problem while being late to class, and the teacher does nothing except record the number of offenses over a given period of time? This is an ethical question that points to the need for other ways to assess the effectiveness of different approval techniques. Finally, Strain, Cooke, and Apolloni[27] argue that behavioral change programs cannot be practically administered by secondary school teachers because of other demands on their time in a classroom.

A second difficulty in using the approval process is the question of fairness and justice. Of course, there are winners and losers in society, but society also makes major efforts to equalize opportunities and rewards. Parents go to great lengths to make certain they treat their children fairly and somewhat equally. The question is not whether the children are actually treated the same; it is a question of intent. That is, are serious attempts made to equalize rewards and opportunities?

While students may understand why some students receive more privileges than others to reinforce appropriate behavior, parents sometimes are less tolerant of this unequal distribution of privileges in schools. For example, in using the approval process, which by its very nature has to be individualized, educators run the risk of creating conflicts with other students who are not in need of constant reinforcement and with the parents of those students. In fact, in some instances students have misbehaved so that they would receive attention when they later demonstrated appropriate or approved behavior. A professional educator may have good reason to extend approval to some and not others, but the expectations of the community may dictate a different practice until those expectations are changed.

A third potential constraint on the application of the approval process is the pupil-teacher ratios in many middle schools and high schools. Society does not provide rewards for every appropriate behavior exhibited by adults, and, similarly, a teacher is limited in what he or she can accomplish. Additional personnel and the use of technology may help, but as an individual the teacher has physical and psychological limitations. If the expectation is fostered that all appropriate behavior will be rewarded, the teacher is creating an illusion.

A fourth concern in the application of the approval process is the overuse of rewards. Redd and Sleater state that:

> Whether something functions as a reinforcer depends upon a vast number of factors, like how we feel, who is giving the reinforcer, and how important the reinforcer is to us. The most important factor is how and when reinforcers and punishments are experienced. If we receive a strong reinforcer every time we do a particular thing, it is highly likely we will continue to do it. If, however, we tire of the reinforcer because we become saturated, the reinforcer will lose its value and our behavior will stop.[28]

Repeated approvals by a teacher can become meaningless to the student and fail to act as genuine rewards for appropriate behavior.

A fifth concern related to the approval process is best expressed in a statement by Deibert and Harmon:

> Many people feel that behavior principles have to be used without the individual being aware of what is happening. They believe that if he knows what's going on (that he's being shaped into behaving in a certain manner) he will not go along with it. When an individual reaches the age where he can understand these principles, to manipulate him without his awareness is a questionable practice. The secrecy of their application should not be a factor in their effectiveness. Knowing we are being rewarded for our appropriate responses in no way reduces the value of the reward.[29]

The potential problem is that once one knows one is being rewarded for appropriate behavior, it is likely that one will come to expect a reward every time the behavior is exhibited.

A sixth concern is related to whether long-lasting behavior changes can result from receiving rewards. Wildman and Wildman,[30] in their review of the long-lasting effect of behavior modification, have determined that it is possible to have generalizable effects (i.e., carry-over of the behavior without the reward) provided certain conditions are satisfied. These conditions are similar to those outlined in this chapter. However, one of the conditions is to teach those with whom the student will work in the future how to maintain desired behaviors. This condition is extremely difficult to meet in any realistic way. Creative methods may be found to involve parents in learning to maintain the desired behavior in the home, but it is more difficult to involve those people with whom students may associate and work after they leave school. A major concern with the approval process is that it may be difficult to meet the conditions for long-range success.

SUMMARY

The penal process is a short-range measure used to reduce the number of inappropriate behavior incidents. It relies on the creation of fear—of being harmed or losing something one desires. The penal process can be effective in schools when it is applied as the logical consequence of the social order. The penalties must be associated with specific incidents of inappropriate behavior. Several other guidelines for using the penal process in the school setting should be observed and its limitations kept in mind.

The approval process works as a long-range (preventive) method for teaching students appropriate social behavior. It has some limitations, but it provides hope for preventing many discipline problems and correcting others. Examples were given of problems that can arise from the overuse or misuse of the approval process. Appropriate behavior can be encouraged through external environmental rewards, but this is not the only method for changing behavior. Together with the penal process, the approval process fosters cause-effect thinking.

The combined thrust of the penal, approval, and reformational processes is to help develop young adults who, while unique in many ways, will achieve satisfaction from behavior that is acceptable to the social order. It is our belief that these processes, when appropriately blended, can aid students in developing their own internal reward system for appropriate behavior.

In addition to the footnote references within the chapter, a list of readings on the subject of behavior modification appears at the end. Elements of the approval, penal, and reformational processes are described in these writings.

NOTES

1. William Redd and William Sleater, *Take Charge* (New York: Vintage Books, 1978), p. 4.

2. William Glasser, M.D., *Schools Without Failure* (New York: Harper & Row, 1969), pp. 129–30.

3. Redd and Sleater, p. 15.

4. R. L. Solomon, "Punishment," *American Psychologist* (1964):239–53.

5. R. Dreikurs and P. Cassel, *Discipline Without Tears: What To Do With Children Who Misbehave* (New York: Hawthorn Books, 1972), pp. 60–63.

6. Deibert and Harmon, p. 22.

7. D. L. MacMillan, S. R. Forness, and B. M. Trumball, "The Role of Punishment in the Classroom" *Exceptional Children* 40, no. 2 (1973):85–96.

8. Solomon, pp. 239–53.

9. G. R. Mayer, B. Sulzer, and J. Cody, "The Use of Punishment in Modifying Student Behavior," *Journal of Special Education* 2 (1968):323–28.

10. Redd and Sleater, p. 15.

11. Mayer, Sulzer, and Cody, pp. 323–28.

12. Deibert and Harmon, p. 73.

13. Ibid.

14. W. S. Davidson and E. Seidman, "Studies of Behavior Modification and Juvenile Delinquency: A Review, Methodological Critique, and Social Perspective," *Psychological Bulletin* 81 (1974):998–1011.

15. Deibert and Harmon, p. 15.

16. Madsen and Madsen, p. 39.

17. K. D. O'Leary and S. G. O'Leary, "Behavior Modification in the School," in H. Lectenbert (ed.), *Handbook of Behavior Modification and Behavior Therapy* (Englewood Cliffs, N.J.: Prentice-Hall, 1976), p. 137.

18. Deibert and Harmon, pp. 23–25.

19. Ibid.

20. Ibid.

21. Redd and Sleater, p. 11.

22. Emilio Ribes-Inesta and Albert Bandura (eds.), *Analyses of Delinquency and Aggression* (New York: John Wiley and Sons, 1976), p. 39.

23. Redd and Sleater, p. 5.

24. Ibid.

25. D. Baer, M. Wolf, and T. R. Risley, "Some Current Dimensions of Applied Behavior Analysis," *Journal of Applied Behavior Analysis* 1 (1968):91–97.

26. J. Zimmerman and E. Zimmerman with S. L. Rider, A. F. Smith, and R. Dinn, "Doing Your Own Thing With Precision: The Essence of Behavior Management in the Classroom," *Educational Technology* (April, 1971):26–32.

27. P. S. Strain, T. P. Cooke, and T. Apolloni, "The Role of Peers in Modifying Classmates' Social Behavior: A Review," *Journal of Special Education* 10 (1976):351–56.

28. Redd and Sleater.

29. Deibert and Harmon, p. 98.

30. R. W. Wildman II and R. W. Wildman, "The Generalization of Behavior Modification Procedures: A Review—With Special Emphasis on Classroom Applications," *Psychology in the Schools* 12 (1975):432–48.

ADDITIONAL REFERENCES

The following are suggested as supplemental readings on behavioral modification. Elements of the approval, penal, and reformational processes are found in these works.

Andrasik, Frank, and Murphy, W. D. "Assessing the Readability of Thirty-Nine Behavior Modification Training Manuals and Primers," *Journal of Applied Behavior Analysis* 10 (1977):341–44.

Altman, K. I., and Linton, T. E. "Operant Conditioning in the Classroom Setting: A Review of the Research," *Journal of Education Research* 64 (1971):277–85.

Davidson, W. S., and Seidman, E. "Studies of Behavior Modification and Juvenile Delinquency: A Review, Methodological Critique and Social Perspective," *Psychological Bulletin* 81 (1974):998–1011.

Drabman, R. S.; Janice, G. J.; and Archbold, J. "The Use and Misuse of Extinction in Classroom Behavioral Programs," *Psychology in the Schools* 13 (1976):470–76.

Glasser, W. "Disorder in Our Schools: Causes and Remedies," *Phi Delta Kappan* (January, 1978):331–33.

Keely, S. M.; Shembert, K. M.; and Carbonell, J. "Operant Clinical Intervention: Behavior Management or Beyond? Where Are the Data?", *Behavior Therapy* 7 (1976):292–305.

McLaughlin, T. F. "Self-Control Procedures in the Management of Classroom Behavior Problems," *Education* 96 (1976a):379–83.

Masters, J. R. and Laverty, G. E. "The Effects of a Schools Without Failure Program Upon Classroom Interaction Patterns, Pupil Achievement, and Teacher, Pupil, and Parent Attitudes: Summary Report of First Year of Program" (Washington, D.C.: Pennsylvania State Department of Education and National Center for Educational Research and Development, 1974).

Silverman, S. and Silverman, H. "Reducing Verbal and Physical Aggression in a Ninth Grade Class Using a Group Contingency," *School Applications of Learning Theory* 7 (1975):20–26.

Thorp, R. G. and Wetzel, R. J. *Behavior Modification in the National Environment* (New York: Academic Press, 1969).

Tsoi, M. M. and Yule, W. "The Effects of Group Reinforcement in Classroom Behavior Modification," *Educational Studies* 2 (1976):129–40.

PART
THREE

Chapters 5 and 6 in Part III describe student and teacher behavior patterns and the extent to which student behavior patterns may be viewed as appropriate or inappropriate. The following questions are answered: What are the motives associated with dominant student behavior patterns? How should an administrator or teacher apply the various methods for changing inappropriate student behavior? What are possible patterns of teacher behavior? What are the interaction problems teachers may experience with each student behavior pattern?

Chapter 5 describes a theoretical model for the relationship between student behavior patterns and the needs these behaviors reflect. It suggests that many patterns of student behavior come from the same basic needs. Chapter 6, on the other hand, describes the specific student behavior patterns in classroom language. Each pattern is seen from two different teacher perspectives—as appropriate or inappropriate student behavior. Chapter 6 explains how teachers can help students replace inappropriate behaviors with appropriate behaviors and speculates that teacher behavior patterns may parallel those of students.

CHAPTER
5

Conceptual Model of Student Needs and Behaviors

When teachers and administrators discuss discipline, they frequently attempt to deal with the crisis of the moment. Often the conversation concerns a single inappropriate behavior and then extends to generalizations about a student's overall behavior pattern. This chapter and the next one examine student behavior typologies, in the interest of providing a common language for discussing student behavior patterns. Chapter 5 relates behavior patterns to their probable causes. Chapter 6 describes specific behavior patterns and recommends methods for improving inappropriate behavior.

MAJOR CATEGORIES OF BEHAVIORS AND NEEDS

There are several different perspectives of the nature of human behavior that relate to student motivation and needs. Our intent here, however, is not to discuss all the theories that have been generated to define specific student behavior patterns, needs, and motivation. Therefore, an extensive discussion of student behavior patterns and their relationship to motivation is not included. Maslow,[1] Herzberg et al.,[2] Vroom,[3] Alderfer,[4] and McClelland et al.[5] provide thorough treatments of needs and motivation. Later descriptions of needs are a synthesis of aspects of these works.

We believe that behavior is most often the result of attempts by students to fulfill specific personal needs or combinations of them. While factors such as health, culture, and environment do influence specific student behaviors, the basic student behavior *patterns* are believed to result from a student's repeated attempts to satisfy personal needs. Such repeated attempts become habitual behavioral responses. Those responses are also influenced by a student's perceptions of potential rewards and punishments and his or her value orientations. This chapter will attempt to relate behavior patterns to needs-satisfying action.

Trait descriptions of behavior tend to group behaviors into patterns.[6] It is useful to stereotype the behavior of a person provided the behavior has been adequately sampled. The use of stereotypes permits inferences and predictions about behavior.[7] However, administrators and teachers must collect an adequate sample of a student's behavior before patterns are identified. The tendency to categorize behavior too quickly can lead to errors and inhibit the teacher's ability to observe the student's behavior accurately in the future.[8] Also quick categorizations by overreacting teachers, according to Brophy and Good,[9] cause these teachers to think of students as stereotypes (troublemaker, good student, slow learner) rather than as unique individuals.

Despite the obvious dangers associated with labeling behavior, an adequate sample of observed behavior can help to determine the student needs which may be causing certain behavior patterns. Ellis[10] writes that the study of normal adolescent development is growing into an independent concern. Behavior patterns described by several researchers provide evidence of this contribution. Licata,[11] for example, discusses student behavior styles in regard to several propositions about the nature of student controls. Licata suggests that students who hassle teachers in a control-designed school setting cause the faculty to institute more rules and regulations, and this action only increases incidents of hassling. Teacher hassling can be categorized into three forms of student brinksmanship: subversive-obedient behavior—rule-obeying behavior carried to the extreme as a means of obtaining some advantages; tightroping—student behavior that is aggravating but not really rule-breaking; and boundary testing—rule-disobeying behavior, including incidents of mass disobedience to avoid punishments and reprisals. Such brinksmanship behavior is designed to shift control from the teacher or school to the student.

In a limited study, Brimm and Bush[12] attempted to identify areas in the school environment with which students felt the greatest satisfaction and dissatisfaction. They also attempted to determine whether there was a difference in the way students categorized as activists and nonactivists felt about their school experiences. Student activists were those who had exerted pressure to bring about change in school policies or regulations; nonactivists were those who had exerted no such effort. The findings suggest that the two groups did have different views of what creates satisfaction and dissatisfaction.

One of the most extensive research projects on the nature of student and adult behavior patterns is found in the work of Isabel Briggs Myers.[13] The manual for the Myers-Briggs indicator describes a variety of typologies of high school students. The Myers-Briggs test is based on Jung's theory that behavior is not random but is actually consistent, orderly, and dependent on the way people choose to use both their perception and their judgment about that which they perceive.[14] "Perception" here means the process of becoming aware of things or people or occurrences or ideas. "Judgment" refers to the process of coming to conclusions about what has been perceived.[15] The Myers-Briggs indicator has separate indices for determining four basic preferences that are the basis of a person's personality. The indices are as follows:

Extraversion or Introversion

Sensing or Intuition

Thinking or Feeling

Judgment or Perception

The possible combinations of these variables provide sixteen typologies of student behavior.[16] Several of the patterns described by Briggs Myers are similar to the student behavior patterns identified later in this chapter.

Frymier[17] established two sets of characteristics for young people whose motives differ in relationship to self-concept, values, time perspective, and personality. These two dimensions were labeled enthusiastic and unenthusiastic as follows:

	Enthusiastic	*Unenthusiastic*
1. Self-concept	Positive	Negative
2. Values	Abstract	Concrete
	Aesthetic	Particular
	General	

3. Time perspective	Realistic Healthy	Unrealistic Unhealthy Preoccupied with the past Afraid of the future
4. Personality structure	Tolerant of ambiguity Open to experience Will suspend judgment	Little tolerance for ambiguity Somewhat closed to experience Polarized thought processes

Offer and Offer described three patterns of growth and behavior in adolescence. Youth in the "continuous growth" group have "smoothness of purpose and a self-assurance of their progression toward a meaningful and fulfilling adult life."[18] They have the ability to integrate experiences and use them as a stimulus for growth. They are described as mentally healthy, that is, content with themselves and with their place in life. They are emotionally secure and able to postpone immediate gratification. Continuous growth students employ problem-solving techniques for coping with difficulty.[19] The "surgent growth" group of students is characterized by a growth cycle of progression and regression. Defenses used by these students include anger and projection. When confronted with crisis situations these students tighten up and tend to overcontrol. Their self-esteem wavers more than that of the continuous growth students. They lack a steady state of working toward vocational goals.[20] Lastly, students with a "tumultuous growth" pattern experience much internal turmoil. They have recurrent self-doubts and often feel much mistrust for adults. They are highly dependent on peers and group members. They search for their identity and look to others as a means of assessing the worthwhileness of their own activities. They are less well adjusted in terms of functioning than are the other two groups.[21]

Research by Kroeber[22] concluded that ego mechanisms may be utilized in either a coping form, a defensive form, or a combination of both. The coping and defensive forms of behavior can be contrasted in general descriptions of student behavior. Students whose behavior is the defensive type are described as follows: their behavior appears rigid and past-oriented and distorts present situations. The process of separating ideas and feelings is difficult for these students; they cannot evaluate situations with complete objectivity. They find it difficult to consider alternative choices or to speculate. These students refuse to face thoughts and feelings that would be painful; hence, their ability to focus attention on difficult events of the past is limited. They blame others for their own uncomfortableness in situations. They have difficulty making decisions because of doubts about their own perceptions and judgments. Problems, they believe, will somehow solve themselves. These students act older or younger than their chronological age to avoid responsibility for personal actions. They also have difficulty modifying aims that lead to socially unacceptable behavior; they usually cannot wait until an opportune time to deal with some of their basic needs.

By contrast, students who have primarily coping behavior can be described as follows: they can separate ideas from personal feelings and make impartial analyses of situations. They can determine causes in situations and can choose and plan from a given set of alternatives. It is possible for these students to ignore unpleasant or attractive diversions in order to stay with a task. They have the ability to deal with unpleasant or attractive feelings and perceptions when ready to do so. These students have the ability to imagine how others feel and to experience these feelings as others do. They are able to tolerate ambiguity in situations—that is, they are able to think in terms of "both" as well as "either-or" when faced with complicated situations. Such students feel enjoyment in being responsible for handling themselves in situations. They can modify their actions until their behavior is socially acceptable. They are able to delay fulfilling basic needs until an appropriate time to do so.

Differences between the defensive and coping typologies are obvious, just as differences between Offer's continuous growth and tumultuous growth patterns are evident. Defensive behaviors are associated with a threat to one's security. Such behaviors are designed to enhance personal security: a student does certain things to protect his or her sense of worth as a person. Coping behaviors, on the other hand, reflect a concern that extends beyond the self. They are caring behaviors: students do things for the satisfaction that comes from the act of caring about another person, a project, a cause, or one's own personal growth. Hence, in our subsequent discussions of behavior typologies and patterns, the terms "security" and "caring" are substituted for "defensive" and "coping," respectively.

Recent research by Martin on the behavior patterns proposed by the authors identified three major patterns. Martin labeled students who exhibited these patterns as mature, cooperative, insecure. She writes:

> The mature pattern is composed of observable variables denoting achievement, autonomy, tolerance, self-discipline, inner direction, acceptance of responsibility, and pictures one who takes an active role in groups. The insecure pattern denotes an inhibited, submissive, hostile, impulsive,

other-directed, anxious person who takes an inactive role in groups. The cooperative, average follower accepts leadership from others, is stable, and tends toward an emphasis on sociability.[23]

The traits of the mature behavior pattern appear to be similar to those of the continuous growth and coping patterns discussed above. Characteristics of the insecure pattern are the same as of the tumultuous growth and defensive behavior patterns. A cooperative pattern seems to reflect some of the surgent growth pattern. The behaviors of the cooperative pattern also appear to combine the coping (caring) and defensive (security) patterns described by Kroeber.

The work of Martin and the Offers suggest that combinations of caring and security behavior displayed by some students produce two additional behavior typologies, impulsive behavior and belongingness behavior. Students who cannot wait until an appropriate time to deal with some of their basic needs are showing impulsive or carefree behavior. They are prone to do what they want when they want, which results in socially unacceptable behavior. These students are daring. It is difficult for them to stay at a task unless it continues to provide change and a sense of extending one's self through a machine, such as a car. Caring and security needs combine to produce students who act on impulse. Belongingness behaviors also reflect a combination of caring and security behaviors. Students reflecting this typology are generally dependent on others for their security. They follow others as long as it helps them fulfill their need to belong to school groups. They care about the feelings of others who belong to the group and can share their feelings. They cannot tolerate a lack of direction. Their mood is subject to change as they experience different feelings and they may be too loud or too quiet at times. In summary, the literature seems to support three major categories of behaviors: security behaviors, caring behaviors, and combinations of these two expressed as belongingness and impulsive behaviors.

BEHAVIOR PATTERNS AND SECURITY NEEDS

Security needs such as physical safety, food, sex, predictability, orderliness, and social acceptance are reflected in a variety of student behaviors. The strengths of the need for security may vary; some students seem to be paralyzed in a constant state of terror and fear, while others seem only slightly afraid and nervous. A primary need for security may be expressed through a need to be accepted by others and a need to control others, and by additional security needs. The lack of food and physical safety may cause the student to feel a need for security. Little attention is given to economic needs in this book, but the need for security may be related to their lack of fulfillment.

The need to control others, one of the two security needs to be discussed, is defined here as the need to predict or influence the future. The elements that comprise this need include the motivation to influence, dominate, and outperform others. The other security-related need, the need for acceptance, is defined as the need to be approved or liked by others. The need to control and the need for acceptance can be experienced in varying degrees of strength and prompt somewhat different student behaviors. Some students may experience a strong need to control while experiencing little need for acceptance. Other students may express a strong need for acceptance and a weak need to control others. When students experience a strong need for both acceptance and control, the primary need for security is also strong. (However, a strong primary need for security does not require the presence of either of the two secondary needs.) As the strengths of the control and acceptance needs vary, the behavior used to satisfy these needs appears to change. For example, as the need for acceptance becomes strong, the tendency to be overcompliant with the desires of others increases.

The strengths of the acceptance, control, and security needs can be depicted graphically. The dimensions would resemble those shown in Figure 5.1. In the diagram, the horizontal line represents a weak-to-strong continuum of the need for primary security. The diagonal lines represent the weak-to-strong continui for the secondary needs of acceptance and control. The "weak" ends of these two continui meet in a right angle. In this diagram, the behavior of a student exhibiting security needs falls within the enclosed area. The continui help to approximate the strength of a particular student's needs. The need-strength a student is responding to at a given time can be represented by two numbers between 0 and 4. The first number is the strength of the control need and the second is the strength of the acceptance need. For example, scores of 1.0 and 1.0 would indicate that weak control and acceptance needs are reflected in the behavior of the student. The overall need for security, of course, would be weak also. A combined score of 2.0 represents a fairly weak need for security, and a 6.0 represents a strong need for security.

The acceptance and control continui can be divided into two equal parts, producing four basic combinations of needs found in student behav-

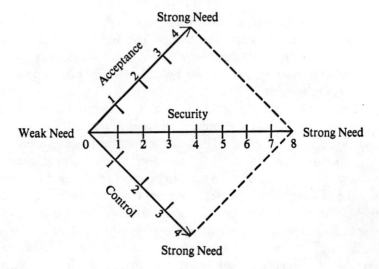

FIGURE 5.1.   *Need–Strength Dimensions for Primary and Secondary Security Needs*

ior. These combinations are derived as shown in Figure 5.2. Student behavior can reflect a strong need for control and a strong need for acceptance and, thus, represent a strong need for security. Or, a student's behavior can represent weak needs for both control and acceptance, and therefore, a weak need for security. A third behavior pattern reflects a strong need for control but a weak need for acceptance, while a fourth pattern shows a strong need for acceptance but a weak need for control. The strength of the security need for the latter two patterns lies somewhere between strong and weak.

Simple terminology denoting the behaviors that reflect these four combinations will be used henceforth. The four patterns of behavior that reflect the different need-strengths have been labeled as follows:

	Behavior Pattern Label
Need-Strength Combination	
Strong control and strong acceptance needs	Onlooker
Strong control and weak acceptance needs	Untouchable
Weak control and strong acceptance needs	Seeker
Weak control and weak acceptance needs	Perfectionist

The four student behavior patterns based on security may be distinguished as follows. *Onlookers* avoid involvement with other students, teach-

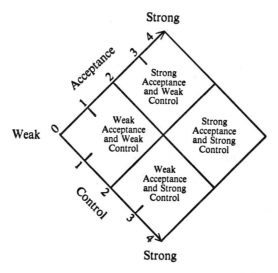

FIGURE 5.2.   *Combinations of Needs for Acceptance and Control in Student Behavior*

ers, and/or work. They prefer to be unnoticed and appear emotionally flat in school classes. *Untouchables* are combative, power-oriented, aggressive, and explosive students. They tend to dominate others, to be judgmental and critical, and to lead exclusive school groups. *Seekers* want to please others, teachers and students, and are overcompliant and very responsive to social pressure. They want to be accepted and included socially. *Perfectionists* are concerned with being competent, with being perfect, with self-improvement, and with beating others in school. They are afraid of failing and try to impress others with their own knowledge and skills. Martin's work tends to support these four student behavior patterns for fifth- and eighth-grade students.[24]

BEHAVIOR PATTERNS AND CARING NEEDS

Caring needs such as the needs for doing well, being creative, experiencing self-development, sharing supportive relationships, leading others, and feeling satisfaction are reflected in a wide range of student behaviors. The need to care varies in strength among different students. For example, some students care intensely, while others reflect a weak concern with caring. The primary need to care may be expressed through two secondary caring needs, the need to care about others and the need to care about a thing (object, cause, or project). These two aspects of the caring need can be experienced in varying degrees of strength and each prompts somewhat different behaviors. Some students may care little about people but may care about the growth of an object, such as a woodworking or computer project. The primary need to care is strongest when the person feels a strong need to care both for others and for a project.

The needs to care for others and for projects are independent because the need for one does not help to estimate how deeply a person feels the other. As the strength of the needs changes, the behavior associated with satisfying these needs also appears to shift. For example, a student who develops a strong need to care about people may work more on other students' projects.

The behavior reflecting a primary need to care and its two secondary needs can be represented by any point within the diagram in Figure 5.3. As in Figure 5.1, the lines meeting in a right angle represent continui for the secondary needs while the horizontal line represents the primary-need continuum. Need-strength scales have been drawn along these three dimensions. A student's general need to care may be represented by two numbers between 0 and 4. The first number indicates the strength of the need to care about a project, while the second indicates the strength of the need to care about persons. Scores of 2.0 and 2.0, for example, would reflect a medium degree of caring about both projects and persons. A 3.5 score on each scale would indicate a strong need to care for people and

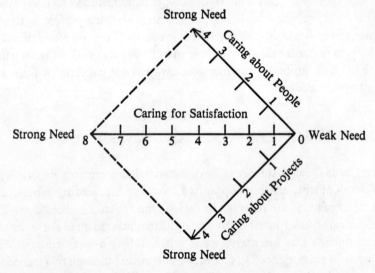

FIGURE 5.3. *Need–Strength Scales for Primary and Secondary Caring Needs*

projects. A combined score of 4.0 represents a fairly weak primary need for caring, and a 7.0 represents a strong primary need.

Division of the two secondary-need continui into two equal segments produces four basic levels of need reflected by students' behavior. The derivation of these combinations is depicted in Figure 5.4. These combinations of secondary caring needs are associated with four rather distinct patterns of student behavior. Convenient labels for the student patterns may be assigned as follows:

	Behavior
Need-Strength Combination	*Pattern Label*
Strong person-caring and strong project-caring	Leader
Strong person-caring and weak project-caring	Developer
Weak person-caring and weak-project caring	Becomer
Weak person-caring and strong-project caring	Performer

The leader shows a strong need to care about both people and projects—strong primary need to care. The becomer, on the other hand, reflects a weak need to care about other people and projects and thereby exhibits a weak primary need. Developers represent a strong need to care

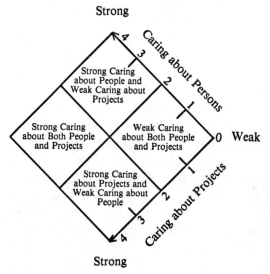

FIGURE 5.4.   *Combinations of Needs to Care about Persons and Projects in Student Behavior*

about people and a weak need to care about projects. Performers primarily care about an object and have a weak concern for people. The strength of developers' and performers' primary caring needs falls somewhere between that for leaders and becomers.

The student behavior patterns that stem from the need to care are distinguished as follows: *Performers* set reasonable goals, make plans, and are persistent in attempting to achieve their aims. They are creative and not afraid of failure, independent in their thinking, and interested in completing their projects. *Leaders* are mature, highly accepting of others and themselves; secure, pleasant, down-to-earth achievers in a school. *Developers* are friendly, relaxed, and popular listeners. As peer counselors in a school, they help others solve the problems associated with maturing. *Becomers* are interested in self-analysis and causes and in the process of becoming. They are "being"-oriented. Seldom are they just themselves, because they are attempting to find out why they are unique and who they want to become. Martin's research on behavior patterns suggests that the leader, performer, and developer patterns can be supported.[25]

BEHAVIOR PATTERNS FOR BELONGINGNESS AND IMPULSIVE NEEDS

The belongingness need is the need to feel part of an organization or group. The belongingness need is one of two motivations that result when a student has both primary security and primary caring needs. That is, the combination of the need to care about people and the need for acceptance explain the need to belong to an organization. Different combinations of the strength of these secondary needs occur in student behavior. For instance, a strong need to care about people, which usually requires putting one's personal aims aside, may coexist with a strong need for acceptance from others. Various combinations of these two secondary needs are associated with varying strengths of the need to belong to an organization. In Figure 5.5, these combinations may be represented as points within the area defined by continui of the need to care about people and the need for acceptance. One specific behavior pattern associated with the varying strengths of these two needs has been labeled the loyalist behavior pattern. *Loyalists* are the cooperative workers in school groups and on school teams. They believe they must contribute independently of others to belong to a group.

The need to be impulsive is defined as the need to act spontaneously

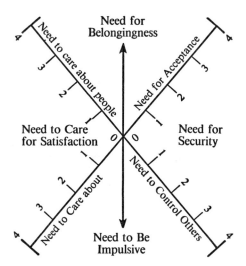

FIGURE 5.5. *Relationship of the Four Secondary Needs to Primary Needs for Belongingness and to Be Impulsive*

in creating excitement. Two secondary needs associated with the need to be impulsive are the need to control others and the need to care about an object or cause. These two needs appear to be independent of each other. For example, when one of these two secondary needs is strong, the other may be weak. A student may have a strong need to care about objects or causes but might also have little concern for controlling people. The strength of a student's need to be impulsive varies according to the combined strength of these two needs (see Figure 5.5). The specific behavior pattern that results from a different strong and weak combination of these secondary needs has been labeled the operator behavior pattern. *Operators* are action-oriented, carefree, and impulsive excitement seekers in schools. They detest drill and repetition but seek new risks with machines and with people to test their own limits.

The labels used in this chapter were selected to reflect the general type of behavior associated with combinations and levels of various needs. The labels are admittedly imprecise and may not define the true patterns in the behavior of students, but they do provide an opportunity to discuss various combinations of behaviors and the needs they may reflect. The usefulness of these behavioral labels for discussion purposes is indicated by Figure 5.6, which summarizes the relationships among the ten behavior patterns, the four primary needs, and the four secondary needs of students. Moreover, these are not meant to convey a positive or negative connotation.

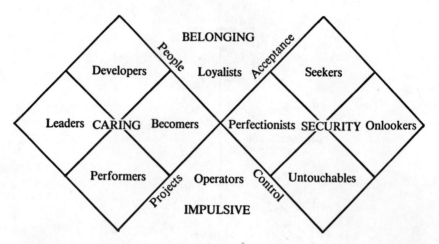

FIGURE 5.6.   *General Positions of Specific Student Behavior Patterns in Relation to Needs Exhibited*

Experience suggests that behavior patterns can be viewed as appropriate or inappropriate depending on particular circumstances. It is important to remember that although the ten patterns do not exist in isolation, they do provide a language for categorizing and analyzing behavior and its causes.

SUMMARY

Ten specific patterns of student behavior are distinguishable within three general typologies. The ten patterns are as follows:

Security Behavior	Security and Caring Behavior	Caring Behavior
Onlookers	Loyalists	Performers
Untouchables	Operators	Leaders
Seekers		Developers
Perfectionists		Becomers

If behavior typologies are to be beneficial, they must help educators identify the probable causes of student behavior. This chapter has proposed a causal relationship between patterns of student behavior and combinations of primary and secondary needs. Additional research is needed to refine the behavior patterns and define the relationship between specific need-strengths and specific behavior patterns.

NOTES

1. Abraham H. Maslow, *Motivation and Personality* (New York: Harper and Row, 1954).

2. F. Herzberg, B. Mausner, and B. Snyderman, *The Motivation to Work*, 2nd ed. (New York: John Wiley and Sons, 1959).

3. Victor H. Vroom, *Work and Motivation* (New York: John Wiley and Sons, 1964).

4. C. P. Alderfer, *Existence, Relatedness, and Growth: Human Needs in Organizational Settings* (New York: The Free Press, 1972).

5. D. C. McClelland, J. Q. Atkinson, R. A. Clark, and E. L. Lowell, *The Achievement Motive* (New York: Appleton-Century-Crofts, 1953).

6. Jerome Seymour Bruner, David Shapiro, and Renato Tagiurie, "The Meaning of Traits in Isolation and in Combination," in Renato Tagiurie and Luigi Petoullo (eds.), *Person, Perception and Interpersonal Behavior* (Stanford, Calif.: Stanford University Press, 1958), pp. 277–88.

7. Frederick McDonald, *Educational Psychology* (Belmont, Calif.: Wadsworth Publishing Co., 1965), p. 528.

8. Ibid., p. 530.

9. Jere E. Brophy and Thomas L. Good, *Teacher-Student Relationships: Causes and Consequences* (New York: Holt, Rinehart & Winston, 1974), p. 35.

10. Eric H. Ellis, "Some Problems in the Study of Adolescent Development," *Adolescence* XIV, 53 (Spring 1979):107.

11. Joseph W. Licata, "Student Brinksmanship and School Structure," *The Educational Forum* (March 1978):345–50.

12. Jack L. Brimm and Doris Bush, "Student Reactions to Environmental Factors in the School," *National Association of Secondary School Principals Journal* 62 (May 1978):65–73.

13. Isabel Briggs Myers, *The Myers-Briggs Type Indicator Manual* (Palo Alto, Calif.: Consulting Psychologists Press, 1962), p. 1.

14. Ibid., p. 1.

15. Ibid., p. 1.

16. Ibid., pp. 70–72.

17. Jack Frymier, *Motivation and Learning in School* (Bloomington, Ind.: Phi Delta Kappan Educational Foundation, 1974): p. 8.

18. Daniel Offer and Judith Baskin Offer, *From Teenagers to Young Manhood: A Psychological Study* (New York: Basic Books Publishers, 1975), p. 40.

19. Ibid., pp. 41–43.

20. Ibid., pp. 43–44.

21. Ibid., pp. 45–49.

22. C. Theodora Kroeber, "Coping Functions of the Ego Mechanisms," in Robert W. White (ed.), *The Study of Lives* (New York: Atherton Press, 1963): pp. 183–88.

23. Mary Martin, "Analysis of Behavior Pattern Composition in the Tri-Student Need and Behavior Model as Related to Behavior Problem Identification and Four Levels of Teacher Acceptance of the Student" (Ph.D. dissertation, George Peabody College for Teachers of Vanderbilt University, 1980): p. 112.

24. Martin, pp. 95–101.

25. Ibid.

CHAPTER 6

Specific Student Behavior Patterns and Their Improvement

Chapter 5 described probable relationships between human needs and the behaviors students exhibit in trying to satisfy those needs. Ten kinds of needs-satisfying behavior were related to distinguishable student behavior patterns. This chapter discusses each of the ten behavior patterns including (1) a synopsis of the need the pattern reflects, (2) a description of the behavior pattern, (3) a contrasting set of teachers' views of the behavior pattern, and (4) an example of how a teacher attempted to change a student's behavior patterns. The four behavior patterns related to security needs, the four behavior patterns related to caring needs, and the two behavior patterns that reflect combinations of security and caring needs are discussed separately. A final section looks at how these ten patterns may apply to the behavior of teachers and examines the conflicts that may occur between the behavior patterns of students and the behavior patterns of teachers.

Educators should exercise caution in classifying student behavior into the specific patterns. A student's behavior is seldom entirely confined to one pattern and one pattern may be only slightly more prominent than another. Moreover, the patterns represent behavioral extremes. The behavior of any student will not usually fit a specific behavior pattern precisely.

ONLOOKERS

Onlookers are students whose behavior is characterized by avoiding involvement in class activities or interaction with others. Their behavior seeks to reduce a strong need for security. Their sense of being a worthwhile person depends upon an absence of criticism and failure. Onlookers are afraid of making mistakes and avoid doing anything that might lead to making a mistake. They cannot separate making a mistake from being a mistake.

Students whose predominant behavior forms the onlooker pattern hesitate to begin conversations with others, are the last in line to do anything, and do not complete homework. Most of the time they appear moody, frightened, and preoccupied with their own thoughts. They are easily embarrassed. They are past- and future-oriented and are seldom in touch with the present. Onlookers look dazed much of the time. Change is viewed as a personal threat. When confronted by authority or possible conflict, onlookers either do nothing or find the easiest escape route. They refuse to take responsibility for their actions with people or with work. When onlookers do school work, they either try to do the impossible or as little as possible.

A teacher who views the behavior of onlookers as appropriate might describe it as follows:

> These students do little classroom work, but they do not bother others in the classroom. They do not argue or disagree with me, nor do they get involved in any type of confrontation with their peers. They also promise to do many things. Onlookers sit in the back of the room quietly staring at me, bothering no one, expecially those of us who are burdened with more than thirty-five students in a class.

On the other hand, a teacher who views the behavior of onlookers as inappropriate can be expected to describe these students as follows:

> Onlookers are simply unresponsive students. They do not do their work. They do not respond to questions in normal conversations. Onlookers frequently appear to be daydreaming. They dawdle and play with instructional materials. They refuse to begin homework and will not complete assignments. They refuse to take responsibility for their behaviors and they avoid involvement with others.

In summary, the onlooker reflects a strong need for security. The behavior of the onlooker can be considered either appropriate or inappropriate in the classroom. Specific descriptors of the onlooker behavior pattern include:

1. Emotionally flat.
2. Always a spectator.
3. Desire to be unnoticed.
4. Isolated from others.
5. Hesitates to act.

Improving Onlookers: An Example

Jack's behavior was classified by his English teacher as fitting appropriately into the onlooker pattern.

> Jack was a bright ninth-grade student who was scared much of the time in his English class. He was always worried about making a mistake. He often found himself embarrassed after he made a mistake. Other students made decisions for him. The teacher tried to motivate Jack to do some classwork, but, most of the time, Jack would simply not do his written assignments. He typically became paralyzed when asked to write anything on paper. When the teacher asked him a question in class, he acted surprised and often said he did not know before he had really understood the question. After several months of Jack's refusing to do his work the teacher talked with Jack, trying to help him get to the point of being at least able to try to accomplish something. The teacher was extremely concerned that even with the assistance of counseling Jack's behavior was not changing.

Chapter 3 outlined three steps for a reformational process that can be used to assist a student who needs to change his behavior. The student must (1) realize that he or she has a problem, (2) express a sincere desire to change the behavior, and (3) describe the appropriate behavior he or she will exhibit in the future. In the reformational process, the student develops a "contract" to produce a specific result. If students are insecure and view themselves as being inadequate, then teachers or principals need to help such students develop contracts that will lead from small to greater successes. A contract for the student who exhibits insecure behavior should include the following elements:

1. Specific, short-range, appropriate behavior goals to which the educator knows the student is committed. The goals need to be relatively easy but not so easy that the student, when the aims are achieved, will say, "Anyone could do that—it was not me; the goal was easy."

2. Short feedback loops. The student must know immediately when he or she has slipped or failed to reach one of the short-range goals.

3. A support system that helps the student try again after having failed to reach one of the short-range goals.

In Jack's case, the English teacher had several meetings with him and together they finally worked out an agreement. Jack would write two or three sentences every day and turn them in before class. The topic of the previous day's classwork would help Jack determine what he would write about. The teacher would not give him a grade on this work but would simply accept the paper, praising his positive accomplishments. They agreed that Jack would receive only a minimum passing grade while the contract was being implemented. For two weeks, he was to turn in a paper based on the previous day's assignments. The teacher and Jack agreed that if he missed a day he would spend a part of his lunch hour making up the work.

The plan was implemented. The teacher consistently supported Jack's effort. The contract was extended until Jack's sentences became paragraphs. Only then did the teacher give him constructive comments as well as positive reinforcement. They renegotiated the contract until Jack began to show signs of becoming confident to write and speak at least enough to do the minimal homework assignments. Jack grew ever so slightly but, by the end of the year, English was the one class in which he received a "C" for the final reporting period. At least in one area of his life, Jack was beginning to reduce his onlooker behavior. He was meeting some of the teacher's and his own expectations. The teacher had helped to build Jack's feeling of confidence or security through small, appropriate steps of successful behavior. Jack's need for security was beginning to be satisfied through appropriate student behavior.

UNTOUCHABLES

The behavior of the untouchable pattern is aggressive, combative, and power-oriented and shows a need to constantly dominate others. This specific pattern represents a strong secondary need for security. The behavior of untouchables appears to be prompted by a great concern for self and little concern for others. These students believe they are worthwhile people only when they are in control of others. They are afraid of what others may do to them.

Leaders of school gangs and some elected class leaders best illustrate untouchables. They order subordinates around, seldom ask for their opinion, and dominate any decisions made in groups. These students sometimes threaten to hurt those who are not loyal to them. They are unpredictable, delegating to others on an inconsistent basis. Yet, the untouchable fears the unexpected and desperately tries to make people behave in predictable patterns. Manipulation of others compensates for a feeling of helplessness. The behavior of untouchables is at times sarcastic and critical of others; they are capable of public denouncement of the accomplishments and errors of others. Untouchables strive to appear self-sufficient and often seem to be rigidly adhering to their set standards. In trying to appear self-sufficient, untouchables avoid class involvement with other students.

The teacher who views the behavior of the untouchable as appropriate may describe the specific pattern as follows:

> These students make my work less difficult in that untouchables help to put controls on the other members of the class. I work the untouchables to my advantage. Students can be controlled through methods of intimidation similar to those I use to control students. When the untouchables work in my class groups, they help direct the action. They get decisions made, and students do not wander aimlessly from the task.

Teachers who reject the behavior of the untouchables as inappropriate in most situations describe these students as follows:

> Untouchables always have an answer even if they are wrong. They physically push other students around. They encourage others to violate the school's regulations or to come as close to violating them as possible without going over the line. Untouchables seek and find ways of "beating the system." They frequently capitalize on my mistakes by trying to intimidate me and to weaken my position of authority.

Some teachers who are most concerned with satisfying their own need for control of others are extremely annoyed by the behavior of untouchables and view their dominating behavior as a threat to the teacher's professional and personal security.[1] The authoritarian behavior of these students is viewed as inappropriate by teachers who believe that all students should be growing in the capacity to become independent rather than following the lead of an untouchable. Specific descriptors of the behavior pattern of the untouchable include:

1. Aggressive.
2. Combative.
3. Puts others down.
4. Easily angered.
5. Oppositional.

Improving Untouchables: An Example

After a brief discussion among Frank's teachers in the faculty room, all concluded that Frank's predominant specific behavior pattern was most like that of the untouchable.

> Frank was a wheel among his loyal followers. He tended to dominate his group. He was always unimpressed with the accomplishments of others and enjoyed talking about the less desirable characteristics of other people. He was generally oppositional. Frank and his home-room teacher were at opposite ends of a continuum much of the time. Frank would not do what the teacher wanted done. He was rebelling against authority and the formal system and taking a significant number of students with him in each instance.

The third step in the reformational process here might be the development of a contract that includes (1) reasonable aims for a student, (2) methods for achieving those aims, and (3) a method for evaluating progress. In this instance, the contract should be designed to help Frank find appropriate behavior to reduce his strong need for control. General elements for a contract to improve the untouchable behavior pattern are as follows:

1. The contract must include provisions for making sure that other students are free to make their own decisions.

2. The student should be able to hold a position in the school that gives him or her appropriate control over others in representing the school. In this way, the need to control is diverted into appropriate behavior, providing appropriate rewards until such time as the need to control is reduced.

3. A portion of the contract should include provisions for helping students recognize and deal with their feelings about themselves and with closeness to others. Specifically, they should learn to express feelings about others in a relatively safe environment. This will take practice.

Frank's homeroom teacher began to work on helping Frank improve his behavior. After a typical homeroom period with Frank challenging the teacher for control of the class, the teacher held a private conference with Frank. Frank and the teacher worked out an agreement that would begin to help Frank find a new way to satisfy his need for control and security. Frank agreed to follow the teacher's instructions for ten days and, rather than argue in class, to meet the teacher after school to discuss in private any areas of disagreement or things he did not understand. Frank agreed that he had to cooperate with the teacher even though he did not always want to, or face the ultimate consequences of being placed on school suspension. The teacher made these expectations clear. After ten days of appropriate behavior as prescribed by the teacher, Frank would begin to work with a small group of students to develop topics for discussion during homeroom period. Frank also agreed to try working with a counselor for a short time.

As the contract was being implemented, Frank's need to control was beginning to be satisfied through the formal school system rather than the informal. He was beginning to take steps toward shaping formal events in school and was becoming responsible for their outcomes. But after five days of working with the contract, an incident resulted in Frank's suspension. The contract was reviewed with his parents. Frank was not returned to his homeroom until he convinced both the principal and the teacher that he meant what he said about adhering to the contract. Frank returned to homeroom to try again.

Some students began to say that Frank was being fooled and manipulated. Others, not loyal to his following, were relieved to have Frank using his influence in a cooperative rather than an oppositional manner. Frank worked with a counselor and several other students trying to learn more about himself. This meant revealing himself and getting close to others, something he wanted but avoided. Upon completion of the second contract, Frank dropped out of the counseling session but did go on to help security personnel control the flow of students at the school entrance. Frank checked student ID cards for a year while working with security personnel.

While untouchable behavior can be viewed as appropriate, it is most often seen as inappropriate behavior in need of being changed. Frank was one of the fortunate few who was able, at least for a while, to satisfy his need for control through appropriate behavior. Frank also received recognition for his appropriate behavior.

PERFECTIONISTS

The perfectionist pattern of behavior reflects a moderate-to-weak need for acceptance in combination with a moderate-to-weak need for control. The perfectionist's behavior is primarily a response to a need for security that can only be satisfied through being perceived by others as perfect at all one does. These students' sense of worth is regulated by the degree to which they are able to attain perfection and to be perceived as better than others. They are afraid of not being the best at everything, and they try to impress people with their knowledge and skills. Their self-image is one of personal inadequacy.

Students whose predominant behavior is perfectionist are concerned with becoming competent, seeking self-improvement, and beating others in school. They are extremely hard on themselves, expecting perfection, as they must be perceived as competent. Improving at whatever they do is essential; they value increased competence in chosen areas. Recreational time is spent attempting to improve with great vigor. Beating others in competition is not enough unless performing with excellence is the source of victory. These students may appear arrogant by questioning statements from authorities. Just because a teacher states something does not make it so. Perfectionists have a high degree of self-doubt—they believe they never do well enough. Sometimes they lack decisiveness because they fear failure.

Perfectionists attempt to impress people with their terse, compact, logical, and profound knowledge. They prefer the exacting and complicated subjects found in the sciences. Perfectionists view all living as work through which improvement and achieving competence are possible. Work is the opportunity to express one's knowledge, skills, and activities. Perfectionists, while trying to determine or analyze what is happening with people around them, are unable to live in the present. They reflect little concern for the feelings of others. Perfectionists project themselves above others to hide their own sense of inadequacy for not being perfect.

Teachers who view the behavior of perfectionists as appropriate may describe the behavior as follows:

> Their "go-get-'em" spirit reflects a zest for living. These students only need a challenge to become committed to a task. They may spend all night on assignments, always trying to do the impossible. Perfectionists attempt to be excellent at everything they do. They put aside trivia and don't get caught up in feeling sorry for those who do not attempt perfection. They create competition with other students and use their energy in such constructive endeavors as winning.

Other teachers view the behavior of the perfectionist as inappropriate. These teachers might classify the perfectionist as follows:

> Perfectionists do not cooperate in a group activity where an individual's effort is diluted in the group. In a group, they try to outdo others and take credit for the group's accomplishments. It is simply not enough for them to beat others; they usually have to make sure that others know that they won. Perfectionists appear not to be genuine as they try to be seen as perfect in front of us. They slam around in classrooms and use strong language in response to a less-than-adequate performance in a competitive situation. These students create games that will help them beat the system. They appear to be particularly boastful after a victory and are concerned about themselves rather than class activities. They set impossible goals for themselves in their attempts to be viewed as perfect or better than others.

Specific descriptors of the perfectionist pattern of behavior are:

1. Wants to do it alone.
2. Concern with competency.
3. Must prove him- or herself.
4. Must be best at everything.
5. "Goes one better" than others.

Improving Perfectionists: A Case Example

Jim's perfectionist behavior pattern, as observed by a teacher who believed such behavior was inappropriate, was as follows:

Jim was the most competitive student in the science class. He was not brilliant but, by working hard, could keep up with many of the students in the class. He typically tried to beat others, and when he did better than others, everyone knew about it. He always tried to appear totally competent and to do the impossible. No matter what the situation, Jim always viewed it as a win-lose situation. When others did better than he on tests, he went into a mood of self-blame, saying that he should have studied more, that he should have studied different things, and so on. In some instances, it would be several days before Jim would again get involved in class activities after someone had outperformed him.

To improve the pattern of behavior of the perfectionist, the contract in the reformation process should include:

1. A reasonable goal that encourages a student to compete against himself or herself rather than others all the time.
2. Short-range goals with feedback to the student at brief intervals. A part of the feedback should be recognition for appropriate behavior.
3. Medium-risk behaviors that are helpful to student and to others and that allow some mistakes.

The teacher, observing Jim's high self-blame and competitiveness, which were hindering his learning and social relationships, decided that he might be focusing too much on perfection and on comparing his performance and that of other students. She met with Jim and worked out an agreement that helped Jim direct his energies toward achieving reasonable expectations. First, the teacher made an arrangement with Jim to estimate before a test a reasonable level for his performance. She asked him to assess the extent of his knowledge and his ability to relate and manipulate the information and concepts. They agreed on the probable number of mistakes Jim might make. For class projects, Jim would submit his aims and time scheme for each project he planned to do. When Jim sought unreasonable aims or standards of performance, the teacher would help modify his goals to reflect Jim's interest and ability. She was always to give him some verbal or written feedback on the reasonableness of his plans. They planned to check Jim's performance to determine his direction of growth.

After Jim took a test or completed a project, the two of them would compare Jim's estimates with his actual results. After the plan was implemented, Jim became less concerned with his lack of perfect performance in comparison to others. He found himself almost always at the top of the class on test scores and project grades. He was able to focus more on his own performance and was able to set more reasonable academic goals for himself.

Not all such contracts or attempts to improve behavior are as successful as the one in Jim's case. The behavior of the perfectionist stems from a basic lack of security, and the behavior can be viewed as appropriate or unappropriate. Helping the perfectionist learn to be moderately rather than severely dissatisfied with a less-than-perfect performance is a difficult task. But perfectionists can learn that they do not have to excel in every venture: perfection may be sought in a selected group of activities rather than every task.

SEEKERS

The seeker's behavior is prompted by a strong need for acceptance by others. Students with this predominant pattern believe they are "okay" only if others indicate approval of their behavior. Their personal sense of worth is determined by the approval or disapproval of others. They fear being rejected.

Students whose predominant behavior fits the seeker pattern basically are easily led by other people. Seekers want to please others, teachers and students alike. They are responsive to social pressure because they want to be accepted and included socially. Seekers are overly concerned with what others expect them to do and can be observed being controlled by others who grant them approval. These students seek out students and teachers who will not reject or disapprove of them in any way. They react to others as if everything others do is a personal attack or criticism of their behavior or person. Relationships with others are almost always one-way relationships; that is, the seekers are always dominated in social relationships. Seekers seldom initiate action unless they have received some indication that it will increase their acceptance. Their actions are always followed by a search for acknowledgement or approval by others. The behavior of such students is marked by a seeming lack of consistency, because a variety of expectations are guiding their behavior. Their behavior is self-seeking, designed to help the student know that he or she is liked or accepted.

Teachers who view seekers as acting appropriately might describe their behavior as follows:

> Seekers talk or listen to me for hours. They are good, helpful, compliant friends to have in a classroom. I make the decisions as to what we will do in the class, and they follow my leads. These students are exceptionally good at doing extra tasks for me. Seekers run errands to the office, tell me how much they like my teaching, and always agree with me. They are outgoing and like to participate in discussions when I want their comments. Seekers do not complain.

Conversely, teachers who view the behavior of seekers as inappropriate describe them as follows:

> Seekers are easily controlled by other students. Seekers often lower their initiative to receive peer approval, seldom make their own decisions, are inconsistent, and usually lack any real sense of direction. Usually, these students are excessive talkers and cannot stand silence. Seekers are unable to think for themselves and incapable of judging their own level of performance. Their self-esteem is tied to the approval or rejection of other persons.

In summary, students who are seekers need approval from others. Some teachers believe that the behavior of seekers is appropriate dependent behavior. Others consider the dependency of seekers as inappropriate. Specific descriptors of the behavior pattern of the seeker include:

1. Conformity.
2. Overcomplicance.
3. Very responsive to social pressure.
4. Seeks approval from others.
5. Easily led.

Improving Seekers: An Example

A teacher categorized Broderick's behavior as being primarily that of a seeker:

> Broderick was a person few students really liked. He was new to the school. He wanted to be everyone's friend. He adopted the values of one group of students. When he behaved as they did it paid off for

him in short-term goals. Other students soon began to use him by getting him to do things that were inappropriate, but which also provided some acceptance and approval from students. Broderick was in conflict with the science teacher's expectations. In that class, he repeatedly used the laboratory equipment for fun and games rather than for experiments. The science teacher was concerned because Broderick did not gain the respect of his peers and teachers. Broderick's teacher conferred with the school counselor and with Broderick on occasion. Finally, a major blowup precipitated a lengthy conference with the science teacher.

A continuous focus on getting approval from others is a major problem for some students who have a dominant acceptance-seeking pattern. Recommendations that might be included in contracts developed in a reformation process are as follows:

1. The aims in the contract should be established by the student and should be reasonable and achievable.
2. The reasons for the aims in the contract should be defined. The student needs to understand why he or she established specific goals.
3. The student should agree to evaluate his or her own behavior. This student needs to become the judge of his or her own progress, behavior, and feelings.

With his parents and the teacher, Broderick developed the following contract.

Broderick established a plan to do three laboratory experiments. These three experiments were fairly simple but could be combined and used in a public science display program scheduled for the next month. He placed in the contract a timetable for completion of each experiment. He agreed to keep the design for the experiment and products intact during the entire science display program. He wanted to do this so others would view his work. Broderick agreed to evaluate his own work and to meet with the teacher to discuss his evaluation of each experiment. He would evaluate both his behavior while doing the project and the effectiveness of his work.

Broderick applied for several new contracts with the same teacher. By the end of the year, he had demonstrated appropriate behavior during science class. Other teachers shared their concerns about Broderick with counseling personnel. Several of these teachers used a similar contract process in dealing with Broderick's problem. His behavior showed an overall improvement, but his desire for acceptance in social relationships led to three years of heartbreak with a wide variety of different girlfriends until he entered into a stable relationship with his wife-to-be!

The four student behavior patterns presented thus far—onlooker, untouchable, perfectionist, and seeker—are designed to provide the student a sense of security. Four different behavior patterns prompted by a student's need for satisfaction were identified in Chapter 5 as caring behavior patterns—those of the becomer, performer, leader, and developer. Discussion of these follows.

BECOMERS

Becomers value their uniqueness; that is, they believe they are different from other people. Their behavior is prompted by the need to care both about people and about impersonal objectives. On occasion, becomers develop an intense commitment to religious causes. The intense caring about the cause often leads to individualist behaviors different from most other students. The crusade for causes marks a concern with self-fulfillment and the imposition of their cause on others, rather than a concern for the growth of some thing or person. Becomers are afraid they may not discover what makes them unique and what they will become. The self-image of the becomer is of one who attempts to be different.

Behavior of the becomer is "being"-oriented and process-oriented. Becomers are interested in the process of becoming. They search for the purpose of their life. When they act, they want feedback from others who may help them review their experience. Every experience is considered personally significant to them. Comments from others help becomers find out who they are trying to become. Becomers contemplate making a decision for a long time. They are attracted to materials and people that help them analyze their own behavior. They tend to make many false starts at doing things, because what they do must fit them. Becomers build ideal relationships with a few people who can help them discover their unique role in school.

Such students may become committed to causes that appear to be significant in the school or world. If the cause loses its significance, so that it does not appear "to move mountains," becomers may search for a different cause with a larger significance or greater application to the students in the school. They are attracted to groups who are interested in transmitting ideas and attitudes. Becomers have a high acceptance level of what others determine to be significant. They know how it feels to have a vital commitment. These students may be the writers, poets, and missionaries of a school.

The teacher who views the behavior of the becomer as appropriate may describe the student as follows:

> Becomers dress differently from other students. In class, they are interested in the lives of "great people" and in the discussion of philosophies. They are captivated by the psychological aspects of behavior. Becomers are extremely accepting of the views of other students but vocal about their own position on a subject. They have an optimistic outlook toward problems I present and encounter in class. They get excited over a variety of topics.

Teachers who view becomers as acting inappropriately characterize them as follows:

> Becomers act differently from other students in the class. They simply do not conform to normal standards and their behavior is oppositional. They are unaware of time. Important assignments do not get accomplished because they do not feel that time is a boundary. Becomers frequently are involved in dreams of greatness for themselves. Without apparent reason they may shift their direction to a different dream. Many projects they start for a class do not get finished. They seem to become emotional at the drop of a hat. This emotional level at times keeps them from reaching closure on anything.

In summary, becomers reflect a weak need to care, and some teachers approve of this behavior while others disapprove. Specific descriptors of the behavior pattern of the becomer are as follows:

1. Centered on self.
2. Seeks self-fulfillment.
3. Attracted to causes; people.
4. Sees good in everything.
5. "Being"-oriented.

Improving Becomers: A Case Example

Joni's behavior was considered by her teachers to be that of a becomer.

Joni had been a "flower child" since ninth grade. She was always in the process of learning. She dressed differently from the rest of her peers and was anxious to hear others tell her about her uniqueness. She worked hard at building relationships with a few close friends who seemed to understand her search for herself. She constantly acted out her role and sought feedback from others on how they regarded her. On at least two occasions, she became intensely committed to two religious groups that had formed among the students. When these causes didn't take, she looked for a higher commitment. Joni frequently was late for meetings and classes because of her dedication to a cause. Teachers and others were concerned about Joni's lack of clear objectives for herself and about her tendency to ignore time limitations. They were afraid that she might be so present-oriented that she would never graduate from high school.

Students such as Joni have a great concern with uniqueness. There are a variety of ways for attempting to improve the behavior of the becomer; Step 3 of the reformational process provides one method. The contract for students with a weak motivation for caring might include the following elements:

1. Specific goals to help a student assess interests, strengths, and weaknesses. The student must begin to become aware of self and long-range interests beyond a major "cause."

2. Specific short-range goals that require closure. The student's behavior needs to become more time-specific and the student needs to experience success with implementing a concrete plan.

Joni agreed in a contract with her teachers to arrive at classes on time. Perhaps the most significant element of the agreement was Joni's willingness to work with the counselor in taking a series of interest inventories and personality tests. Joni stuck with her agreement for two weeks. Thereafter, Joni still had difficulty disciplining herself to be on time. Through feedback on herself from friends and the inventories, Joni began to discover her strengths and weaknesses. She began to believe she knew herself and where she might be going with her life.

PERFORMERS

Performers set reasonable goals and plans and are persistent in their attempts to achieve their aims. The performer behavior pattern reflects a strong need for caring about the growth of a project. Performers need to achieve growth in an impersonal entity for the sake of accomplishing a task. Their sense of worth is derived from contributing to the growth of a project. Performers are afraid of not being able to complete tasks. The self-image of the performer is of one who has success accomplishing tasks. They believe that they are capable of controlling and manipulating the environment.

Students whose behavior reflects the performer pattern tend to set goals in which they accept responsibility for their actions. They evaluate work carefully and select aims that include risk, but not too much. Performers seek immediate feedback on their performance and adjust their actions or goals based on information on their performance. Rather than share their work, performers try to do it all themselves. They look for opportunities to achieve self-set aims using their own effort.

Students of this type aim to improve their own records of performance without a major concern for "beating" other students. Defeats are viewed by performers as opportunities to improve. These students accept their past performance as history that is impossible to change. Performers avoid situations that lack clarity of their responsibility to others. They discuss their preferences in a direct and open manner and work as team members when specific goals are established.

A teacher who views the behavior of performers as appropriate in school might describe them as follows:

> Performers are self-starters, persistent, and able to achieve assignments in classes. They are the movers and stimulators in class projects and extracurricular activities. They act while others talk about acting. They write up plans and determine materials needed for a project. Performers use initiative on assignments and are anxious to receive feedback on how they are doing. They are quick to adjust their behavior to be more successful.

Conversely, teachers who view the behavior pattern of performers as inappropriate might describe them as follows:

These students are primarily selfish, wanting to do their own thing most of the time. Performers set their own goals and do not accept the assignments and activities the teacher defines. Performers act independently of others in groups, are uncooperative at times in working with teams, and are self-seeking. They are insubordinate, refusing to do easy assignments and reluctant to take on extemely difficult tasks if I define them.

In summary, performers are task-oriented students concerned with orderly planning and project work. They reflect a strong need to care about an impersonal entity. Descriptors for the behavior pattern of the performer include:

1. Sets reasonable goals.
2. Plans ahead.
3. Creative.
4. Perseveres.
5. Project-oriented.

Improving Performers: An Example

The inappropriate behavior pattern of a performer and a contract developed to improve the student's behavior are provided in the following account:

> Jane was a task-oriented student and very effective at completing the work she laid out for herself. She was a determined person, knowing what she wanted to do most of the time. She had the ability to set reasonably challenging goals for herself and to evaluate the extent to which tasks appeared to be relevant for her own growth. She planned far in advance on her own and usually created plans with alternatives. Her major problem revolved around a class in physical education and her lack of involvement with other people. She was always told what to do in physical education class, and she refused to do some of the assigned exercises that involved others. The teacher became concerned about her uncooperative attitude toward working with other students.

In using the reformational process with performers, one must be mindful that such students prefer setting their own goals with little concern for sharing responsibilities with others. Thus, the following should be observed:

1. The contract must include goals that include sharing responsibilities with others.

2. The third step of the reformational process should include a procedure for involving other students in the evaluation of the progress the group is making toward some goal.

3. The contract should include time to be spent by the student just conversing with others.

4. As an alternative to items 1–3, a student might contract just once to do what other students want done, thus helping others achieve their goals.

The P.E. teacher met with Jane and they formulated a contract.

Jane would be paired off with another student, and together they would determine their desired level of team performance in gym class for one month. A month later, Jane would work with a group of three students. Once a week, in lieu of a study period, Jane would work with several students in P.E. classes. The teacher and the older students would plan the classes together to provide individual attention to the younger students. Jane would spend some of these other periods sitting on the gymnasium benches and, rather than studying, would converse with members of the P.E. class. Jane and the teacher agreed to talk once a week for a few minutes to review the progress she was making.

The plan was implemented, but it did not work. Jane had too many personal goals to achieve and simply could not be bothered with other students in the physical education class.

LEADERS

Leaders are emotionally secure, pleasant, and down-to-earth achievers. The behavior pattern of the leader reflects a balance between a strong need to care about the growth of a project and a strong need to care about the growth of people who may be involved or affected by the project. Leaders believe they are worthwhile people when they can get things accomplished through and with others. They fear very little. The self-image of the leader is positive and grounded in the belief that he or she can be successful with social interactions and in project-related tasks.

Students whose predominant behavior fits the leader pattern are cooperative, mature, accepting of others, and task-oriented. Leaders are not likely to be threatened by the unknown and at times they are attracted to it. They are comfortable with confusion. These students are seldom shaken by an unfortunate turn of events. They have the ability to accept their feelings and seldom suffer from extreme guilt or shame. Leaders rely on their own judgment and inner feelings to make decisions. They are open to suggestions, capable of weighing alternatives, and willing to accept the responsibility that accompanies decision making. These students accept others as they are, not as they wish others to be. Because they accept others, they establish selected caring relationships with others while working toward the achievement of their long-term tasks.

Leaders are spontaneous, focus on things outside themselves, and usually have well-thought-out, long-range plans for their lives. Short-term setbacks such as a failed test or a lost match are viewed as small incidents in the activities designed to achieve the long-term mission. Being rejected by others does not substantially alter their behavior, and they continue to reach out in a caring manner. The teacher who views leaders' behavior as appropriate describes them as follows:

> Leaders are sensitive to situational factors and are successful at a variety of school-related tasks. They are comfortable in new situations, communicate effectively, and use realistic judgment in situations. Leaders are sensitive to the feelings of others. They respond to their own emotions but use logic and reasoning in making the most of their decisions. Leaders respond to the behavior of others by acknowledging how a person is feeling and, on occasion, by aiding a person in confronting a problem. These students exhibit a wide range of adaptive behaviors in situations. Remaining calm in stressful situations and handling responsibility in an adult manner are perhaps their most notable characteristics. They represent the resources of another adult when I am working with students.

Other teachers view the behavior of the leader as inappropriate. A likely expression of such an attitude is as follows:

> Leaders act too much like adults in the classroom setting. They refuse to follow the teacher's directions and resist going along with the rest of the class for the sake of going along with the crowd. They simply accept mistakes they have made rather than apologizing for what they have done.

It is difficult to bring them into line in situations where the control of others through anxiety is essential. They make judgments (often accurate) about situations before I can assess a situation and react to it.

In summary, the leader shows a high need to care for both projects and people. The behavior of the leader reflects a sensitive but stable emotional base. A teacher views the behavior of the leader as appropriate depending on the needs of the teacher. Specific descriptors of the leader behavior pattern are as follows:

1. A good listener.
2. Steady.
3. Accepts self and others.
4. High emotional security.
5. Pleasant facial expression.

Improving Leaders: An Example

Cheryl's case is one in which leader behavior was considered inappropriate by her social science teacher.

Cheryl has always been a step ahead of her friends in both physical and mental maturity. She was elected president of her class for three of her four years in high school. As a senior in school, she was ready to enter the adult world. Cheryl was having difficulty with her teacher in an advanced social science class. The class was studying typical problems faced by communities. The teacher had brought in speakers from the local community to present community problems. Cheryl believed that the class was ready to participate in a series of problem-solving simulations built around these community problems. She had suggested that the class be divided into teams for attacking ten critical community problems. Other students picked up on her suggestion. The teacher found himself in conflict with the students. He felt that Cheryl did not know enough about education and social studies to make such decisions. This was not the first time he and Cheryl had disagreed. She was simply too outspoken and opinionated to meet his expectations of what a student was supposed to be.

It is difficult to create a recommendation for improving Cheryl's behavior, because it may be the behavior of the teacher that needs to be altered. However, some educators do view the leader pattern as inappropriate for students. Therefore, a contract for improving the behavior of the leader might rest on the following:

1. The contract should include an agreement for the student to be concerned about his or her individual performance rather than that of other students.

2. The contract should include provisions for the student to make suggestions to the teacher on a one-to-one basis rather than during class.

3. The contract should encourage the student to help the teacher perform instructional roles only when asked to do so.

A contract designed to help Cheryl meet the expectations of the social science teacher was developed.

Cheryl would work on a problem-solving project, but it would not include other members of the class. Because Cheryl had her own judgments about how she and others learned, she would meet with the teacher on a one-on-one basis and write out suggestions she had for the class as a whole. Cheryl would have an opportunity one day a month to make presentations to the class or to involve them in an activity that she and the teacher had designed. The contract was implemented and Cheryl and the teacher reduced the obvious tension that had created the problem for both of them. The teacher was not really open to suggestions, as Cheryl soon discovered, but Cheryl was able to become less visible in class and to get some suggestions accepted through the contract. In the next year, however, the teacher's class included several of Cheryl's suggestions and student interest in the class, particularly that of leaders, increased.

It is hoped that teachers review their own behavior and attitudes while attempting to change those of their students.

DEVELOPERS

The behavior of developers reflects the strong need to care about others. Developers are concerned about the status and growth of other people. They assist others in solving problems associated with maturing. The developer's behavior pattern is a reaction to the need to contribute to the lives of others and his or her self-worth is attached to actions that help others achieve the things they want. They are afraid of having to spend too much time on their own work. The self-image of the developer is that of a person who likes him- or herself and who has the capacity to help others achieve the goals they establish for themselves.

Students with the predominant pattern of the developer appear to enjoy relationships that help others grow in the ability to make decisions. Developers like the support of others and the warmth that is returned to them from others. They avoid working alone and setting unilateral goals, since satisfaction is derived from the process of sharing with others. They like to participate in both group and team situations. They enjoy self-development as it contributes to the team effort. Developers have empathy and seem to have unlimited time to help others. In their view, time is an endless commodity, and they often engage in long conversations. They are friendly, relaxed, and popular listeners. Establishing wholesome relationships with others is the developer's primary aim. Impersonal tasks are not attractive to the developer.

Some teachers view the behavior of developers as appropriate in the school situation. For example, some teachers describe developers as follows:

> Developers are extremely helpful to other students. They are excellent team members and work with me and other students to complete their work. Emotionally upset students seek them out for peer counseling. Developers are perceptive receivers of nonverbal signals that come from me. Developers help me not simply for a grade or for my approval, but because I am a person.

Other teachers view the behavior of developers as inappropriate. For example, some teachers view this behavior as follows:

> Developers spend time listening to their friends and other students. They seem to serve as crutches to students who should be thinking for themselves. The long conversations developers share with other students take them away from the academic work. They are people-oriented rather than

task-oriented. Developers are simply concerned about the growth of others rather than with creating a work of art, for example, or with mastering scientific concepts.

Specific descriptors of the behavior pattern of the developer are as follows:

1. Friendly.
2. Close relationships.
3. Popular with others.
4. Does not make quick decisions.
5. Relaxed, comfortable appearance.

Improving Developers: An Example

A middle school math teacher regarded the developer behavior of one student to be inappropriate for learning.

John was a student who enjoyed being with other people. He was concerned about the welfare of his friends, listened to them, and was popular as a student. His interest in people was intense and appeared to be the source of a problem with his math teacher who was subject-matter–oriented and less concerned with human relationships. John constantly engaged in long but helpful conversations with other students. He expressed a genuine warmth toward his classmates. His problem, as the teacher viewed it, was that he talked too much and was far too interested in being popular, although he really did not disturb the other students. He did his own work and then tried to be of assistance to others. At times, students in the class would seek his assistance rather than that of the teacher. The math teacher thought that John was simply not doing as well as he should in handling detail and time, even though John was in the top one-fourth of his math class. She expected to see John "put his hand to the task" more often and to get all of his work in on time. She encouraged John to go deeper into the material rather than talk to others so much. John resisted this and the situation became a struggle.

Considerations for a contract to apply the reformational process to the inappropriate behavior of the developer are as follows:

1. The student should include as part of the contract specific task-related aims that do not involve relationships with others.
2. Specific methods of receiving feedback should be included in the contract to help monitor the student's progress toward the aims specified.
3. The contract should include specific deadlines for accomplishing some tasks.

After several brief encounters, the teacher and John developed a contract.

> John was to identify several aims beyond classroom assignments each day for a three-week period. These aims might involve working with others on math-related projects after class, but not during class. He would be responsible for submitting the final product on time as mutually predetermined. This extra work would take the place of his talk time in class. John would pay particular attention to detail in his work. After each extra assignment was turned in, John would receive feedback on his work and on whether he had met the planned deadlines. He would talk to other students only after he had permission from the teacher.
>
> The contract was implemented and John fulfilled the agreement. His interest in math class decreased, although his achievement levels increased slightly. By the end of the year, he was able to define his work more effectively and pay close attention to detail. For a while, John resented not being able to provide more assistance to others. There appeared to be an increase in his out-of-school involvement in others centering on non-school–related projects.

To John, learning away from school on a cooperative basis was now seen as appropriate, but learning in school was something you did alone, particularly mathematics.

The four patterns of caring behavior exhibited by students—becomers, performers, leaders, and developers—arise to satisfy intrinsic needs to care about people, impersonal entities, or both. Combinations of the secondary needs associated with the need to care and the need for security lead the student to feel the need to belong to an organization and the need to be impulsive. Student behavior patterns produced by these resultant needs are discussed next. The need to belong to an organization is seen in the loyalist and the need to be impulsive is seen in the operator.

LOYALISTS

Loyalists are the cooperative workers in the formal and informal organizations of a school. Loyalists reflect a strong primary need to belong to an organized group. They may have a need to be accepted, a need to care about others, or a combination of both. They believe they must contribute through work to belong to a group and that group status is earned through a person's efforts. Loyalists believe they are worthwhile people when they are in place in an organization. Loyalists are afraid of not being a part of one. The self-image of the loyalist is that of a follower in an organization.

Loyalists value belonging to a group or unit. They value accomplishments that they may achieve by cooperation with the group and membership that is earned through cooperatively serving independently of others. Loyalists look for what they are supposed to do, believing if they do "the oughts" they will find and maintain a place in the organization. The loyalists, although followers, are interested in positions of status, and they express concern for establishing and maintaining groups. The loyalists follow the norms established in the group for purposes of attaining rank in the organization. Loyalists enjoy responsibilities associated with rank. They are oriented toward duty, authority, and obligation. Their time orientation is the past, and that is reflected in their occasional moodiness. The immediate or spontaneous has little appeal for loyalists.

A teacher who believes the behavior of loyalists is positive might describe the person as follows:

> These students work on committees and in groups to keep the school organization operating. They are obedient, independent contributors to their group(s). Loyalists decorate the gym for dances, help to prepare for homecoming and graduation, and participate in organized rituals. They assist in maintaining school organizations and also contribute to groups that are not formally recognized by the school. They are nice, cooperative students who, at times, value the group above themselves.

Other teachers do not hold a positive view of the behavior of the loyalist. They describe the inappropriate behavior of the loyalist as follows:

> Loyalists are joiners. They devote themselves to work designed to attain status in an organization. When it comes to a choice between doing their school work and doing work for their organization, they choose the latter. They neglect their academic work for the sake of the school group. They satisfy the expectations of group members rather than my concerns. Loyalists are concerned with the title they get in a school group.

Specific descriptors of the behavior pattern of the loyalist are as follows:

1. Rule-oriented.
2. Concerned about status.
3. Believes in fundamentals.
4. Reliable and dependable.
5. Nice, cooperative person.

Improving Loyalists: An Example

The loyalist behavior of Jenny in school organizations caused teachers to attempt to modify her behavior.

> Jenny liked the security of belonging to a variety of school organizations. She believed that hard work leads to success and membership in clubs. She worked on tasks that contributed to the goals of the organizations. Jenny always did what the group thought she should do. She was obedient and abided by all group rules to the letter. The result was that Jenny frequently did not do the things that led to success in many of the classes. But Jenny had not been elected to a position of status in any organization to which she belonged. Several teachers were concerned about her overwhelming need to belong to organizations and the strong authority the members in the groups had over her.

When contracts are written with loyalists as a means of changing their behavior, the contracts should include the following elements:

1. Self-development aims should be included that may or may not contribute to the organizations to which a student belongs.
2. Specific times should be scheduled for non-organization–related work.
3. A mechanism for recording the balance between time devoted to organizations and self-development should be arranged, if the self-development activities are not making a direct contribution to the

organizations. (Note: It may be possible in the contract to encourage student contributions to the organizations, in a way such that the student can develop personal skills, knowledge, and maturity at the same time.)

Jenny and her biology and social studies teachers worked together on the development of a contract.

> Jenny agreed to work on her classwork during instructional time rather than on other projects. She would not ask to leave class early on occasions to work in activities associated with the organization as she had done in the past. At the end of each week, Jenny would submit a sheet showing the amount of time she had devoted to her class work and to her organizations. After two weeks, Jenny was upset about not fulfilling the expectations of those with whom she was associated in two organizations. The biology and social studies teachers conferred with the faculty advisers for these organizations to explain the problem. Jenny then met with the faculty advisers and the presidents of both organizations. She worked out an arrangement with the advisers and presidents to do a specific, limited amount of work for each club. She was assured that this reduction in work would not jeopardize her standing in the school organizations.

Six months later, Jenny had dropped out of one organization but was excelling in the other. Her classwork had also improved. But in the next year, Jenny had to repeat the process, as she had again become overcommitted to organizations.

OPERATORS

Operators' behavior is a response to a strong need to be impulsive. This primary need may reflect a secondary need to control others or to care about impersonal entities. Action-oriented operators need to test their own limits as part of the need to be impulsive. They constantly seek new risks with equipment, such as automobiles, and with people as a test of their own limits. Operators' sense of worth is tied to the extent to which they can control themselves and equipment in high-risk situations. They are afraid of being denied the opportunity to be involved in the action. Their self-image is that of a spontaneous gambler who believes he or she can bring anything in the environment under his or her control.

Operators are action-oriented, carefree, and impulsive excitement seekers. They detest drill and repetition. Operators would rather not practice, even though they can get caught up in action that is so rewarding that they stay with it for a time. Operators want to do as they wish, when they wish. They prefer randomness and an opportunity to do a variety of things. They are impulsive, yielding to sudden urges to do things. These students really like to test the limits, take the chance. They are able to respond effectively in crisis situations and may create a crisis if things are too quiet. They create an atmosphere of excitement in a group.

Operators prefer action, but not for the purpose of achieving an end product. Their enjoyment comes from the process. Operators frequently complete their work without reading the assignments, as they strive to be independent and free and to reach closure. They may desert groups or organizations in favor of their own interests. Success is measured by the extent to which they obtain satisfaction through an adventure in which they elected to participate. Life is seen as play, not work.

Some teachers believe the behavior of operators is appropriate in the classroom. For example, a teacher might describe the operator as follows:

> Operators are the "doers" in the vocational education program. They use initiative, learn by trial and error, and actively engage in the use of technology. Operators have brief conversations with others. They ignore the mundane. In cocurricular activities, these students complete the difficult, high-risk tasks—like climbing to the roof of the building. Operators are adaptable in that they can exercise options when their plans are not working. They enjoy evaluating alternatives and trying something they have not done before.

Other teachers deplore the behavior pattern of the operator, regarding it as totally inappropriate. They describe the operator as follows:

> Operators are freewheeling, thoughtless daredevils who take unnecessary chances with their own lives and the lives of others. They drive too fast, create danger with explosives, and enjoy seeking thrills. They are unable to, or will not, follow a routine with their work and do not achieve excellence through practice. Frequently, their work is not done unless it is something new and exciting to them. In groups, operators stir up the rest of the students to create a crisis.

Operators are responding to a need to be carefree. Attempts to change operators through contracts may be difficult, as the next case account will demonstrate. Specific descriptors of the behavior of operators are:

1. Carefree.
2. Considers alternatives.
3. Always a participant.
4. Action-oriented.
5. Lacks empathy.

Improving Operators: An Example

The predominant behavior pattern of a student in a large suburban school was characterized as being that of an operator. A vocational education teacher was concerned about the student's carefree spirit, lack of dependability, and his avoidance of doing things that did not appeal to his fancy. He was described by the teacher as follows:

> Ken does what he wishes when he wishes. He believes that each day is to be enjoyed and that life is too brief to let pass by. His spice of life is variety. He feels no loyalty to any groups or to individuals. Ken avoids practice but likes to test the limits. His work is seldom done, particularly if it involves repeating the same task. He drives a car somewhat recklessly and looks for opportunities to do daring things with modern electrical technology. Ken creates an air of excitement whenever he enters a classroom or joins a group of students. He creates crises in school in order to do something daring.

The components to be included in a contract designed to improve the behavior of an operator are as follows:

1. Short-term classroom tasks of a significant nature should be defined as aims to which the student is committed.
2. The precise quantity and level of expected performance of the work should be identified.
3. Several appropriate risk-taking activities should be identified and integrated into the other less exciting tasks, but participation in

the risk-taking activities should depend on successful completion of the regular classroom tasks.

After a rather heated discussion involving Ken's parents, the principal, and the vocational education teacher, the first steps were taken to complete a contract with Ken.

The most difficult problem associated with the development of the contract was obtaining commitment from Ken to carry out the contract. Ken finally agreed to complete the written portion of his work in vocational education even though he preferred the laboratory work. He agreed to set specific aims for each day of one week for the completion of his written work. The contract also included the provision for on-the-spot review of Ken's work by his teacher for purposes of determining the extent to which quality and quantity were being met. It was also agreed that at least two days a week Ken would help other students do work that involved Ken's taking some risk in providing this assistance.

In less than seven days, Ken had slipped back into his old habit of ignoring the daily written work. The contract was renegotiated. More controls on Ken's time were built into the agreement. Three months later, Ken was suspended from school for burning up an engine. By the end of the year, Ken had been excluded permanently, awaiting a judge to rule on whether he should be readmitted to the school.

In summary, the predominant behavior of students may be categorized into one of ten specific behavior patterns. Recognition of the dominant behaviors that constitute the patterns provides a means of identifying the needs to which students are responding. Satisfying students' needs through appropriate behaviors in school may become possible when the reformational process is employed.

TEACHER BEHAVIOR PATTERNS

Discipline problems in school can be more easily understood when one identifies the contributions that teachers as well as students make to the conflict. This section should help to identify the possible contributions that teachers may be making to a conflict situation; it should also be of assistance to educators who search for the causes of, and cures for, conflict between teachers and students. The writers propose that teachers' classroom-management behavior can be categorized into patterns similar to the ten student behavior patterns. Extensive documentation of this assertion cannot be provided since research on teacher patterns is insufficient at this time.

Security Behavior Patterns

Onlookers as Teachers.   The onlooker pattern as manifested by teachers is characterized by an avoidance of responsibility, commitment, involvement, or communication. Teachers who behave in this manner believe they are incompetent and that survival can best be attained by ignoring the behaviors of students and keeping to oneself. Their awareness of others and of situational factors is very low, and their personal anxiety and stress are high. They find it difficult to really know what is going on around them, because they are preoccupied with their own thoughts of past failure and fantasies of what may happen. They lack confidence and harbor extremely high self-blame. As a consequence, onlookers as teachers find it extremely difficult to develop relationships with students or other faculty.

Such teachers give the complete responsibility for learning to the student. This posture allows a teacher to avoid becoming personally involved in the process. When these teachers sense inappropriate student behavior, they either act as though it is not there or they overreact by using penalties that do not fit the miscue. Their absenteeism rate may be high.

Onlookers are particularly susceptible to students who use fear as a means of gaining control over teachers. Untouchable students seem to be extremely threatening to onlooker teachers. Pickhardt, in discussing how students are able to create fear in teachers, stated the problem: "The sophistication of some of these students is impressive; they are 'people wise' beyond their years. Keenly observant, they notice the slightest tremors or insecurity or fright and move with incredible speed and accuracy to exploit their momentary advantage. They do not 'see' fear so much as they 'sense' it. And they know how to use it."[2]

Untouchables as Teachers.   Teachers whose behavior predominantly reflects the untouchable pattern have a strong power orientation. They view people as being subject to manipulation, criticizing almost everyone except a few loyal supporters who join them in denouncing teachers who do not belong to their group. They set themselves above those outside of their own group, sneak around creating distrust, and secretly or publicly denounce others. In many instances, this pattern leads to self-inflicted wounds. Teachers with this pattern more often than not lose the influence they need so desperately.

The behavior of the untouchable teachers reflects a lack of concern for students. Untouchable teachers view students as subordinates and expect them to follow orders. Untouchable teachers are reluctant to forgive students for mistakes. They get students to do what they want by making them fearful. Increased levels of anxiety resulting from fear can interfere significantly with a student's ability to learn. The teacher with an untouchable orientation may be unaware of many of the expectations that exist in a situation; hence, the teacher may act inappropriately in dealing with students. The social effectiveness of these teachers is reduced to the extent that they try to impose their will on others who do not expect or want to be controlled. It appears as though untouchable teachers view students who exhibit the leader, operator, and untouchable behavior patterns as acting inappropriately. Conversely, they probably enjoy the dependency of seekers and seldom view them as discipline problems.

Perfectionists as Teachers.   Teachers with perfectionist behavior patterns are extremely concerned about being right, appearing perfect, and beating others, both students and teachers. Conflicts with students are viewed as win-lose confrontations in which the teacher must win. Losing in any type of perceived contest is followed by feelings of not being a worthwhile person—much less a worthwhile teacher. Any sign of error is a symbol of weakness to the perfectionist. The perfectionist is anxious to fix blame for failure on oneself or others. After failing at a task, perfectionists are sometimes simply not aware of what is occurring around them because they are in such a high state of self-blame. Perfectionists enjoy exposing the weaknesses of students as they compare the performance of students to their own efforts.

In faculty relationships, perfectionists seem always to maintain a hidden agenda. Cooperation with other members of the staff in dealing with discipline problems is difficult for them to achieve.

Perfectionists do tend to help improve the performance of students who attempt to achieve perfectionist standards. The students' performance may show marked improvement as teacher approval is received for their drive for perfection. Perfectionist teachers appear to have difficulty with students whose behavioral pattern is that of developers, onlookers, and operators.

Seekers as Teachers.   Seekers as teachers do not regard themselves as acceptable people. They continually set their goals to get approval from others. One elementary teacher said, "If the students do not say they love me at least once during the day, I go home feeling bad." Although this may be an extreme case of the seeker teacher, it does identify the basic acceptance problem exhibited by these teachers. Seeker behavior in teachers is subject to the control and influence of the untouchable student. Seekers can be talked into reducing assignments and lowering standards in their classes. They do not maintain a consistent approach to discipline. Seekers may let students off too much of the time. Some students describe these teachers as soft. In some instances, seekers take several weeks to correct and return homework or tests to students. Seekers as teachers prefer being involved with teachers rather than completing desk work. These teachers are also likely to try to carry out sometimes impossible tasks.

Seekers appear too flexible with students. Behavior patterns of leaders, performers, and operators may be viewed as inappropriate by teachers whose pattern of behavior is that of the seekers. Sometimes the behavior of untouchable students may also be viewed as inappropriate.

Caring Behavior Patterns

Becomers as Teachers.   Becomers as teachers are interested in the process of their own development. They often are the social activists on the faculty concerned with how decisions are made rather than the decision itself. They teach students the importance of being unique and the value in discovering and developing all of their potential talents. These teachers are understanding of the plight of students who are attempting to discover themselves, and they accept a wide variety of student behaviors and reasons for behavior. They are likely to discount rules and regulations for situational or social ethics in instances of inappropriate student behavior. In so doing, they sometimes "lean over backwards" to find a student innocent of inappropriate behavior. Becomer teachers frequently trust their feelings about students rather than accumulated objective data. They are concerned with the behavior of perfectionist students who are always doing rather than just being. The becomer teacher is also concerned about the behavior of students who are performers and loyalists. They see performers as too concerned about their organization to govern their behavior.

Performers as Teachers.   Performers as teachers are the "taskmasters" of the profession. They enjoy professional responsibility and are industrious and committed to reasonable tasks. They value time, and they believe in efficiency. Performers take constant soundings from students regarding the effectiveness of themselves as an instructor. Performers set high standards and goals for students. These teachers tend to evaluate both the quality and quantity of student work. They expect students to be finishers of their work. They express concern about students who are not able to define a problem and develop a plan for solving the problem. Performers upset students who want to share some of the responsibility for what will be learned and when it will be learned. These teachers may have difficulty working with some students and other teachers who have behavior patterns similar to the performer. Performers seem to view as inappropriate students whose behavior patterns are those of the developer, becomer, onlooker, and seeker. Neither time nor task is emphasized in these student behavior patterns.

Leaders as Teachers.   Leaders as teachers have a broad perspective on student growth. That is, they believe students may be at different learning levels and have different learning styles. Leaders are concerned about students as well as subject matter. They are able to keep these two sometimes conflicting concerns in balance. Leaders are emotionally stable and able to cope with most student behavior patterns, varying learning styles, and different classroom teaching strategies. These teachers know themselves; they are open and secure. They maintain a high level of situational awareness, paying close attention to the present as opposed to the past and future. Students seldom fool leaders by their actions, as these teachers collect and quickly process situational data. The behavior of the leader teacher is not entirely predictable and students are sometimes caught off guard by the teacher's mixture of project- and people-oriented behaviors. The leader teacher considers the student behavior pattern of the onlooker, seeker, perfectionist, and untouchable to be inappropriate. Leaders as teachers view the behavior of insecure students as inappropriate, but they also seem to sense the needs reflected by such behavior.

Developers as Teachers.   Teachers whose behavior is predominantly that of a developer are concerned about the growth and development of individual students. They enjoy working with students and are able to be involved in cooperative relationships. They do not need to receive complimentary feedback from students or other teachers. Developers as teachers are particularly sensitive to the nonverbal behavior and feelings of students. Developers prefer students who like to become members of teams and students who have good interpersonal skills. They are concerned about students whose patterns of behavior reflect a need for security and an overconcern for tasks. They sometimes perceive the behavior of onlooker, untouchable, operator, and perfectionist students as inappropriate.

Combinations of Security and Caring Behaviors

Loyalists as Teachers.   School organizations cannot function without faculty members who are loyalists. These teachers typically act as followers in organizational affairs. They follow routinely the procedures and guidelines established for teachers. Sometimes they are so overly concerned with following the orders of authorities that they are not sensitive to classroom changes that may require a deviation from policy or accepted practice. Teachers with this pattern may not feel secure enough to take the initiative, such as suggesting new methods, policies, or procedures for the organization. They are easily swayed by the opinions of others and do not want to be outside the teachers' group. These teachers expect students to be cooperative and to complete assignments as given to them. They expect detailed, precise answers to questions during class or on tests. Loyalist teachers are extremely concerned with self-control. Loyalists as teachers may view the behaviors of student operators, untouchables, becomers, and leaders as inappropriate. Spontaneity and student initiative bother the loyalist teacher.

Operators as Teachers.   Operators as teachers are spontaneous and action-oriented. They may be absent from work on occasion to attend or participate in a sporting event or some other exciting happening. Operator teachers seem to encourage students to take risks and to become active participants in all phases of life. They do not encourage mere membership in organizations. They emphasize learning survival skills in the action-oriented world, but provide little opportunity for student growth through practice and preparation. These teachers expect students to complete assignments with a minimum of instruction. They believe that students can learn to solve problems that confront them with a minimum of assistance. Operator teachers have little compassion for those who are timid and shy; hence, they are concerned about the behaviors of students whose patterns are of the onlooker, seeker, loyalist, and developer.

Research on Teacher Behavior

No attempt was made by the writers to test the ten teacher behavior patterns in actual school situations. While none of the teacher behavior patterns are believed to exist in pure form, the patterns do seem to represent associated elements in observed teacher behaviors.

In general, the security-related teacher patterns—onlooker, untouchable, perfectionist, and seeker—would appear to be negative teaching patterns. Situational factors, however, may make some of these patterns appear quite appropriate. For example, a community and school administration that stress teaching students to obey authority may prefer teachers who act in the manner of untouchables, intimidating students and creating dependent seeker and onlooker behavior patterns in students. An untouchable principal who is viewed as acting appropriately by the board of education may hire teachers whose behavior is primarily dependent on receiving approval from the principal. The principal in such a case would view seeker teachers as appropriate.

Even though there may be some situations in which security-related behavior appears appropriate for teachers, research indicates that teachers who exhibit those behaviors may experience more problems with classroom discipline than teachers whose patterns reflect caring behaviors. For example, Kounin's[3] research revealed several findings pertinent to teacher behavior patterns and discipline. He discovered five dimensions of teacher behavior that correlated with good student discipline: (1) teacher "with-it-ness," or awareness of what is going on in the classroom at all times; (2) smoothness in changing from one instructional activity to another; (3) task focusing, or keeping all students working on an activity; (4) ability to stimulate and challenge students; and (5) ability to individualize instruction for students who are doing work at their seat.[4]

Doyle[5] indicates that teacher behavior prior to the occurrence of inappropriate student actions is critical in determining overall disciplinary success. Doyle listed four dimensions of classroom managerial skills needed by teachers to improve discipline. These skills, similar to Kounin's teacher behaviors, were as follows: (1) "with-it-ness," the teacher's ability to communicate to students his or her awareness of what is happening in the classroom; (2) "overlap," the teacher's ability to perform two or more activities at one time; (3) "movement management," the teacher's skill in maintaining momentum; and (4) "group focus," the teacher's confidence in involving all class members in each classroom event.[6] Teachers who have security needs—as reflected by the onlooker, untouchable, perfectionist, and seeker behavior patterns—are unable to stay in touch with the realities of their classrooms. Hence, their "with-it-ness" is reduced. A teacher's ability to have and to communicate "with-it-ness" seems extremely important if the teacher is to be effective in dealing with discipline. If students detect a lack of teacher "with-it-ness," influencing the students' behavior will obviously be a more difficult problem. Hence, in comparing the teacher patterns that reflect the need for security and the teacher patterns that reflect the need for caring, the lack of "with-it-ness" or situational awareness that accompanies strong security needs, suggests that teacher behavior reflecting the need for caring is more effective than teacher behavior associated with the need for security.

Cheser's[7] recent study sought a method to determine the disciplinary styles of school teachers. He identified four basic disciplinary patterns that he labeled the Battler, the Freezer, the Progressor, and the Eliminator.[8] The Battler typically uses behaviors designed to dominate and intimidate the student as a means of changing inappropriate student behavior. The Battler seems to view the student as irresponsible and in need of strict supervision and may enjoy dominating and confronting students. The Eliminator, by contrast, avoids confrontation with students and uses problem-solving techniques to work out social and written contracts with students. The Eliminator also uses rewards as a means of influencing positive behavior. The Eliminator appears to view students as being capable of solving their own problems with a little assistance from the teacher.

The Freezer and Progressor patterns fall between the behaviors of the Eliminator and the Battler. For example, the Freezer's behavior seems designed to penalize and punish students as a means of correcting or preventing inappropriate behavior. Freezers do not use rewards to influence behavior nor the intimidation and domination techniques characteristic of the Battler. The Progressor, on the other hand, is interested in applying preventive methods such as rewards to control pupil behavior. When inappropriate behavior occurs, the Progressor uses penalties as a last resort but, unlike the Eliminator, the Progressor gives less attention to helping a student assume personal responsibility for his or her own behavior.

Cheser's disciplinary styles appear to be related to the ten teacher patterns outlined earlier in this chapter. For example, the behavior of the Battler is similar to that of the untouchable teacher and, perhaps, the onlooker teacher. The Eliminator seems to parallel the leader and the Freezer may be similar to perfectionist and seeker teachers. The Progressor appears to be similar in behavior pattern to teachers termed becomers, developers, and performers. Research is currently being conducted to determine (1) the extent to which teacher behavior patterns can be verified in local schools and (2) the extent to which conflicts occur between the behavior patterns of teachers and students. Additional research is needed to determine relationships that may exist between Cheser's disciplinary styles, Willower's ideology-of-control continuum, and the ten behavior patterns of students and teachers proposed here. Patterns of behavior provide an avenue to examine causes of behavior and potential conflict situations between and among students and teachers. In this way, they aid the study of discpline in the schools.

NOTES

1. Mary Martin, "Analysis of Behavior Pattern Composition in the Tri-Student Need and Behavior Model as Related to Four Levels of Teacher Acceptance of the Student and Behavior Problem Identification" (Ph.D. dissertation, George Peabody College for Teachers, 1980).

2. Carl E. Pickardt, "Fear in the Schools: How Students Make Teachers Afraid," *Educational Leadership* (November 1978):109.

3. J. S. Kounin, *Discipline and Group Management in Classrooms*. (New York: Holt, Rinehart & Winston, 1970), p. 79.

4. Ibid.

5. Walter Doyle, "Helping Beginning Teachers Manage Classrooms," *NASSP Bulletin* 59 (December 1975):41ff.

6. Ibid., p. 41.

7. Donald B. Cheser, "Development of Instrumentation for Determining Disciplinary Styles of School Teachers" (Ph.D. dissertation, George Peabody College for Teachers, 1980), p. 110.

8. Ibid., pp. 80–81.

PART
FOUR

Chapters 7, 8, and 9 in Part IV are written specifically for the principal. This section answers the following questions: What methods and assets do principals have to attain the organizational aims related to school discipline? How should these assets be utilized and what are their limits? What is the nature of the problems a principal may encounter in dealing with discipline and how can these be prevented or reduced? What are the legal parameters within which a principal operates to maintain discipline?

Chapter 7 proposes several types of leadership assets that principals may use to improve school discipline. Practical examples of the use of these assets are presented. For instance, methods are discussed for changing the established norms of teachers and/or students in a school. Chapter 8 aids the principal in understanding why someone might select one asset rather than another in bringing about changes in teacher and student behavior. It also discusses many of the problems principals may encounter in attempting to improve discipline. Examples of techniques for avoiding these problems are provided.

Chapter 9 is a detailed but brief reference guide for determining the legal constraints and opportunities within which discipline must be considered. Specific suggestions are made for establishing policies. The functions of a principal are discussed in relation to the law and various court cases involving students.

CHAPTER 7

The Principal
and Leadership Assets

The following comment from a 1963 book by Harl Douglass directed toward the secondary principal, can still apply to elements of the current situation regarding discipline:

> If for no other reason, school principals and teachers must give careful consideration to the problems of discipline because of the increased criticism of the schools, teachers, and administrators with respect to what many parents seem to think is inferior discipline and student behavior today. . . . Although many parents insist that teachers and principals should be stricter and more severe with youngsters, many of these same critics are quick to protest vigorously when their own children are punished. Nevertheless, the individual principal is faced with the problem of seeing that there is less basis for criticism of his [or her] school on this point.[1]

The principal, regardless of school responsibilities, is almost always held accountable for the behavior of the students. The manner in which student discipline is handled is important since one measure of a principal's effectiveness is achieving success with discipline.

This chapter examines how the principal can use leadership assets for the improvement of school discipline. These assets are (1) the penalties the principal can use to influence behavior; (2) the rewards that the principal may give as a means of influencing behavior; and (3) the reformational assets that the principal can utilize to change the behavior of individuals and groups. The integration of the penal, approval, and reformational assets by the principal through working with members of the school to change behavior is leadership. It is possible to plan for the effective use of these leadership assets. The planned use of leadership assets to improve discipline is illustrated in the following account.

After using the Discipline Organization Effectiveness Inventory (discussed in Chapter 1) to assess the effectiveness of discipline in the school, a principal met with the faculty to review the gaps between their expectations for discipline in the school and their perceptions of discipline as it existed. Faculty discussion confirmed the information generated by the DOEI; namely, over one-half of the faculty did not believe they should be responsible for improving discipline—discipline was the vice-principal's responsibility, not theirs. The principal considered his leadership assets. He devised and promoted a plan that included faculty involvement for changing the expectations of those teachers who did not believe they should be responsible for improving discipline. A year later, DOEI results reflected a change in teachers' expectations—from half of the teachers believing someone else was responsible for improving discipline to all teachers believing that they were responsible for improving it.

In this case, through his leadership the principal either directly or indirectly changed the norms among the faculty.

THE NATURE OF LEADERSHIP

Before discussing the three types of leadership assets, a few terms need defining: formal and informal organization; leadership and power; and penal, approval, and reformational assets. Etzioni[2] describes two types of organizational structures, formal and informal. Formal organization generally refers to the organizational pattern designed by management.[3] Informal organization refers either to "the social relations that develop among the staff or workers" or to "the pressures of the interpersonal relationships among the participants."[4] The formal organization in schools is represented by the organizational charts and position descriptions indicating domains of authority. The informal organization consists of the relationships and norms that exist among teachers, students, and the principal. Exercising leadership to improve discipline in a school must occur through an understanding of both the formal and informal aspects of the organization. Many times it is the informal relationships and norms that must be altered before improvement in discipline can occur.

Katz and Kahn define leadership in behavioral terms as "any act of influence in a matter of organizational relevance." They contend that the "essence of leadership has to do with that influential increment which goes beyond routine and taps bases of power beyond those which are organizationally decreed."[5] Burns[6] makes several statements about leadership and leaders that are relevant. Burns conceives of leadership as tapping people's potential motives and existing power bases to achieve "intended change." Its function is to activate the energies of all persons so they engage in a joint effort. Leadership is not defined as power. Leadership emerges from people who assess individual and group motives, values, and needs and then exploit the potential energy in each person as they move toward an intended direction.[7] Once the collective aims or motives of people are determined and the organization begins to move in a direction, leadership then includes the use of psychological and institutional resources to maintain the movement toward change.[8]

Leadership in this book is broadly defined as the mobilization of potential followers through the integrated use of leadership assets to achieve an intended aim. Leadership in this context involves assessing the latent individual power bases residing in each person and group. This assessment includes estimating the values, motives, and moral levels of followers to determine which aims they will pursue. Leadership not only includes establishing aims that will move potential followers to action, but the use of penalties and rewards not as naked coercive power, but as a means of moving followers toward an intended change that is generally agreed upon by those being led.

Leadership and leadership assets are, however, partially derived from the concepts of power and influence. A simple definition of power that seems to be appropriate for the principal's role is that of Goldhamer and Shils. A person may be said to have power to the extent that he or she strongly influences the behavior of others in accordance with his or her own intentions.[9] Power indicates the use of strong influence and persuasion to achieve one's own aims, whereas leadership integrates the influence of leaders and followers to achieve their mutual aims. In discussing the exercise of power, Hersay and Blanchard differentiate between "position power" and "personal power."[10] Position power is described as being derived from the position held in the organization. The principalship is a relatively high office in the school organization. Thus a principal always has position powers. Personal power is defined as the ability of a person to induce others to change their behavior or to follow his or her lead. For example, students or teachers change behavior because they believe a personal relationship will be damaged if no change in behavior occurs. Hersay and Blanchard also describe how a person may have both positional and personal power.[11] Individuals who are able to influence the behavior of others because of their position in an organization have position power and individuals who derive their influence from their personality and behavior have personal power.

Etzioni describes three kinds of power used to make subjects comply. One kind is "coercive power," the application of sanctions or the control through force of the satisfaction of needs.[12] French and Raven state that one source of power is the perceptions others have of the number and type of rewards the person can deliver. They label such power "reward power."[13] Etzioni calls this "remunerative power," or the control over material resources and rewards through the allocation of financial benefit, services, and commodities.[14] Remunerative power involves the manipulation of behavior through the use of rewards. "Normative power," according to Etzioni, involves the control of symbolic rewards and the distribution of "acceptance" and "positive response."[15] Etzioni states that normative power could be termed persuasive, manipulative, or suggestive power.

The concepts of coercive, remunerative, and normative power are all directly or indirectly related to the leadership assets. The three types of leadership assets available in varying degrees to the principal are the penal, approval, and reformational assets. These same assets are also available, to some extent, to teachers and students. Penal leadership assets, in their simplest form, are defined as the penalties a principal can invoke against others in the school organization. Coercive power is similar to the penal leadership assets.

Approval leadership assets are defined as the rewards the principal can directly or indirectly deliver to others in the school organization. Remunerative power and normative power parallel the approval leadership assets. Both the penal and approval assets of leadership provide direct ways to influence the behavior of others and may be used on occasion to impose the principal's will.

Reformational leadership assets are the skills, techniques, and resources a principal uses to encourage members of an organization to participate in decision making. Members involved in decision making may solve problems, set aims (goals which may not always be the principal's priorities), and plan. Participation in decision making helps people develop a sense of responsibility for, and control over, their own behavior. It also develops the members' feelings of ownership of an organization. The principal uses resources to mobilize the existing and potential motivation of teachers, students, and community members. Besides assessing the needs, values, and moral stages of others, the principal may also use the influence of charisma, inspiration, and quiet lobbying to achieve aims the principal desires. These particular resources are extremely valuable in an organization, if the person can exhibit such qualities.

The principal's effective application of the penal, approval, and reformational assets will result in changes in behavior and improved discipline. Costs to the principal, however, may result from the use of each of these assets. The principal's ability to influence behavior in desired ways is enhanced or diminished by the selection and management of leadership assets. Some leadership assets may be liabilities when applied inappropriately. For example, suspending a student whose needs are satisfied by being out of school serves to reinforce the inappropriate student behavior.

The three types of leadership assets are discussed separately in the following sections. The appropriate and inappropriate use of each of the leadership assets is also discussed.

PENAL LEADERSHIP ASSETS

The leadership assets labeled penal assets include those of a positional and personal nature. The principal can utilize positional penalties or personal penalties as a means of punishing, preventing, or changing inappropriate behavior. Such penalties may inflict physical pain or psychological discomfort on students and/or teachers. Penalties almost never satisfy teachers' or students' motives or needs. In fact, a penalty will usually further block the satisfying of a particular need, because it may be designed to create frustration and anxiety.

Positional Penal Assets

Positional penalties might include, for example, the establishment of more rules for a group of misbehaving students and reduced opportunities for independent decision making by students. Adding more rules (penalties) seems to be a common response to a problem of inappropriate behavior in schools. Consider the following case:

> A principal working with a few advisors tried to reduce the number of incidents of use of alcohol in the school. The principal instituted a series of rules about the use of student rest rooms. Additional supervision from teachers was necessary to assure that students were obeying the rules. After a month, the rules were dropped because there was substantial evidence that the frequency of alcohol use among students was increasing, as was the number of students using alcohol for the first time. It is possible that the increased supervision provided more accurate information about the use of alcohol, but comments from teachers and students indicated that there was in fact an increase. Tension between students and teachers was also increased through attempts to apply these rules.

The cost of the use of positional assets such as establishing rules and more controls may outweigh the benefits. Gouldner indicates that the intent to obtain control of students through increasing bureaucratic rules may have the reverse effect.[16] When rules are spelled out they are typically minimum acceptable standards. In many schools, teachers and administrators expect more from students than meeting the minimum acceptable standards for appropriate behavior. It is also possible that the increased supervision necessary to make certain the rules are being compiled with makes the power relations more visible, thus producing more interpersonal tension between students and their supervisors. Establishing more rules and regulations increases the need for control devices and may have negative rather than positive consequences. Gouldner suggests that rules should have the following characteristics: (1) rules should be initiated and supported by both students and educators; (2) rules should be enforced by the educators and obeyed by the students; (3) violations of rules should be viewed as a lack of information; (4) attempts to educate violators about the rules should be initiated.[17] The Gouldner model examines one of the assets associated with the use of such positional assets. Other positional assets, such as increased workloads and undesirable assignments for teachers and students whose behavior is not appropriate, may also have costs as well as benefits. The costs and benefits must be considered in the use of positional penal assets in improving discipline.

Some principals believe that positional penal assets can be utilized an infinite number of times. But once a principal has resorted to the use of positional penal assets to influence behavior, their potency as a force to change behavior may be decreased. The person(s) who received the penalty may no longer fear the shock effect of its use. For example, consider the case of a principal in a suburban school.

A principal, frustrated with noise during an assembly, walked to the front of the auditorium, turned facing the group of 700 students and shouted, "There will be no more assembly programs in this school unless the noise in this auditorium ceases!" The students quieted down immediately. Authority—the office of the principal—had spoken. The principal had changed the inappropriate behavior of the students in that setting. After the incident, the principal in discussion with the vice-principal concluded that it would not be possible to repeat that action and receive the same compliant response. Alternate leadership-asset responses were used to improve behavior in future assemblies.

The supply of positional penalties is limited with a particular group of students or faculty during a specific time period.

The use of positional penal assets also tends to produce student and faculty alienation.[18] The penalty-receiving members of the organization complain, and become generally dissatisfied about the contribution they have to make to the school. The long-term effects or costs of continuous student or faculty alienation need to be considered in exercising the use of positional penal assets. Candid conversations with faculty and students about how they feel toward their school may help the principal become aware of the level of alienation.

The use of positional penalties, moreover, can create fear among members of an organization. When people perceive threats, according to Machiavelli, they may behave to avoid the threat. He believed, however, that some fear, if not overextensive, is essential if a leader is to be effective over a long period of time.[19] Machiavelli thought it desirable to be both loved and feared. Use of positional assets can create fear, but the principal must remember that once used on a group or person their potential for influencing the behavior of the same group may be reduced.

In determining the benefit to be gained and the cost to be incurred through the use of these assets, the principal must accurately anticipate participant response. Is achieving compliant behavior through the penalty used worth the loss of the positional penal asset as a potential threat? Is its use worth the alienation the students and faculty may come to feel toward the organization? Does the use of the positional penal asset make it a liability?

Personal Penal Assets

The personal penal assets of leadership are derived from the relationships that students and faculty share with the principal. One of the primary penal assets a principal has is not to accept a person or the person's behavior. Teachers are generally concerned about their relationships with other people, some more so than others. The principal who fails to speak to a teacher in a corridor or who fails to communicate informally with members of the faculty as one has done in the past may be perceived as punishing that person. Granted that most educators would agree that this is not a desirable method of influencing behavior, it is, nonetheless, one that principals may use on occasion. Another example of personal penal assets is making decisions for teachers who enjoy making their own decisions.

A serious problem caused by the use of such penalties is the long-range effects on faculty-administrator relationships. Some teachers may become extremely stressful as a result of apparent rejection by the administrator. This stress may significantly affect the health and performance of these teachers in the classroom. Thus, the asset may become a liability. Another problem is that teachers may attribute the administrator's penalizing behavior to an entirely different set of behaviors on his or her part. That is, a teacher may not know why the administrator is unfriendly. If the teacher makes an inaccurate guess about being rejected, it could lead to more inappropriate behavior rather than less (as the principal views it).

Many personal penal assets are designed to affect the recipient's feeling of being a worthwhile person. Teachers who are secure are less apt to be influenced by the principal's use of such personal assets, but for those teachers whose self-worth is tied to receiving approval from others such as the principal, the loss of approval from the principal or some other personal rebuff will be viewed as a serious problem by that teacher. The following account is such an instance.

In a junior high school, the principal was extremely concerned about the dress of his faculty. Over the years, women had been accustomed to wearing dresses and men typically had worn shirts and ties. Several of the faculty decided that with the advent of negotiations and their own striving toward professional independence they would wear clothes that differed from these norms. Several of the women began wearing pants suits; several men wore open shirts with no ties. The principal was concerned about the dress of those faculty members but was reluctant to verbalize his outrage. Instead, he complimented the teachers whose dress was, in his judgment, appropriate, and he frowned at those who were violating the dress norms for the faculty. Several of the teachers who had been wearing the open shirts and pants suits became concerned about their relationship with the principal, since he seemed to be ignoring them. After two weeks, three of the five teachers returned to the prior mode of dress, while two of the teachers were not intimidated by the lack of the principal's approval for their behavior and continued to wear clothes they thought appropriate in the classroom.

In this instance, the principal used penal personal assets to influence the behavior of three faculty members. The two nonconforming faculty members may have felt uneasy about the lack of approval of their attire, but not enough to change their manner of dress.

Groups as well as individuals can be affected by the use of personal penal assets. A principal's failure to attend a committee meeting can be perceived as relating to his or her dislike for some of the committee's actions. If the principal uses the personal penal assets frequently and does not identify the reasons for the behavior, the principal may be viewed as a "game player." The principal who uses these assets to influence the behavior of others without being explicit as to his or her actions runs a risk of being disliked for a lack of candor in relationships with people and groups in school.

In summary, the use of personal penal assets reduces the potential assets a principal has to influence behavior. It also can seriously affect the perceptions and relationships that exist between an administrator and other people in the organization. In most instances, the use of such assets creates blocks between the administration and the faculty. Such blocks may lead to a closed problem-solving climate, lack of trust between teachers and principal, and a feeling among the faculty of being manipulated. Positional penalties at times can cause student and teacher alienation. If teachers or students believe they are being forced to do things they do not want to do, they may lose motivation and effectiveness in their respective work.

When to Use Positional and Personal Penal Assets

Exercising positional and personal penal assets may at times be necessary; but, because of the potential for damage to the organization, their use should be considered with care. When a situation demands immediate change in the behavior that students or teachers are exhibiting, it may be appropriate to use positional and personal penalties. For example, if the health of students is endangered and the teachers involved do not have time to change the students' behavior through the use of other leadership assets, the principal may have to exercise penal assets. In such cases, the principal judges that the time necessary to use other approaches is not available and considers the issue involved to be extremely important to the school and the community.

Another occasion when the principal may want to exercise penal assets might involve enforcing rules for faculty or students that they believe are unfair. Sometimes, through contract negotiations, faculties find that informal norms they have established are not in keeping with the regulations of the negotiated contract. The passage of time may not make these regulations acceptable to the faculty. Hence, the principal may choose to enforce the contract's requirements through the use of penal assets.

A third occasion for the use of penal assets may occur in a situation in which the faculty or students expect to be punished for inappropriate behaviors or mistakes. Until these perceptions are changed, the principal will need to use some penalties in order to be perceived as effective. In summary, penal assets may be used when time to involve people in decision making is limited, when unpopular changes in behavior must occur, and when others expect the principal to use penal assets in fulfilling the responsibilities of the position.

APPROVAL LEADERSHIP ASSETS

Approval leadership assets are the rewards a principal may provide to members of the school organization as individuals or in groups. Acts of influence by the principal that satisfy the needs of an individual may be perceived as rewards by the individul. Approval assets may be positional approval assets or personal approval assets.

Positional Approval Assets

Positional assets are organizational or career rewards. They take such forms as promotion, financial increases, special citations, work load or schedule changes, and expanded responsibilities. All of these rewards are associated with the formal organization. Consider the following example:

A principal had been attempting to select a new vice-principal for several weeks. The central-office selection committee had identified two prospective candidates for the position. One person was a teacher in the same building in which the vacancy existed. The other was a teacher with recommendations and credentials equivalent to those of the teacher already in the same building. The principal selected the teacher from his building because that particular teacher had the skills to do the vice-principal's work and because the teacher had done much more than most others in the school to help improve discipline in the school. The new vice-principal was elated with the appointment.

The principal's role within the organization is one of recommending teachers for promotion. This is a function of the position or an approval leadership asset. Positional approval assets can serve to reward those whose behaviors meet the principal's expectations. They can be promised to those who act appropriately as a means of enticing the appropriate behaviors.

Positional approval assets reinforce appropriate behaviors that may produce benefits for the school organization. These assets may have associated costs also. For example, if the principal delegates tasks that he or she prefers to accomplish, the principal may suffer the loss of some enjoyment. Delegation of tasks may necessitate the principal's spending an inordinate amount of time helping others learn how to perform effectively. Some principals share administrative tasks with groups of responsible students as a means of rewarding them for their appropriate judgments and mature behaviors. These same students may call upon the principal to explain actions and decisions that seem to violate the norms of fairness and consistency in the school organization. The principal may find such explanations to be time-consuming and not worth the effort. Hence, assigning administrative tasks to students may cost the principal the privilege of making decisions without being questioned.

Perhaps the most serious cost of using positional assets is that they can lose their meaning as motivators if rewards are given to too many people or are given out too frequently. Consider the following account.

A principal of a small, rural, K-12 school gave out awards to students in assemblies throughout the year. The categories of awards seemed endless and almost every student received one. Students supported these awards and were pleased to see all students received something for their efforts. Parents became disturbed because the awards appeared to have lost their meaning. Because everyone received an award, the really deserving students, in the parents' judgment, did not obtain the recognition they should have received. (The real problem may have been that those parents' egos were not being fed through the limited distribution of rewards to students.) The principal was asked to leave his position several years later. The student response to the board of education's decision was one of disbelief and dismay. The parents of students who had not received awards in elementary school but did so in the high school turned out in large numbers to support the possible reinstatement of the principal. The parents of students who had been accustomed to being recognized with rewards in the elementary grades did not want the principal reinstated. Some of these parents were influential in the community. The principal was not retained.

The distribution of too many rewards (positional assets), even though substantially different for each child, may have cost the principal his position.

Personal Approval Assets

The personal approval assets are the informal rewards a principal may give to members of the organization to satisfy some of their psychological needs. These rewards include, for example, verbal and nonverbal compliments, behaviors that indicate a liking for the person, responsiveness to the other person, and the extension of trust and autonomy to another person. The use of personal assets in leadership is illustrated in the case of a principal who had to convey the same message to two different department chairpersons.

In one conference, the principal moved from behind the desk to sit next to Chairperson A. Before discussing the message to be conveyed, the principal joked with A and complimented A on doing well as a chairperson. The principal transmitted a high degree of acceptance of the person through smiles and through being close physically. The conversation was a shared discussion with little indication of dominance by the principal.

Chairperson B received the same verbal message, but the principal stayed behind the desk, did not establish eye contact with B, and got right to the point. The principal slumped back in the chair and occasionally looked at B from the corner of the eyes. The principal transmitted a low degree of acceptance of B as a person. The lack of smiles, distance from B, and general air of superiority demonstrated a high degree of dominance over B by the principal. Also, the conversation tended to be one-way communication from the principal while B sat at attention fulfilling the role of the dutiful subordinate.

The principal's behavior toward the two chairpersons was quite different despite the similarity in the words used to convey the message. This principal's behavior shows how personal approval assets may be utilized in school administration. The personal assets included the liking for and acceptance of Chairperson A by the principal. If Chairperson B needed to be accepted and liked, and not dominated, the behavior of the principal was probably viewed by B as being penal in nature.

Personal approval assets, which often take the form of nonverbal messages, are also strong reinforcers of behavior. They are most effective when the teachers and students have high needs for approval. For example, one principal in a large city school met daily with four vice-principals. Two of the vice-principals described their activities from the previous day as a means of determining the appropriateness or inappropriateness of their behaviors. The principal, who was a person of few words, conveyed feelings through facial expressions. The principal nodded and smiled when their reported behavior appeared appropriate. This nonverbal approval almost always prompted more of the same behavior from the two vice-principals on succeeding days.

The absence of approval assets can sometimes be viewed as the presence of penal assets. Personal approval assets may be applied by eliminating colleagues and students from some normal interpersonal interactions. When a principal withholds looks or words as a means of penalizing faculty, those whom he or she does speak to or look at approvingly may feel rewarded. Those who receive the normal interpersonal signs of approval view them as personal recognition. When a principal attempts to manipulate behavior through the use of personal approval assets, damage may be done to the interpersonal relationships. This result seriously impairs the principal's ability to use persuasion and other reformational assets. (These assets are discussed later in this chapter.) When the potential damage to interpersonal relationships is estimated to be serious, as may be the case when members of a school organization expect to be rewarded for every contribution made, then personal approval assets become liabilities. Regardless of these potential costs, approval assets are powerful instruments for reinforcing appropriate behavior when used in a proper manner. Chapter 4 described the process for the proper use of rewards to improve the behavior of students. The principles of that approval process also apply to the use of rewards with teachers to effect improvement.

When to Use Approval Leadership Assets

Approval leadership assets should be used in situations where the aim is the continuance of appropriate behavior. Positional and personal approval assets can be utilized in a variety of school situations. They are perhaps best used in situations (1) where maintaining relationships between the administrator and teachers is important, (2) when accumulating social credits is viewed by the principal as important, (3) when teachers or students are trying out new behaviors in the organization, and (4) where faculty have determined what the approval assets are going to be.

In summary, the approval leadership assets are effective forms of reinforcing or changing behavior. The perception that a reward will be forthcoming can also influence teachers and students to act in a manner to warrant rewards. The positional and personal approval assets are both subject to specific conditions, and the user of these assets should recognize guidelines outlined in Chapter 4. Moreover, the number of positional assets a principal may use is limited. Each one awarded may be one less that the principal may use as a future reward. Finally, the principal may not benefit when approval assets are misused.

REFORMATIONAL LEADERSHIP ASSETS

The reformational assets of leadership are those positional and personal assets designed to encourage participation in decision making by organization members and to place responsibility for a person's behavior in the organization on that individual. Positional reformational assets include the responsibilities of the principal to organize the formal structure of the faculty and to influence the assignment of individual roles and responsibilities within the organization for purposes of mobilizing the power bases of individuals and groups. Personal reformational assets include a principal's personal ability to influence others to participate in problem solving and in establishing and achieving organizational aims.

Importantly, the personal assets include the encouragement a principal may use in helping teachers and groups work through problems using steps similar to those described in the reformational process (see Chapter 3). The steps are: aiding students in defining a problem; helping students develop a desire to solve the problem with appropriate behavior; and developing a social or written contract that both student and educator must approve. The personal assets include helping a group of teachers with problem identification, with reaching agreement on a solution, and with developing a plan to achieve the solution. The reformational assets extend beyond the immediate process to help groups select choices, work through conflict, and collectively move to change behaviors.

Reformational Assets and Group Norms

Shared relationships in a group provide the basis for the use of reformational leadership assets. Bobbitt has written, "A group is a collection of individuals among whom a set of interdependent relationships exist (that is, the individuals influence each other)."[20] Members of any group share norms. Norms, as social contracts, "represent the group's consensus of what is proper and expected behavior."[21] A group is not a group until these norms for behavior are established. The concern for relationships and the norms of the group provide the glue that keeps the members of a group in the group. Failure of a member to conform to group norms leads to the perceived breach of a social contract. Violators of group norms are prosecuted by members of the group or by the leader of the group who is expected to enforce some group norms. Prosecution includes the use of penal assets or the approval and reformational assets to bring the deviants' behavior back into line. In many instances, when a group has a strong commitment to the norm violated, the members of the group will react swiftly and strongly to rectify the deviant's behavior. If there is a weak commitment to the norm violated, group members may leave correction up to the school administration.

The fact that norms control the behavior of members in groups is often overlooked by administrators. One of the major secrets to leadership success with discipline is the use of the positional and personal reformational assets to set and change the norms for groups of students and teachers. When members of student or teacher groups are committed to appropriate behavioral norms, the need to use either penal or reward assets is almost nonexistent. When penal or reward assets are used, they are issued as a means of influencing the norms of the group.

A principal who understood the principles of group behavior applied reformational leadership assets in the following manner:

Students were leaving food on the cafeteria tables. The principal met with the student leaders of the school to discuss the problem, just as he had met with them the week before to plan for the winter carnival. The students suggested several things, including group discussions with all students about conduct in the cafeteria. The principal met with the faculty executive committee which also suggested discussing the topic with students.

The plan eventually adopted included teacher-student discussions in homerooms through which students would help construct a code of conduct for student behavior in the cafeteria by developing a list of appropriate cafeteria behaviors. The plan did not include adoption of a set of rules and regulations to apply to the various situations in the cafeteria; it only asked that students in each homeroom reach some degree of agreement about appropriate cafeteria behavior. Each homeroom, with the help of the teacher and student leaders, submitted a list of appropriate cafeteria behaviors to the principal. For ten weeks the behavior of the students in the cafeteria was appropriate. Peer pressure was instrumental to improved conduct. Periodically, new norms were established and old ones reinforced in each homeroom. No formal rules or regulations were necessary nor was increased supervision required. The principal and teachers had understood enough about group norms to implement the plan. A year

> later, the faculty repeated the process using the reformational lead-
> ership assets on involvement in decision making and added another
> component to the plan. Teachers periodically reinforced the appro-
> priate behavior that followed and penalized repeated offenders.
> Group norms remained intact at least one-half of the school year.

Establishment and reinforcement of the group norms were accomplished through the interrelated use of the reformation and approval leadership assets.

Positional Reformational Assets

The positional reformational assets include a principal's direct steps to
establish an organizational structure that enables teachers and/or students
to become part of the decision-making process and to participate in problem
solving. Establishing the organizational structure includes the defining of
roles and responsibilities with or for the faculty. As the principal and
faculty define and redefine the organizational structure and associated roles
to capture the reservoirs of motivation in each person, the principal uses
positional leadership assets. Consider the following example:

> One school had established a set of rules for student behavior that
> included statements as follows:
>
> No petting
> No balloons and water pistols
> No cutting of classes
>
> The list included some 35 items. A consultant working with the
> school principal and vice-principals determined that (1) the emphasis
> was on actions that constituted inappropriate behavior and that (2)
> while it was important to make students aware of what was consid-
> ered inappropriate behavior, students should also be informed of the
> expectations for appropriate behavior. The principal appointed a fac-
> ulty study group to determine what to do about the overemphasis on
> listing inappropriate behaviors. He selected committee members who
> had a need to be recognized and who could reflect both the positive

and the negative aspects of student behavior. The principal structured the committee, not the outcome. The committee eventually
eliminated two-thirds of the rules about inappropriate behavior and
listed a set of general statements about student behavior. The study
group recommended that the faculty adopt its appropriate-student-
behavior statements as policy in the school. After the faculty slightly
altered the statements, the principal declared them school policy. But
the policy took two years to implement. In retrospect, the principal
believed that the committee should have included students and that
the committee should have set in motion a process of student body
review and approval before making the policy.

The principal in this situation used his positional reformational assets to
establish the committee. The principal also used his position to help establish the mandated contracts or policy necessary to implement the change
in student guidelines.

Personal Reformational Assets

The personal reformational assets of leadership include the personal skills
and qualities a principal has in encouraging others to share in decision
making in the organization. They may or may not include the principal's
personal influence to move others in a desired direciton. The principal uses
personal leadership assets when he or she encourages others to use their
own resources in achieving intended changes in the organization. Such
facilitation leads to accurate problem identification, consideration of alternative solutions to problems, and a plan to implement solutions to problems. The successful implementation of these personal assets depends on
the extent to which the principal understands how groups function and the
nature of the relationships the principal maintains with others.

A principal who was about to retire had worked with a small faculty
in an inner-city middle school. For years, the principal had not
wanted to shift from a letter-grade marking system to a numerical
marking system. Six months prior to retirement, the faculty, many
of whom had worked with the principal for years, complained loudly
about the letter-grade marking system. The matter was placed on the

agenda for the January faculty meeting. The principal encouraged the establishment of a study group to review once again the issue of marks, but the principal did not appoint or establish the committee. The faculty set up a committee that defined the problem with the administrator's assistance. During the course of the study, the principal met with committee members one at a time, pointing out the pros and cons of each of the two marking systems, and suggested to each person how the present marking system achieved one or more of each teacher's several aims. Ultimately, in the discussion with each person, the person would ask the principal for her judgment about which of the marking systems was better. The principal always pointed out the reasons for maintaining letter grades. In a meeting of the entire faculty in June, before the principal retired, the study committee asked for and received the strong commitment of the entire faculty to maintain the present marking system. Although the faculty did not vote on the issue, the study committee ascertained that everyone was in partial or full agreement with their recommendation.

Two years after the principal retired, another study group was formed to consider changing the marking system. A numerical grading system was adopted a year after the study was initiated. The new principal left the decision in the hands of the faculty and did little to personally facilitate or influence the decision.

The foregoing example illustrates the principal's use of the reformational process. Initially, the problem was defined by a faculty group. The principal encouraged the faculty to participate in the activity. The desire to maintain the letter-marking system was strengthened through the personal persuasion of the principal. Social contracts were established among faculty members when they agreed with the recommendations of the study group. These contracts were broken two years later with the decision to adopt a numerical system.

When to Use the Reformational Leadership Assets

Burns[22] comments on the determining of when to use reformational leadership assets. He writes:

> The leader is dealing with persons—potential followers—who have their own power bases, however small, and their own hierarchies of motives.

In this process, both behavior and structural variables are converted into two sets: (1) the motive bases—hierarchies of want, need, aspiration, etc.—that can be mobilized by competing leaders, and (2) the actual power that can be mustered through these motive bases—power that rests in economic, social, and other resources centered in institutions, technology, coalitions, constitutions, rules, traditions, ballots,' money, information, intelligence, genius, skills. The leader eternally must deal with the double interrelated questions: What can these persons do for (or against) me in a pursuit of collective goals and what will these persons do for (or against) me? Hence, leaders must assess collective motivation—the hierarchies of motivations in both leaders and followers—as studiously as they analyze the power bases of potential followers and rival leaders.[23]

Reformational leadership assets can be utilized as a means of controlling or changing a group member's behavior, School administrators, in general, lack an understanding of the power of a group to control a student's behavior. It also seems that they lack understanding on how the reformational assets may be used to improve discipline. The following account demonstrates the use of the reformational leadership assets to improve discipline.

A principal and four vice-principals in a predominantly inner-city school were especially concerned about the number of times students were cutting classes and being tardy. One solution to these problems called for more rigid rules and regulations with strict enforcement. A similar plan had been implemented the previous year. But the number of classes cut and tardinesses had increased. The administrators were extremely concerned that teacher morale would drop even lower if something different from their proposed plan was not initiated soon.

After much discussion with a consultant, they decided to plan a two-day "leadership retreat" for the faculty and seventy-five student leaders to be held prior to the opening of school. The inclusion of the students in this retreat was a major step toward beginning to place some of the responsibility for the problem on the students. It was determined that students should also be included in planning the leadership retreat. If improvement was to occur in that school, it meant the establishment of a new set of student norms. If change was to occur, the student body would have to eventually accept a social agreement among themselves that cutting class and being late to class were not appropriate. Changing the present social agreements through which peer approval rewarded cutting and tardiness was the goal. Including students in planning the retreat and in dealing with the problems in the two-day conference was a turning point for the school. In two years, students had accepted a different set of social agreements among themselves that disapproved of those who were not prompt and did not reward those who skipped classes. The suspendable incident rate was reduced 50 percent over previous years, and the average daily attendance increased from 85 percent to 93 percent during the two years.

This account illustrates how students can influence the behavior of other members of the student group. It also illustrates that social agreements that define a group can be changed through the use of the reformational leadership assets. When using reformational assets to change or reinforce norms, an administrator may not always control which appropriate behavioral norms the group adopts, but helping the group determine the agreed upon "norms" creates an environment in which alternatives may be considered.

Reformational leadership assets are designed to tap the power bases of individuals and should be used whenever a principal determines that the process of choice, priority-setting, and conflict should and can be utilized by others in the organization. Whenever time is limited or the principal believes that there is only one possible intended change, which others will not support, other leadership assets should be exercised. When both individual growth and commitment to the collective effort are desired, however, the principal should consider using the reformational leadership assets including inspiration, charisma and/or involvement in decision making. If it is important that each teacher feel responsible for moving toward the intended change in the school, the principal should consider the use of reformational leadership assets. In this process, the principal will help the group determine the specific intended change, and will help the group seek to satisfy some individual and group needs and values.

REFORMATIONAL ASSETS USED FOR STUDENT LEADERSHIP DEVELOPMENT

Principals and faculty share the responsibility for helping student leaders become effective in leadership roles. One of the most productive ways a school can do this is by involving students in organizational decisions through their participation in a leadership corps. Some educators believe that students do not need to be represented in school decisions, and that the reformational leadership assets should be used with faculty but not with students. They believe, moreover, that the best way to control students is to make sure that they do not get organized. It is doubtful that the students in such schools will view themselves as belonging to the school. Other administrators use reformational assets only when they believe a problem exists in the school. "When in trouble, involve the students" is their motto. It is doubtful that feelings of student ownership of the school can develop from crisis involvement. They did not in the 1960s. The writers believe that one of a principal's best uses of reformational leadership assets is the establishment of a leadership corps in the school.

Shortcomings of the Student Council

Historically, the "student council" has been considered the vehicle for representative student government in secondary schools. Usually, the students in each class or homeroom elect one of its members to represent them on the student council. Unfortunately, these large, schoolwide organizations can become cliquish and nonparticipatory, resulting in injustices to some students or organizations in the school.

Numerous other problems are associated with the council form of student government. In many schools, for instance, councils tend to foster an authoritarian atmosphere wherein council representatives assume that other students are not to be held responsible for their own behavior. In these schools, the student council is viewed as the governing body trying to run everything. Instead of fostering students' individual responsibility to govern themselves, the council encourages students to leave authority to student council members. Such councils fail to assume responsibility for helping to lead or to aid other students in self-governance.

A second major problem of student councils is the distance that often separates the administrator of the school from the council members. Teachers acting as student council advisors are frequently ill-advised on their role and function. All too often the untrained advisor fails to communicate with the administrator about the weekly operations of the council. As a result, the principal is unaware of its activities until a crisis of sorts is pending. When council advisors do not confer with the principal or other appointed administrative representatives, the status of the council and its functions relative to the school governance comes into question.

But the chief deficiency of student councils is that they often are not greatly concerned with helping to manage the institution. It is common for student councils (1) to help provide for election of pupil representatives, (2) to help set up extracurricular activities, and (3) to help in scheduling school events. In recent years, student councils also have been active in establishing student study areas within the school building. In some cases, they have helped to monitor the financial accounts of other student organizations. On the whole, however, the development of councils as student organizations whose major concern is the administration of the school has not been promising.

The Student Leadership Corps

A leadership corps is an organized group of student leaders in a school that works with the administration and faculty in leading the entire school organization. The broad purpose of such an organized group of student leaders is the development of a student body that believes it has responsibilities for achieving the goals of the school. A school's goals should include the learning of appropriate social behaviors and self-governance. One major way of achieving this purpose is for the leadership corps to assist school personnel in solving problems and in defining, achieving, and evaluating the goals of the school organization. Another important way is for the leadership corps to provide assistance to student leaders in carrying out the functions of their specific roles. A second general purpose of the leadership corps is that of helping students learn skills and attitudes that will enable them to participate effectively in public affairs as members of a democracy. School is a large part of the student's public and, in this sense, its affairs are "public." In addition, an effective leadership corps helps to develop and sustain appropriate student norms. These norms include a commitment to the school and its students, to protect school property, and to preserve the individual rights of faculty and students. When a strong commitment to the school's aims is the norm, it becomes extremely difficult for a student to violate the norm.

Carrying out the purposes of the leadership corps requires scheduled meetings of the school administrator with the members of the leadership corps. The principal should meet with the corps at least one hour per week on a regular basis. These weekly meetings should convey to students the importance of the group and, at the same time, provide the principal with an opportunity to establish a close relationship with the elected representatives of the school. At the first few meetings of the corps, the principal should include several items on the agenda that deal with skills in handling large groups (e.g., learning how to conduct effective meetings, acquainting students with simplified parliamentary procedures) and problems of immediate concern to students. Students should become accustomed to helping set the agenda for the meetings as the year progresses. Taking time in the initial meetings to look at the school as a total organization is essential. As the year progresses, the administrators and students can begin to function in a problem-solving manner to deal with the important problems that keep the school from achieving its goals.

The leadership corps' role regarding school discipline may be approached from several perspectives. The corps may focus attention on problems that arise from common student infractions. It is legitimate from time to time for the corps to consider the behavior of groups of students who are violating school regulations. For example, smoking in the boys' rooms and girls' rooms will periodically become an issue in any school. Smoking in the lavatories is an appropriate problem for the corps to address. Lunchroom misbehavior is another area the corps can consider. A leadership corps should be expected to suggest actions that student leaders, administrators, and teachers can take to improve these kinds of school situations.

The corps, however, generally would not concern itself with any one individual who violates the regulations of the school. The leadership corps cannot become a court for handling matters of individual discipline. Parents generally do not approve of such courts because, in most instances, the student court members lack the depth of understanding to deal properly with the situation. Responsibility for determining individual punishments and corrective measures should not be delegated to students by administrators.

The leadership corps may involve itself in an individual case when students' opinion is that an arbitrary or capricious punishment may have been given to a student. The corps may raise questions about actions that are perceived by many students to be unjustified. When the fairness of the principal or faculty is in question, the corps may try to find out why certain action was taken against a particular student. In this sense, while the corps cannot prosecute discipline cases, it can on occasion act as an informal defender.

The number of times that the actions of administrators and teachers are questioned may tend to increase as the corps' feeling of school ownership increases. It is legitimate for student leaders to question decisions that appear to be in conflict with the stated purposes of the institution and with their understanding of the expectations for students and faculty. In one case, for example, a student who had never been disciplined was suspended from school for the commission of a particular offense. A representative of the corps questioned the administrator about this decision. The principal explained that the case was serious and that details could not be discussed with him or anyone else except the student's parents. Even though corps members did not fully understand the administration's point of view, they did not express more concern. Sufficient trust had been developed between the administrator and corps members to lead to acceptance of the decision.

As students grow in their abilities to share responsibilities for achieving the organizational goals, incidents of give-and-take between the corps and the administration and teachers will increase. Students who help to establish some policies and procedures in schools can be expected to approach the school administrators about other school regulations. Students may ask particular questions about requirements and other things that are included in the school program. Experience has indicated, however, that once students understand the reasons for the goals, procedures, and policies, they will accept them even though they may disagree.

In many schools, students or teachers will not be accustomed to being in an organization where reformational leadership assets are applied in decision making. The principal in such instances should be aware that it will take time for the faculty and student body to change their expectations for how decisions will be made and, subsequently, to build commitment to different methods of making decisions. Students, for instance, when suddenly thrust into group problem-solving situations, may view the group as an opportunity to obtain their personal, short-range desires. They may have little orientation toward the collective goals of the school. The principal will need to ward off any temptation to rush the use of reformational leadership assets with the corps. The level of responsibility can be increased as corps members demonstrate their ability to balance their own desires with the broad goals of the school.

Finally, concern may arise among the faculty about the functions and deliberations of the corps. The administrator, as part of the advisor's role to the corps, must keep the faculty informed of the activities of the corps. One ground rule that should be established with the corps and communicated to the faculty advisors is that the corps, as a body, will not discuss an individual teacher or a teacher's performance. Concerns about the school program are to be discussed in terms of the program rather than the individuals in the program. Individual student concerns about a teacher may be discussed with the principal or guidance personnel on an individual basis.

Corps Membership and Student Elections

The composition of the leadership corps will vary from school to school. It appears that the membership should include at least the presidents and vice-presidents of each class and the president of the student organization. The remaining composition of the leadership corps may depend upon the traditions and orientation of the particular school. Most schools have some provision for student elections, a useful mechanism for determining some, if not all, corps membership. School elections, however, vary widely in their conduct and results.

Striking differences between schools may be found in the climate in which school elections are conducted. In one school, elections were treated as a silly game and were viewed by most students as insignificant. In another school, the elections were seen as important decisions that students had to make regarding the future of their school and themselves. In the former, students elected the most popular students and, occasionally, the most ridiculous students to serve in leadership capacities. In the latter, students elected, in almost all instances, were responsible and mature and able to exercise reasonable, intelligent, decision making styles.

Why the difference between the two schools? The differences were due, in part, to the behavior of the administrators and teachers toward the student-elected leadership. In the first school, students were not given any responsibility once elected, were not trained to handle their responsibilities, and received little or no recognition for being elected. In the second school, elected students were placed in positions of some authority, provided opportunities for training, and recognized as being in positions of influence. The second school emphasized reformational leadership assets, whereas the first school did not stress student involvement in decision-making.

Differences in school climates for student elections are further illustrated by a situation involving the merger of two schools having similar populations. Prior to consolidation, students in one school had to be encouraged to run for office because holding office was not perceived to be a worthwhile activity. Student leaders were not involved in school problem solving nor in planning with teachers and administrators. In the other school, students were viewed as important to the school organization. It was difficult to eliminate candidates for office. When the two high schools of equal size were merged, twenty-seven candidates ran. Of these, twenty-four were students from the school whose staff had fostered a three-year program of student participation in the governance of the school. It took two years in the consolidated school before the field of candidates for office equally represented the two former student bodies.

The election of student representatives as corps members who are accorded legitimized authority in decision making is an ideal way to help students become a part of the school organization. It may be necessary for administrators and teachers to work with students to make certain that all segments of the school population are represented. Some schools, for instance, may encounter special problems with the elective system in terms of multiethnic and socioeconomic representation. Administrators have reported that, in most instances, the elective process has been able to bring about good representation of the entire student body once reformational leadership assets were used with the leadership corps.

SUMMARY

Penal leadership assets are penalities that force teachers and others to make the behavioral change desired. Whenever the principal uses these assets, faculty or student alienation usually occurs. Approval leadership assets are the rewards a principal uses to induce or reinforce individual behavior among members of the school organization. Both penal and reward assets reflect the use of power by the principal. Reformational leadership assets include the methods and skills the principal uses to tap the energy of others through involving them in problem solving and goal setting and implementation. Use of these assets encourages commitment to agreed-upon aims and to feelings of personal responsibility for satisfying personal needs while achieving the collective goals of the organization. Penal and approval assets are external to the people in the organization and, as such, are finite and may become liabilities in some situations. Reformational leadership assets tap the internal resources of people. Although not infinite, they have great potential for bringing about change.

One of the most important ways that reformational assets may be used with students is through the creation of a leadership corps. An organized group of leaders, many elected by their peers, can help the faculty and administration in pursuing school goals and promoting self-governance and norms for appropriate social behavior.

NOTES

1. Harl R. Douglass, *Modern Administration of Secondary Schools* (New York: Ginn and Company, 1963), p. 318.

2. Amitai Etzioni, *Modern Organizations* (Englewood Cliffs, N. J.: Prentice-Hall, 1964), p. 40.

3. Ibid.

4. Ibid.

5. Daniel Katz and Robert Kahn, *The Social Psychology of Organizations* (New York: John Wiley and Sons, 1966), p. 334.

6. James MacGregor Burns, *Leadership* (New York: Harper Colophon Books, Harper & Row, 1978), pp. 435–61.

7. Ibid.

8. Ibid., p. 438.

9. H. Goldhamer and E. A. Shils, "Types of Power and Status," *American Journal of Sociology* 45 (1939):192.

10. Paul Hersey and Kenneth H. Blanchard, *Management of Organizational Behavior: Utilizing Human Resources* (Englewood Cliffs, N.J.: Prentice-Hall, 1977), pp. 40–41.

11. Ibid.

12. Amitai Etzioni, *A Comparative Analysis of Complex Organizations* (New York: The Free Press, 1969), p. 61.

13. John R. P. French and Bertram Raven, "The Bases of Social Power," in Darwin Cartwright and A. F. Zandler (eds.), *Group Dynamics*, 2nd ed., (Evanston, Ill.: Row, Peterson & Co., 1969), pp. 607–23.

14. Etzioni, p. 61.

15. Ibid.

16. Alvin Gouldner, *Patterns of Industrial Bureaucracy* (New York: The Free Press, 1964), pp. 162–80.

17. Ibid., pp. 215–27.

18. Etzioni, p. 68.

19. Niccolo Machiavelli, "Of Cruelty and Clemency, Whether It Is Better to Be Loved or Feared," *The Prince* (New York: New American Library, 1952), p. 90.

20. H. Randolph Bobbitt, Jr; Robert H. Breinholt; Robert H. Dalton; and James P. McNaul, *Organizational Behavior Understanding and Predictation.* (Englewood Cliffs. N. J.: Prentice-Hall, 1974), pp. 110.

21. Ibid., p. 109.

22. Burns, p. 435.

23. Ibid.

8

Aspects of the Principal's Use of Leadership Assets

The principal makes choices about how to lead the school organization. The selection of one type of leadership asset over other types may result in the change intended. It may also result in an unintended change. Previous chapters discussed how situational factors can determine the type of leadership assets used. This chapter explores why a principal might prefer the use of one type of asset over others. It should help principals conceptualize their own value orientations. It should also help principals analyze why teachers, students, and parents strenuously debate some of the issues inherent in the aims, processes, and climate factors of school discipline. This chapter also discusses six problems that principals may encounter in achieving discipline effectiveness and ten errors to avoid in using organizational change to improve discipline.

VALUE ORIENTATION

Many decisions made by principals are related to the selection of specific leadership assets. This selection process should be governed by the situational factors present at the time in the organization and the personal preferences of the administrator. The situational factors were explored in Chapter 7. The focus here is on the role of personal beliefs that affect a principal's preference for the different leadership assets. The principal's selection of leadership assets may be influenced by one or more of five value orientations that are present in some form in all individuals and groups. According to Kluckhohn and Strodtbeck,[1] these value orientations are: human-nature orientation, people/nature orientation, time orientation, activity orientation, and relational orientation. It must be assumed that a principal's value orientation is the dominant force in the selective use of leadership assets just as it is in other decisional options.

The five value orientations, while appearing complex, are easily understood when each is stated in the form of a question. For example, the question crucial to the principal's orientation to human nature is:

1. What is the character of innate human nature? Or, what is the innate goodness or badness of human nature?

The range of possible answers to this question are predictable and universal, according to Kluckhohn and Strodtbeck. Answers may take three different forms: (a) students and/or teachers are basically evil but perfectible; (b) students and/or teachers are both good and evil, (c) students and/or teachers are basically good but corruptible.[2] If a principal believes that teachers are basically evil but perfectible, they would need close supervision and a climate that does not permit them to take responsibility for their own behavior. Students, for instance, cannot be trusted to act appropriately. Since they cannot be trusted, students must be controlled primarily through the application of penal leadership assets. Principals who view faculty in this manner are likely to avoid extensive use of reformational leadership assets to improve discipline in the school. But if a principal believes that others are both good and evil, then it is likely that both penal and approval leadership assets will be used. The principal would place some responsibility on students and teachers for their behavior through the use of reformational leadership assets.

Principals who believe that others are basically good but corruptible are likely to use the reformational leadership assets as their primary method of improving discipline. They view students as capable of being trusted and as having the resources to be responsible for their own behavior. These principals believe that a high degree of external manipulation through the use of penal and approval leadership assets is not necessary. McGregor's descriptions of "Theory X" and "Theory Y" may be compared to the human nature value orientation.[3] Theory X closely parallels the view of administrators who believe man is basically evil but perfectible, while Theory Y is similar to the belief that man is basically good but corruptible.

The question that determines a second value orientation of the principal is:

2. What is the relationship of people to nature?

Kluckhohn and Strodtbeck allowed three possible responses to this question: (a) people are under the authority of nature or controlled by nature; (b) people are in harmony with nature and both share the authority; (c) people are nature's conqueror, and people have authority over nature.[4] Principals whose dominant belief is that people are reactors to their environment and can do little to control or change the course of events in a school are likely to use the penal and approval assets to improve discipline. Since these principals believe people are controlled by external forces, they use punishments and rewards rather than self-controlling leadership assets such as the reformational assets. Such principals are not likely to use reformational assets because these are based on a belief that others have the resources to control themselves and not just react to an overwhelming environment.

Other principals believe that people live in harmony with nature, rather than being controlled by it, and share the authority for their behavior with their environment. Such principals tend to place less emphasis on the use of penal and approval assets. They maximize the use of the reformational assets as a means of changing behavior, since people have both the authority and resources to deal with discipline problems.

Principals whose dominant belief is that people are conquerors over nature can be expected to use both the penal and reformational assets. These principals will use reformational leadership assets when they appear to be a "sure bet" to produce an outcome that they desire. They believe that people, as a part of nature, are subject to the influence of external controls. This belief centers around one's ability to manage the elements (people) in the environment. When a principal holding this belief is confronted with a major disciplinary problem, the solution to which requires a concerted effort from the faculty, the principal moves quickly to demand cooperation from others in implementing his or her solution to the problem. The use of reformational leadership assets takes time and is risky in terms of the principal's goals. It is the time factor that the principal most often fails to consider when he or she tries to use reformational assets.

The third basic value orientation concerns the perspective principals have toward time. The key question is:

3. What is the temporal focus of human life; or, what is the meaning intuitively attached to time?

The range of responses to this question is as follows: (a) people are oriented toward the past; (b) people are oriented toward the present; and (c) people are oriented toward the future.[5] Those principals whose primary orientation is toward the past tend to rely on the use of penal leadership assets to improve school discipline. The penal leadership assets used are typically positional leadership assets related to penalties issued for the failure to obey rules and regulations about student behavior.

Principals who are oriented toward the present apply few leadership assets to student problems and are likely to accept discipline in the school as it exists. They do not believe in developing plans for the future and appear to learn little about cause and effect through application of penal and approval assets. They do little to influence behavior other than to model toleration for a large variation in human behavior.

Principals whose primary time orientation is toward the future tend to use all three leadership assets to improve school discipline. These principals focus on change and methods for preventing inappropriate behavior. The reformational leadership assets provide opportunities to plan for the future.

The activity orientation governs the manner in which people choose to express themselves. The determinative question for this value orientation is:

4. What is the modality of human activity?

Possible responses to this question are as follows: (a) people choose to participate in activities that are spontaneous, nondevelopment expressions of impulses and desires ("being-oriented"); (b) people choose to spend time developing all aspects of their self ("being-in-becoming–oriented"); and (c) people choose to participate in activities oriented toward measurable results or accomplishments ("doing-oriented").[6] Principals whose dominant orientation is toward being-oriented activity tend to use reformational assets to improve discipline. They become enthralled with the process of decision making itself. In general, such principals believe that the fewer assets used the better, since behavior should be spontaneous, impulsive, and unplanned. On the other hand, principals whose dominant value response is for being-in-becoming activity are likely to emphasize the approval leadership assets with some reliance on the reformational assets. Such principals are concerned with self-development and becoming responsible for one's own behavior, but they also believe that coordination among individuals must occur in a positive manner.

Other principals value doing and planned activities with measurable outcomes. They tend to use the reformational leadership assets. The use of the penal and approval assets may be included in the plans to achieve an intended result. These principals believe students and faculty should take responsibility for correcting their own inappropriate behavior. A tendency among principals holding this belief is to use the penal assets occasionally, since the threat of penal assets is perceived as being able to "shake people up."

Finally, a relational orientation indicates the nature of a person's relationship to other people. The key question for a principal is:

5. What is the priority a person places on individual versus group goals?

Possible answers to this question are: (a) a person places a priority on autonomous action and individual goals; (b) a person places a priority on the goals of the immediate group with which the person is associated; and (c) the person places a priority on the goals of the groups that are associated with the continuity of that group through time.[7] The principal whose relational orientation is to the goals of the individual and the goals of the immediate group with which the individual is associated will primarily utilize the reformational leadership assets. The penal and approval assets are viewed as attempts to manipulate the behavior of other persons—disregarding the individual goals of those persons. The principal whose dominant value orientation is to achieve the goals of the group will emphasize reformational assets in determining what is to be achieved. However, principals with this orientation may use both penal and approval assets when individuals fail to contribute to the aims of the group. Principals whose orientation values maintaining the group through time will focus on penal and approval assets. These principals, for example, are concerned with keeping a school organization intact for several decades. The principal's personnel decisions will be based on this aim. The principal may also use the reformational leadership assets as long as he or she perceives others in the organization as sharing the aim of extending the organization through time.

Each of the five value orientations influences how the principal uses leadership assets. Further research is needed to determine the precise relationships between the value orientations and the use of the leadership assets. This discussion of value orientations should aid an administrator in considering what he or she believes and how beliefs and assumptions may influence the selection of leadership assets. If the principal extends the understanding of value orientation to the beliefs of teachers, students, and parents, it may be possible to explain some of their discipline behaviors.

THE PRINCIPAL AND EFFECTIVENESS

The principal's effectiveness or ineffectiveness in using leadership assets to improve school discipline may be viewed in a number of different ways. This section describes six different problems a principal may experience. The problems are directly related to the lack of:

1. Expectation fulfillment.
2. Expectation awareness.
3. Perception awareness.
4. Expectation consistency.
5. Perception consistency.
6. Perception congruency.

Expectation fulfillment describes a problem the principal may have when he or she is viewed by others as not being effective in school discipline matters. It is illustrated by the following case:

> The vice-principal in a midwestern high school was viewed by the faculty as being inconsistent, soft, and unfair in administering penalties for inappropriate behavior. The expectation faculty members had for the vice-principal was that he be firm, fair, and consistent in

administering such penalties. The vice-principal had many ties to the community, had been there a long time, and was reluctant to offend the parents of students with whom he had been associated. He received discipline position effectiveness data showing the faculty's concern over his use of the penal process. Given this information, the vice-principal had several options. First, he could work with the faculty in trying to change their expectations. Secondly, he could change his behavior to more closely fulfill their expectations. Thirdly, he could modify faculty expectation slightly and, at the same time, change his behavior slightly. Fourthly, he could do nothing or, finally, he could leave. This vice-principal retired the following year simply because the agony associated with trying to close the gaps between the faculty expectations and perceptions was too great. The vice-principal confided to the principal that he believed he could neither change his behavior nor change the expectations held by the faculty. Furthermore, he did not believe he wanted to change his behavior.

This account demonstrates the problem an administrator can experience when he fails to meet the expectations that teachers hold. In short, it is a problem of expectation fulfillment. The solution that the vice-principal selected was an option. But more often, persons who are concerned about their discipline effectiveness will want to study the possibilities of changing the faculties' expectations or their own behavior, or both. The methods used for changing the expectations of others rely heavily on extensive discussion of expectations related to discipline. Often the expectations that teachers have are not verbalized or communicated to administrators. Sometimes administrators are negligent in assessing the expectations that the faculty maintain. Moreover, faculty expectations change from time to time and the principal needs to be aware of these shifts.

Principals are sometimes unaware of the expectations others have for discipline in the school organization. This problem is exemplified in the following situation.

The principal was new, having been transferred from an inner-city school to a suburban setting. During the first three weeks, five students were sent to the principal's office because of inappropriate behavior in the classroom. The principal, in four out of five cases, gave the students severe tongue lashings and wrote letters to their parents.

Copies of those letters were forwarded to the teachers. The students were sent back to class the next day. The principal expected the teachers to view his actions as supportive and appropriate. The teachers involved were in the teachers' lounge and were discussing the behavior of the principal. They all agreed that the students had not been sent to the office to be reprimanded nor to have letters sent to their parents. The teachers had sent the students to the office to cool off before they continued with the rest of their classes that day. In the past, it had been common for teachers to do that with students who were angry and in danger of losing control of their behavior.

Principals can have difficulties because they simply "guess" the expectations others have for the way they should handle discipline rather than communicating with the faculty, community, or students to assess the expectations held for the way in which discipline should be handled. In the foregoing case, the principal was simply not aware of the reason students were sent to the office and of the teacher's expectations for how students should be handled in the office. This problem is one of expectation awareness—knowing what others expect. A principal should continually assess the expectations for discipline of the faculty, community, and students.

A third problem is a principal's unawareness of the perceptions teachers have of his or her behavior. This awareness problem is evident in the following episode:

The principal of a high school established a steering committee as a means of planning for improved discipline. After three or four meetings, the committee was still not functioning effectively. It had not developed a plan to improve the discipline problem. Several committee members were talking prior to the principal's arrival at the fifth meeting. One said, "Our principal believes that we see him as an effective leader in our school, especially when it comes to discipline. But the truth is, he couldn't be further from reality. We see our principal as trying to spread out the responsibility for discipline, when that is primarily his responsbility. Therefore, we see the principal as not being effective in dealing with school discipline." The principal, on the other hand, said to his vice-principal the same day, "I believe the teachers think I'm doing a good job in handling disci-

> pline. Certainly, they know that I am concerned about improving discipline and they must view me as attempting to bring all the resources of the school to bear on this important problem. My use of their resources must be viewed in a positive manner, since they are continuing to participate in the task force meetings."

In this situation, the principal was almost totally unaware of the perceptions of his behavior. The principal's perception awareness was low. This principal would benefit from the feedback of an informal sounding board within the faculty relative to perceptions of his behavior.

A fourth problem that sometimes plagues principals is conflict between their expectations and others' expectations for how they should handle discipline. Consider the expectation inconsistency in the following case.

> Students had smoked in the school restrooms for many years. The principal felt, as did some faculty, that this situation had gone on too long and that something should be done to correct it. The principal and faculty recommended to the superintendent and board of education that a smoking area for students be established. After some rigorous debate, the board of education approved a small area outside the building. Students who wished to use the smoking area were required to present a slip giving their parents' written permission to do so.
>
> In January, the principal worked with counselors and teachers to reduce the frequency of inappropriate behavior and to reduce the number of study halls for which the students were scheduled. By June, the principal concluded that he had been successful in reducing the number of incidents of inappropriate behavior and especially smoking incidents in the restrooms. By these measures, the principal was effective in dealing with school discipline. The principal's expectations were perceived by him as having been achieved. A majority of the faculty, however, felt that its expectations for the principal's role in discipline had not been met. Teachers were specifically concerned about the lack of any attempt to place responsibility for student behavior on the students themselves. Students had not been included as members of the school organization. The faculty was not at all satisfied with the leadership the principal had provided in dealing with discipline.

It is not uncommon for administrators and faculty to have differing sets of expectations for the role that the principal should play in improving discipline. Such lack of expectation consistency leads to differing views of effectiveness. The principal in the foregoing account believed that discipline personal effectiveness had been achieved; that is, the principal had accomplished what he had hoped to accomplish. The faculty, on the other hand, argued that the principal had not achieved discipline position effectiveness; that is, the principal was perceived as having failed the expectations which the faculty held for discipline. When administrators and faculty share the same expectations for the role of the principal, a high level of expectation consistency exists.

The problem of differences between position and personal effectiveness often involves the principal's lack of awareness of others' expectations for his behavior and/or of how his behavior is perceived. Discussions with the faculty tend to help identify the variations in expectations. Moreover, the principal may be aware of the differences between personal effectiveness and position effectiveness and choose to maintain the expectations he or she holds for success rather than to alter his or her behavior in accordance with the expectations of others. In instances of principle, the principal may ultimately lose the principalship due to the lack of position effectiveness, but the person may maintain his or her personal integrity.

A fifth problem the principal encounters results from differences between the way principals view their behavior and the way others view it. Consider the following example.

> A middle school principal described herself as trusting, warm, somewhat unstructured, and not likely to go by the book in every case. Teachers who completed the DPEI (Discipline Position Effectiveness Inventory) indicated that the principal was highly structured, untrusting, and extremely rule oriented. When confronted with these results, the principal argued that the teachers simply did not view her as she is. It was several months before the teachers began to admit that their perceptions of her behavior were somewhat distorted.

In this situation, the perceptions of the principal and the perceptions of others regarding the principal's behavior were not the same. Perception inconsistency was the problem in this case. When a principal is simply unaware of the perceptions of others, the problem is the lack of perception awareness. The principal was aware of her own behavior and knew that others viewed her differently. She attributed the judgments of others to their limited observations of her behavior.

When both faculty and the principal perceive the principal's behavior in the same way, a high level of perception consistency exists. The lack of perception consistency is best resolved through increasing the visibility of the principal's actions. Reliable faculty, whose perceptions are believed to be accurate by other members of the faculty, should be placed in a position to observe the principal's actions.

A sixth problem that principals may encounter is one of incongruence in perceptions. Incongruence can occur when a principal attempts to guess how he or she is perceived and makes comparisons between those guesses and the way in which the principal views him- or herself. Consider, for example, the following case.

A principal believed that he rewarded students frequently for appropriate behavior. He saw himself as encouraging students and providing opportunities for them to receive recognition for appropriate behavior. He believed that the faculty saw him in the same way. Through use of the DOEI and subsequent discussions with faculty, it became evident to the principal and other faculty members that this principal was not, in fact, perceived to be supporting and rewarding student behavior. The principal concluded that he had not shared with the faculty the actions taken with students on an individual basis from time to time. Subsequently, whenever the principal rewarded a student for appropriate behavior, he communicated this event to the faculty.

Other solutions for the differing perceptions of the principal and the teachers could have included discussions with the faculty members and students about the actions of the principal. It might also have been useful for the principal to engage in candid conversation with several faculty members who would share their perceptions of the principal's performance.

A principal needs to remain open to feedback to detect the existence of any of these six potential problems. When such feedback suggests that the principal is involved with one of these problems of discipline effectiveness, some decisions need to be made about what can or should be done. The first decision the principal should consider is related to the accuracy of the feedback. Do others share the view one person is expressing? If others report that the feedback is accurate, then the principal needs to determine the extent of his or her own concern about the problem. For example, does the principal either need or want to satisfy the expectations of others? Perhaps the principal's ethical standards would be altered in meeting the expectations of others.

Thirdly, a principal should assess the areas of greatest concern for change. Are others concerned primarily about the principal's personal characteristics, behaviors, or outcomes? The principal may want to consider the probable impact a change in one of these areas might have on the other two components. For example, if behavior is altered, how will this affect the perceptions of the principal's personal characteristics? A fourth consideration for the principal is to determine whether one should attempt to alter others' perceptions or expectations for the principal. Perhaps both perceptions and expectations should be altered at approximately the same time. The principal also needs to estimate the influence these changes may have on still other perceptions and expectations.

There are two requirements the principal should address in making decisions about improving effectiveness. The principal who is planning improvement should establish criteria by which the person can assess the level of improvement at a later date. These criteria provide the measures for assessing changes in expectations and perceptions. Secondly, during the time the principal is attempting to change perceptions or expectations, selected individuals should provide a personal support base to the principal. They can aid the principal during the period of change. These considerations and requirements may be incorporated into a self-development plan for the principal. The reformational assets may be applied by the principal to the development of this program for improving the principal's discipline effectiveness.

ERRORS TO AVOID IN THE USE OF LEADERSHIP ASSETS

Whenever a principal uses leadership assets to improve school discipline, there are potential errors to be avoided. Reddin has listed ten errors he has made while working with organizations to bring about change.[8] These errors, if made by principals, can lead to serious problems for discipline in the school. The first error is to use the leadership assets to effect the management of discipline without either informing or involving the central-office staff in the intended change. Central-office approval and support are usually essential if leadership assets are to be effective. Support such as money, time, and district-wide cooperation may be necessary to penalize, reward, or involve a faculty and others in program improvement.

A second error a principal may make is to attempt to help people change their behavior too fast. The norms of the school groups took time to form; they will take time to change. Since people are comfortable with habits, demands for change in those habits frequently create stress, and too much change can cause intolerable stress. An example of gradual change was found in a large school. Data from the DOEI in a high school indicated significant gaps on six of the seven profiles. The principal, working with the staff, spent the first of a three-year improvement plan devising a process for collecting accurate discipline data for the school. Teachers implemented this data system and began working on the second and third phases of the plan in subsequent years. The faculty did not experience much stress from this gradual approach. Principals will need to assist faculty and others in setting realistic aims that do not create an overload on the people involved in making changes.

The third error for principals to avoid is the raising of unrealistic expectations. Designs for improving discipline do not produce miracles. Short-range aims that are realistic and attainable will preclude the staff's having dreams that cannot be realized. (In some schools, it may be extremely difficult to raise teachers' expectations ever so slightly because they believe nothing will ever improve their situation. While this point does not address the potential error, it does suggest that care should be exercised in making certain such faculties experience success with steps taken toward improving discipline.)

Another error that is made by principals is providing in-service training for improved discipline to teachers without planning to reward the new behaviors expected when they return to their daily activities. The establishment of new norms among the faculty must be reinforced. If the principal does not implement a plan to reward those teachers who exhibit changes in behavior, their former behavior will dominate.

The principal may make the error of not identifying the need for assistance outside of school personnel. At times, an outside consultant's assistance is essential to the effective use of leadership assets for improving discipline. In seeking such assistance, the principal should look for someone who has expertise and "a good track record" in the area of need by checking into such matters as:

1. The general quality of previous work performed by the consultant.
2. The satisfaction of other organizations for whom similar services have been performed by the consultant.
3. The consultant's ability to work with teachers.
4. The consultant's ability to meet deadlines and fulfill contractual obligations.
5. The consultant's accessibility.
6. The consultant's publications in the area in question.

The principal should reduce to writing the obligations of both parties—the school and the consultant. What services will be provided—when, by whom, and for how much? How often will the teachers be made available? What data will the school provide? A definite termination date should be established at which time the services of the outside consultant will cease.

Lastly, some principals attempt to use leadership assets to improve discipline but fail because they make the mistake of becoming emotionally involved with their faculty. Respect for professional leadership is earned by principals who are able to experience feelings in relationships with teachers but who are able to maintain professional detachment when applying the leadership assets. Some emotional attachment may lead to the humanistic caring concern for others in the organization, but too much emotional influence in the principal's decision making can lead to serious mistakes in the judgment of the principal.

SUMMARY

Mistakes and problems can occur in the principal's use of leadership assets to improve school discipline. The penal, approval, and reformational leadership assets when used effectively can produce changes in school discipline. A principal needs to know how and when to use these assets and must know his or her value orientations well enough to ascertain why some assets and not others are used. Difficulties in improving discipline can be avoided when the principal is aware of some of the perception and expectation problems and the potential for error.

NOTES

1. Florence Rockwood Kluckhohn and Fred L. Strodtbeck, *Variation in Value Orientations* (Evanston, Ill.: Row, Peterson and Co., 1961), pp. 10–11.

2. The questions and responses reflecting the value orientations are significantly more complex than depicted in this chapter. The reader interested in this topic is encouraged to review reading in anthropology, including Kluckhohn and Strodtbeck's work described in *Variation in Value Orientations*.

3. Douglas M. McGregor, *The Human Side of Enterprise* (New York: McGraw-Hill Book Co., 1960), pp. 33–57.

4. Kluckhohn and Strodtbeck, p. 13.

5. Ibid., pp. 13–15.

6. Ibid., pp. 15–17.

7. Ibid., pp. 17–20.

8. William J. Reddin, "Confessions of an Organization Change Agent," *Groups and Organizational Studies* 2 (March, 1977): 33–41.

CHAPTER
9

Legal Parameters
Affecting Discipline

Existing laws, constitutional provisions, and court decisions determine the legal parameters within which the public schools must function. Discipline to be effective must operate within the law as it exists at any point in time. The legal framework of a society changes over time, but at any particular moment the framework is usually rather well defined.

In recent years, students and parents have been quick to challenge disciplinary actions of school officials that they believe fall outside of the existing legal framework. Litigation involving public school students has increased rather dramatically with the advent of court decisions that explicitly state that students no longer "shed their constitutional rights to freedom of speech or expression at the schoolhouse."[1] As a result of this basic change in outlook on student rights, practitioners in public education are seeking guidance for their efforts to control student conduct in positive, meaningful, and effective ways.

The authors acknowledge Mr. Robert Sharp, J.D., legal counsel for the Tennessee State Department of Education, for his substantive and editorial comments relative to this discussion of school law.

This chapter purports to provide a set of readable guidelines and a concise overview of legal areas relevant to student conduct. The chapter is organized into two main sections. The first section deals with the conduct of students or, in legal parlance, "substantive due process." A number of problem areas in student conduct are explored in detail. A concise legal overview is presented for each problem area. These overviews examine the types of student conduct that are constitutionally protected and outline the resources school officials have at their disposal. The second section deals with "procedural due process." Procedural due process comes into play after a student has been accused of a wrongdoing and/or given a punishment. The rights to which a student is entitled at this stage are presented. Some general procedural due process guidelines for the practitioner are suggested.

SUBSTANTIVE DUE PROCESS

The First and Fourteenth Amendments of the United States Constitution provide the legal derivation of student rights as currently established. The First Amendment reads as follows:

> Congress shall make no law respecting an establishment of religion, or prohibiting the free exercise thereof: or abridging the freedom of speech, or of the press; or the right of the people peaceably to assemble and to petition the Government for a redress of grievances.

and the Fourteenth Amendment holds that:

> All persons born or naturalized in the United States, and subject to the jurisdiction thereof are citizens of the United States and of the State wherein they reside. No State shall make or enforce any law which shall abridge the privileges or immunities of citizens of the United States; nor shall any State deprive any person of life, liberty, or property, without due process of law; nor deny to any person within its jurisdiction the equal protection of the laws.

Public school systems and teachers are agents of the state and their actions are actions of the state; consequently, their actions are subject to constitutional scrutiny as provided by the Fourteenth Amendment. Thus, the freedoms granted in the First Amendment, such as symbolic speech in the form of the wearing of buttons and arm bands, petition, assembly, and freedom of the press, are made applicable to students through the Fourteenth Amendment.

The general problem involved in substantive due process is that the students' constitutional rights are weighed against the duty of the school board to control and protect the school system and to protect the rights of other students to obtain an education.[2] Within the framework of checks and balances of substantive due process, many educational practitioners make initial decisions in dealing with students that prove very troublesome at a later date. For instance, a school may attempt to enforce a regulation that is unconstitutional, or it may attempt to enforce a regulation that is vague and thus open to different interpretations. In still other instances, a school may take rather severe action to prevent possible student behavior when, in fact, the school may not have enough evidence to warrant such action. If practitioners are aware of the legal limitations within which they operate, their initial decisions will be realistic and they will pursue an orderly process of finding positive solutions to student conduct problems.

Regarding the substantive rights of students, two guidelines for practitioners have general applicability to student conduct situations. These guidelines are:

1. Will the actions of the student cause substantial disruption to the educational process and/or the normal operation of the school?
2. Will the actions of the student be an invasion of the rights of others?[3]

Even if school officials judge the answer to either of these to be affirmative, they must remember that the burden of proof rests with them. Courts have been critical of school officials who took disciplinary actions to prevent student misconduct based on presumption and speculation.

Good rules, regulations, and policies regarding student conduct established by the board of education and individual schools greatly help practitioners—if they are consistent with existing legal thought. Courts have looked with favor on school systems that have established such guidelines and have communicated them to their students. (Preferably, students and parents will have been involved in their formulation.) Conciseness and clarity in these guidelines cannot receive too much emphasis because regulations that are open to different interpretations are very difficult to enforce. As an example, a dress code that states that "Student dress must be of the caliber and taste expected at Stylish High School" is a policy that is entirely too vague. The key phrases are "caliber" and "taste expected." The meaning of these words may vary considerably in the minds of different individuals.

Legal Problem Areas

Many areas of student rights have caused legal difficulties for school districts. The following sections provide a summary of the legal context for the regulation of student conduct based on court decisions. References given for each section head direct the reader to the actual cases that have thus far contributed to the legal complexities in school discipline.

Symbolic Speech.[4]   Symbolic speech has been defined by the U.S. Supreme Court to include such things as words and slogans, protest buttons, arm bands, writing on T-shirts, and writing on book covers. Students can use these means to express their opinion as long as their message isn't obscene or libelous and doesn't threaten to substantially disrupt the school. It must be remembered that the burden of proof is on the school to show that substantial disruption would occur before the school may legally impose limits on or proscribe the display of such symbols.

Distribution of Literature and Demonstrations.[5]   School authorities may by prior regulation establish the time, manner, place, and duration for students who wish to distribute literature or hold demonstrations on school grounds. Officials may regulate the content of literature to be distributed on school grounds only to the extent necessary to avoid substantial interference with the operation of the school. If guidelines are set up for submitting literature to be distributed for prior approval, these guidelines ought to identify to whom the material is to be submitted, specify how the material will be evaluated, and set a time-limitation for making the decision.

Student Newspapers.[6]   Student publishers have the right and responsibility to print all sides of an issue. However, newspaper comments may not be libelous or obscene. School officials may be held responsible for defamation of character, obscenity, and the like if the student newspaper is not supervised properly. Students who are not on the newspaper staff must also have access to publishing in the paper. In recent years, some students have chosen to publish an "underground" paper not associated with authorized school activities. In such instances, the school is not held responsible for the paper's content. The distribution of unofficial newspapers falls within the same category as any other non-school–related literature.

Speakers and Programs.[7]   The time and location of speeches and assemblies may be regulated by school authorities. School authorities may also require advance notice in order to promote the efficient administration of the school. Authorities may not deny speakers the use of school facilities solely because they are deemed controversial or undesirable. If some outside speakers are allowed to use the school facilities, then the same guidelines must be applied to all speakers. Officials may prohibit the use of school facilities by outside speakers if they suspect disruption or violence will result. But they must be able to show that there is a very great probability that such actions will be precipitated. Schools may establish guidelines which prohibit the use of school facilities to speakers who advocate such actions as civil violence or the overthrow of the U.S. Government.

Use of School Facilities.[8]   The legal criteria for the use of school facilities are much the same as those for speakers and programs. Essentially, school officials must treat all individuals or organizations uniformly. If one individual or group is allowed to use a school facility, then all who desire must be given the same opportunity. Religious organizations often ask to use school facilities. Schools are not required to let religious organizations use school facilities; however, if they do provide the use of a school facility to such organizations, the guidelines for outside groups using the facilities must be applied. Schools that do let religious organizations use their facilities often limit the usage to a special event or to short-term emergency situations. Use of a facility over an extended period of time as a regular place of worship may lead to a problem with community members.

Patriotic and Religious Ceremonies.[9]   Students may not be compelled to recite the pledge of allegiance, salute the flag, or participate in any other patriotic ceremony. Conversely, a student who chooses to refrain from such participation may not interfere with the rights of others to participate. The student must either remain respectfully silent or leave the classroom during the time of the activity. Currently, the public schools are not permitted to sponsor or require religious ceremonies.

Exclusion from Extracurricular Activities.[10]   Any exclusion of a student from extracurricular activities for disciplinary reasons must not be arbitrary, capricious, or unreasonable. A student may not be prohibited from participation because of his dress or appearance unless it impairs his ability to perform or constitutes a danger to his health or safety or that of others. Marriage, pregnancy, or parenthood may not be used (in and of themselves) as a reason for exclusion from extracurricular activities or from regular classroom activities.

When a student is suspended or expelled from school, he or she also loses the right to participate in all school-related activities. However, if the student shows up for a football game after school hours with money to purchase a ticket, he or she must be treated the same as any other citizen in the community coming to the ball game. Should the student misbehave during the ball game, he or she may be excluded from attendance because of it.

Search and Seizure.[11] Problems in this area are often associated with the search of a student's locker. Before performing a locker search, school officials should have reason to believe that articles in violation of school regulations or articles that would be detrimental to the efficient operation of the school are contained in the locker. It is not necessary that students be present when their locker is searched, although the student's presence is advisable whenever possible. A school official should have a witness when searching a locker. Evidence confiscated from the locker that the school official did not have sufficient reason to believe would be in the locker probably will not be admitted as evidence in a court proceeding. However, such evidence could be used as the basis for administrative action and the courts would sustain such discipline measures.

A search of the person of an individual is a slightly different matter. School officials are charged with operating an orderly and safe school. When they have reason to believe that a student is carrying an item that could be dangerous to the student or to others (such as a gun or knife), action must be taken. Preferably the student's consent should be obtained for the search. If a student does not give consent, a school official may wish to take actions other than a search due to the unclear legal issues that surround searching a person. Possible actions include securing a search warrant, calling the parents or police, excluding the student from class, or detaining the person in the principal's office until the police arrive to conduct the search.

Searching a student's car can present another problem since the car is property owned by the individual. A car parked on school grounds may be searched only with the permission of the student. A student who refuses to give permission may be prohibited by school officials from parking the car on school grounds. A car parked off school grounds should not be searched by school officials. Instead, they should contact the local police authorities if there is reason to believe that illegal activity involves the car.

Police in the Schools.[12] Police officers come onto the school grounds under the same conditions as they do any other premises. They may not search a student or the student's locker unless they have a valid warrant to do so or they have probable cause to believe that the student possesses contraband. In the absence of a warrant or probable cause, the police do not have the right to interview students in the school or to use the school facilities in connection with their official work. By the same token, the board of education does not have an obligation to make students available to the police.

In most instances where the police are involved with a student regarding nonschool activities, they should take the matter up directly with the student's parents. If a student is interrogated by the police on school property, he or she should be afforded the same rights as any other citizen— e.g., be informed of the right to remain silent. School officials have the duty to protect students from coercion from outside sources. A school official should always be present when a student is interviewed by the police. It is advisable to notify the parents and give them the opportunity to be present during the interrogation. At the very least, the parents should be informed that their child is being interrogated.

In no instance should a student be taken from the school by the police without a valid warrant because school officials are charged with the safekeeping of the student during the day. This phase of school operation can be rather delicate since it is essential that good relations be maintained between the police and the schools. Usually, if prior communications have taken place between the school and the police, common understandings with respect to the duties and obligations of each party can be reached.

Married and/or Pregnant Students.[13]   Married and/or pregnant students must be afforded the same opportunities as any other student. They may not be barred from participating in extracurricular activities, from marching in the commencement line, from becoming a candidate for student council, or from other school doings. Pregnant students cannot be suspended from school for being pregnant except for health reasons. Some states have legislation that specifically mentions pregnancy as a condition that brings the student under the definition of a "handicapped child" and, thus, makes the rather extensive provisions of some special education acts applicable to the pregnant student.

Student Records.[14]   In recent years, the contents of and access to student records have become items of concern. These concerns relative to student records led Congress to pass the "Family Educational Rights and Privacy Act of 1974" (often referred to as the Buckley Amendment). In general, the Act provides the parents or guardians of students under eighteen years of age with the right to see all records maintained on them by the school. The school may set a reasonable time and place for access to the records. The school must let the student and/or guardians make copies of the records (at students and/or guardians' expense) or let them copy information from the records. A summary of several other salient points of the Act is given in the sections that follow. Some items have been omitted; readers are urged to study government regulations for further details.

Parent means the parent, guardian, or person acting as parent of a minor child who is or has been a student in the school. *Eligible student* means a present or former student who has attained eighteen years of age or who is attending a postsecondary institution. *School* means any educational institution or agency receiving federal funds under any USOE program. It includes all individual schools operated by a recipient agency even though a particular school may not be a direct recipient.

Records. Student records refer to all records, kept in whatever form, containing personally identifiable information directly related to a present or former student and maintained by a school or agent thereof *except:*

- —records of professional personnel maintained by them for their sole use, kept in their exclusive possession, and not available to anyone else except a substitute;
- —records pertaining to the student's employment by the school;
- —records maintained by a law enforcement unit of a school and not available to school personnel;
- —records of an eligible student created and maintained by a licensed physician, psychologist, or other such professional and used only in treatment of the pupil;
- —directory information of a nonconfidential nature such as name, address, age, studies, achievements, or athletic activities, which may be released to anyone, provided that the releasable categories of directory information have not been objected to by the parent or eligible students.

Student records can be released only on specified conditions of access.

Access. The school shall not permit anyone except the parent or eligible student to have access to protected information without written consent, except:

—other school officials with a legitimate educational interest;

—officials of other schools or systems in which the student intends to enroll, provided that the parent or eligible student shall be notified that records are to be transferred, shall be given a copy of all records so transferred, and shall have opportunity for hearing to challenge the content of the records;

—state and local officials to whom the information is required by statute to be reported;

—authorized federal officials;

—persons in connection with the student's application for financial aid;

—testing bureaus and services if confidentiality can be preserved;

—accrediting agencies;

—parents of dependent students, i.e., claimed for income tax purposes, even if eighteen or attending a postsecondary institution;

—persons in compliance with a judicial order or subpoena on condition that a reasonable effort is made to notify the parent or eligible student prior to release;

—appropriate persons in connection with an emergency to protect health or safety.

Information released to persons granted access under these conditions can be provided only on condition that such persons protect the confidentiality of the information so obtained, except if a record is kept of any redisclosure. A record of access must be kept in the student's file and disclosed to the parent or eligible student upon request. A parent or eligible student shall be granted access to the record within forty-five days of his request, with explanations provided, under appropriate conditions.

Notice.   The school is required annually to notify the parent or eligible student of:

—its policy of protecting confidentiality of student records, and of eligible student's right of access;

—the types and locations of records and information contained therein related to the student and maintained by the school, and the title of the responsible official;

—the persons having access thereto and the purposes for which such access is granted;

—the policy for reviewing and correcting records;

—procedures for inspecting the records, challenging the contents thereof, and securing copies, together with any cost thereof;

—the categories of nonconfidential information designated as directory.

Hearing. Parent or eligible students who doubts the accuracy, relevancy, or completeness of records contained in the student's file may request appropriate amendment or correction. If they are denied such request, they may then demand a hearing, to be held within a reasonable time before a disinterested party, at which they are afforded an opportunity to present evidence. If the decision is adverse to them, they may place in the record a statement explaining their disagreement, which must also be disclosed to anyone to whom the record is disclosed.

Destruction of Records. Records that are not required by law to be kept may be destroyed. However, access shall be granted to a parent or eligible student prior to destruction where either has requested such access. Moreover, explanations and records of disclosure shall be maintained as long as the records are. Records that are required by law to be kept may not be destroyed except under the terms of the pertinent federal law or state statute.

Waiver of Rights. Although a school may not require either parent or student to waive rights under the regulations, either may do so with respect to all or a part of the records. Such waivers must be in writing.

Some concluding comments on student records are in order. First, it is desirable to have a school official present at all times when student records are being scrutinized to provide any needed explanation. Secondly, school personnel *who do not have a legitimate need* for information contained in the records may not browse through the records at their leisure. Thirdly, student files should be continually reviewed for the relevance of data included. When a student permanently leaves school, data without further usefulness should be destroyed.

Personal Appearance.[15] It may generally be said that students are entitled to groom themselves as they choose as long as their appearance is not a health hazard or is obscene (which must be explicitly defined). Thus, a student may be compelled to wear shoes in school for health reasons and may be required to maintain a reasonable degree of cleanliness. Societal styles at the time must be taken into consideration when dealing with personal appearance.

While the U.S. Supreme Court has ruled on hair and dress code issues for employees, it has refused to do so for students. Lower federal courts have ruled on these issues as they relate to students but have not been consistent in their rulings. Thus, administrators should be familiar with the rulings of the courts that have jurisdiction over their school district.

Clubs and Social Organizations.[16]   Courts have traditionally upheld the right of school officials to prohibit and to regulate high school organizations such as fraternities, sororities, and secret societies. The basis for these decisions has rested on the tenet that these organizations promote an undemocratic spirit of caste and cliques and, in many instances, show a contempt for school authority. This issue bears close scrutiny in the future, for court decisions could begin to deviate from this position. A recommended school policy requires all proposed organizations to submit to school officials a constitution that, among other things, outlines the purposes of the clubs, their activities, and their modes of operation. If any clubs are allowed to organize, then all responsible clubs should be given the same opportunity.

Self-Defense.   School personnel, as is the case with any citizen, have the right to defend themselves against physical harm. Thus, an educator may take steps that are reasonably necessary to bring a situation that threatens physical harm under control. However, the educator, again as with any citizen, does not have the right to continue to inflict physical punishment once the possibility of physical harm to the educator has been removed. The force used cannot be unreasonably excessive, given the nature of the attack, the age, sex, physical condition, and aggressiveness of the student.

PROCEDURAL DUE PROCESS

Procedural due process comes into play when a student has violated a school regulation or in some other way has committed a wrongdoing in the eyes of school officials. As this point, procedural due process provides the student with the opportunity to defend himself against such accusations.

Thus, procedural due process is, as the terminology implies, an orderly process for arriving at a just and impartial settlement of conflicts between school personnel and students.

A rather serious question arises as to when a student is entitled to full procedural due process; for unlike defendants in legal proceedings, students in school are not universally entitled to all the safeguards of procedural due process. The seriousness of the proposed penalty determines the due process protections to which the student is entitled.[17] The seriousness of student misconduct ranges from extremely minor infractions (such as whispering in the classroom) to extremely major infractions (such as those that are capable of inflicting bodily harm on others). The number of procedural due process protections that must be afforded the student increases with the severity of the penalty imposed. (An explanation of procedural due process protections is given in the next section.) As an example, even a teacher who makes a sixth-grade pupil stand in the corner for talking in class should be assured that the pupil being punished is the one who committed the offense. And even though the processes here may be entirely mental, the teacher should go through them before inflicting the punishment. In this case, an impartial hearing is not appropriate. But as the seriousness of the violation increases and the punishment becomes more severe, more and more of the due process protections should be added. In every instance where the potential punishment for the alleged misconduct is of such a nature that it could seriously affect the student over an extended period of time, and perhaps even has the possibility of changing the student's whole lifestyle, he or she is entitled to full protection under procedural due process.

In all instances where exclusion from school for an extended period of time is involved, the student should be provided full recourse to procedural due process proceedings. With respect to short-term exclusions from school of ten days or less, the Supreme Court ruled in Goss v. Lopez that the student must be given an oral or written notice of the charges against him or her; and that, if the student denies the charges he or she is entitled to an explanation of the evidence. The student must also have the opportunity to respond to the suspension proceedings. However, the Court did rule that in instances where the pupil's presence constitutes an immediate danger to persons or property or poses a threat to disrupt the learning process, he or she may be immediately removed from school. In such instances, the pupil must be given the necessary notice and hearing as soon as possible. In Goss v. Lopez, the Court did not grant students the right to counsel nor to confront and cross-examine witnesses in their own behalf.

The Court did not address the question of procedural rights in regard to long-term exclusions from school.

In another decision, Wood v. Strickland, the Supreme Court created the possibility of monetary damages being levied against school board members and, by implication, other school personnel for acting with malice or in violation of a student's clearly established constitutional rights. Thus, through the Wood decision, the Court established the possibility of monetary liability for failure to follow the due process guidelines established in its Goss v. Lopez decision.

Rules of Thumb

Each piece of procedural due process legislation has its own peculiarities. Most of the legislative differences lie in the time frames which are allowed for the respective parties to make their requests and responses. It would not be useful here to summarize all of the details of varying legal codes. However, the general guidelines presented below indicate the conditions that fulfill the intent of procedural due process. In specific cases, of course, these guidelines should not be taken as a substitute for the actual legislation.

1. *The individual must be made aware of the rules and regulations he is to follow and the potential penalties for their violation.* It is important that rules and regulations be stated in precise terms. Reasonable methods must be established to ensure that the students are made aware of the rules and regulations and potential penalties. Many schools attempt to accomplish this by discussing school regulations in homeroom or assemblies. The age of a student and the length of time he or she has been enrolled in the school can be factors in determining whether the student should be expected to be aware of a regulation. There must be a correlation between the penalty and the type of regulation that has been broken. However, past or repeated infractions by the student can be taken into account when determining the penalty.

2. *The student must be given a written statement of the charges and the nature of evidence against him.* In this phase of procedural due process, it is extremely important that the student and/or the parents fully understand the contents of the written statement. The complexity of this statement and the background of the individuals involved must be taken into account when determining whether

the written statement should be reasonably understood. Under some conditions, merely mailing the written statement to the individuals involved may not be adequate. Personal delivery of the statement giving the student and/or the parents the opportunity to ask clarifying questions might be more appropriate in these cases. Specificity in the written statement is extremely important. The individual must be informed precisely of the charges and nature of the evidence. The record shows that vague rules and imprecise charges have resulted in more reversals of school board decisions by courts than any other single defect.

3. *The student must be informed of his or her procedural rights.* Rights are of no use unless the student has knowledge of their existence. Therefore, one of the requirements of procedural due process is that the student be informed of the appeal and defense process available. The information given should include such things as to whom the appeal should be made, how it should be made, the time limit under which it can be made; and the rights of the student to present evidence on his or her own behalf, to confront the accusers, and to produce and cross-examine witnesses.

4. *The individual must be given adequate time to prepare his or her defense.* A student may not be informed of a suspension from school in the morning and asked to appear at a full scale board hearing in the afternoon. The definition of adequate time varies according to the circumstances; however, in most instances, five days is adequate time and, in every instance reviewed to date, ten days have been deemed adequate.

5. *At a hearing, the student must be provided the opportunity to present a defense.* Specifically, the student must be allowed to do the following:

   Present his or her case to an impartial hearer. The school officials who are bringing the charges may not also act as the hearer. On occasion, boards of education get into trouble on this matter for they first expel the student and then attempt to act as an impartial hearer. Thus, students should be given the opportunity for a hearing before they are expelled.

   Present evidence on his or her behalf. This, in essence, means that students get the opportunity to put forth their side of the situation. Evidence can be in any form such as an oral presentation, the producing of witnesses on the student's behalf, or written statements.

Confront his or her accusers. This means that students have a right to know who brought the charges against them and to question those who have brought charges.

Produce and cross-examine witnesses. This procedural right is rather self-explanatory. The important thing is that the student be given the opportunity to disprove the accusations of a hostile witness and to include the testimony of witnesses explaining the student's side of the affair.

The right to counsel.[18] While a U.S. Supreme Court decision on this issue has not been rendered, it seems that a public-school student has a right to counsel only at an expulsion hearing. The student does not have a right to counsel at other hearings, such as a "guidance conference" hearing. If the student has legal counsel, it is highly advisable that the school board also be represented by counsel.

The use of counsel at a formal school board hearing should not be confused with the use of counsel in meetings that are held with the student and/or the parents in attempts to resolve the conflict prior to the board hearing. School personnel working with the student and the parents to bring about a positive solution of the problem are not required to admit counsel to these proceedings. However, it should be stressed that the goal of these meetings is to bring about a positive solution to the situation and not to harass or in other ways intimidate the student.

It needs to be mentioned that when "special education" students are under consideration for disciplinary actions, special due process procedures may be in effect. This is particularly true if the reasons for the disciplinary actions are in some way related to the student's handicap. At present, these special procedures are being developed at the state level, so it is not possible to give rules of thumb that might be applicable nationwide.

Corporal Punishment[19]

The U.S. Supreme Court has rendered a decision that states that neither the Fourteenth nor the Eighth Amendment is applicable to corporal punishment in the public schools. The decision indicates that corporal punishment is not a matter of constitutional jurisdiction but, rather, is a matter of state and local jurisdiction. Any school board approving or permitting the use of corporal punishment should have a policy relative to its use. Any such policy must be at least as restrictive as the state mandate. If a board policy is more restrictive than the state mandate, the policy takes precedence over the state mandate and must be obeyed by teachers and other board employees. To do otherwise would make them subject to insubordination.

Often a school district has neither a state requirement nor a policy pertaining to corporal punishment. In Baker v. Owens, a North Carolina Federal Circuit Court affirmed the legality of a North Carolina statute that permitted a school system to use corporal punishment in spite of parental objections. The recommended guidelines for the administration of corporal punishment issued by the court in this decision are well thought out and logical, and lacking state and/or local policies, they can be used for guidance at the local level in administering corporal punishment. These guidelines are as follows:

1. In all but those acts of misconduct that are so antisocial or disruptive in nature as to shock the conscience, the student must have received prior notice that specific misbehavior could occasion the use of corporal punishment.

2. Corporal punishment must not be used as a first line of punishment, but only after attempts to modify behavior by other means have failed.

3. Corporal punishment must be administered only in the presence of a second school official or teacher, as witness.

4. The witness must be informed beforehand, and in the student's presence, of the reason for the punishment to allow the student to protest, spontaneously, an egregiously arbitrary or contrived application of punishment; but there is no requirement that the student be afforded a formal opportunity to present his or her side to the second person.

5. Upon request, the parent must be provided a written explanation by the person administering the punishment of the reasons for the punishment and of the name of the witness.

A school system must operate within legal parameters in establishing an effective and efficient discipline process. According to the law as it is now being interpreted by the courts, students must be afforded both substantive and procedural due process in matters of school conduct.

NOTES

1. Tinker v. Des Moines Independent School District, 383 U.S. 503 (1969).
2. 16 Am. Jur. 2d, Constitutional Law #550.
3. Tinker v. Des Moines Independent Community School District #21, 89 S. Ct. 733 (1969).
4. Tinker v. Des Moines Community School District, 383 U.S. 503 (1969); Butts v. Dallas Independent School District, 306 Fed. Supp. 488 (1961); Guzick v. Drebus, 305 Fed. Supp. 472 (1971); Hernandez v. School District No. 1, Denver, Colorado, 315 F. Supp. 289 (1977).
5. Eisner v. Stamford Board of Education, 314 F. Supp. 832 (1971).
6. Lee v. Board of Regents State Colleges, 306 F. Supp. 1097 (1969); Scoville v. Board of Education of Joliet Tp. H.S. District 204, 425 F. 2d 10 (1970); Antonelli v. Hammond, 308 F. Supp. 1329 (1970).
7. Payroll Guarantee Assoc. v. Board of Education, 27 Col. 2d 197 (1945); ACLU v. Board of Education of City of Los Angeles, 59 Col. 2d 167 (1961); Ellis v. Allen, 165 N.Y. 2d 624 (1946); East Meadow Community Concerts v. Board of Education, 18 N.Y. 2d 129 (1966); National Socialist White People's Party v. Ringers, 473 F. 2d 1010 (1973).
8. Merryman v. School District #16, 43 Wyo. 376 (1931); Mr. Knight v. Board of Education, 365 Pa. 422 (1969); Southside Estates Baptist Church v. Board of Trustees, Tax Dist. #1, 115 So. 2d 697 (1959).
9. Zorach v. Clausen, 343 U.S. 306 (1952); Abington v. Schempp, 374 U.S. 203 (1963); Engel v. Vitale, 370 U.S. 421 (1962); Mangold v. Albert Gallatin Area School District, 438 F. 2d 1194 (1971); W. Virginia Board of Education v. Barnette, 319 U.S. 624 (1943).
10. Bentley v. Board of Education of Harrodsburg, 383 SW. 2d 677 (1965).
11. Preston v. United States, 376 U.S. 364 (1964); United States v. Blok, 188 F. 2d 1019 (1951); Johnson v. United States, 333 U.S. 10 (1963); Frank v. Maryland, 359 U.S. 360 (1959); People v. Overton, 20 N.E. 2d 360 (1969); People v. Stewart, 313 N.Y.S. 2d 253 (1970).
12. Moore v. The Student Affairs Committee of Troy State Univ., 284 F. Supp. 725 (1968); State v. Stein, 203 Kan. 638 (1969); Overton v. Reiger, 311 F. Supp. 1035 (1970); Piazzola v. Watkins, 316 F. Supp. 624 (1971); Chimel v. Calif., 395 U.S. 752 (1969).
13. Ordway v. Hargraves, 323 F. Supp. 1155 (1971); Holt v. Shelton, 341 F. Supp. 821 (1972); Davis v. Meek, 344 F. Supp. 298 (1972); Bentley v. Board of Education of Harrodsburg, 383 S.W. 2d 677 (1965); Shull v. Columbus Municipal School District, 338 F. Supp. 1376 (1972).
14. Title 45 CFR Part 99 (1975).

15. Pugsley v. Sellmeyer, 250 S.W. 538 (1923); Wallace v. Ford, 346 F. Supp. 156 (1972); Massie v. Henry, 455 F. 2d 799 (1972).

16. Passel v. Ft. Worth Independent School District, 453 S.W. 2d 288 (1970); NAACP v. Butler, 371 U.S. 415 (1962); Waugh v. Board of Trustees of Univ. of Miss., 237 U.S. 589 (1915).

17. Goss v. Lopez, 43 USLW 4181 (1975); Wood v. Strickland, 43 USLW 4293 (1975).

18. Givens v. Poe, 346 F. Supp. 202 (1972); Madera v. Board of Education of the City of New York, 386 F. Supp. 778 (1967).

19. Ingraham v. Wright, 525 F. 2d 909 (1977); Baker v. Owen, 395 F. Supp. 294 (1975); Ware v. Estes, 328 F. Supp. 657 (1971).

APPENDIX A

Discipline Organization Effectiveness Inventory

FORMS I AND II

Instructions for Completing the Discipline Organization Effectiveness Inventory I

To respond to Inventory I, you must first select a particular school population (building or district) with which you are especially familiar in terms of discipline practices. Your selection may be your current school or school system or one with which you have had recent experience. Then, respond to each set of inventory items according to the specific directions below.

1. On a blank sheet of paper, write DOEI I at the top and then list numbers 1 through 28 down the left-hand margin.

2. On your numbered sheet, you will record your response to each of the 28 items on the inventory by writing one of the letters A, B, C, D, E, F, or G after each number, 1–28. *Do not respond on the inventory itself.*

3. Letters A, B, C, D, E, F, and G represent seven possible responses to complete the following statement:

I believe the discipline processes in my school are:

A–Very much like the item on the left

B– More like the item on the left than the one on the right

C– A little more like the item on the left than the one on the right

D–A balance between the two items

E– A little more like the item on the right than the one on the left

F– More like the item on the right than the one on the left

G–Very much like the item on the right

4. An example of the 28 items in the left and right columns of Inventory I is shown by the following:

| Not penalizing students who constantly misbehave. | A Ⓑ C D E F G | Penalizing students who constantly misbehave |

The selection of response "B" means that the respondent believes that students who constantly misbehave are seldom penalized.

5. In each instance select the letter that most closely represents your perceptions of discipline and how it is practiced in the school you have selected. The responses you select should reflect your *current and personal views of how discipline is actually addressed* within your selected school, not your expectations or preferences for how the discipline processes should be implemented. There are no right or wrong answers.

A–Very much like left

B–More like left than right

C–Little more like left than right

D–Balance between left and right

E–Little more like right than left

F–More like right than left

G–Very much like right

I believe the discipline processes in_____school are:

1. Developing students who do not rely on their   A B C D E F G   Developing students who rely on their own judgment in making

own judgment in
making decisions.

decisions.

2. Creating students
   who do not trust
   their own feelings
   in making
   decisions.

   A B C D E F G

   Creating students who
   have learned to trust
   their own feelings in
   making decisions.

3. Penalizing students
   who constantly
   misbehave.

   A B C D E F G

   Not penalizing students
   who constantly
   misbehave.

4. Selecting a special
   reward for students
   who act
   appropriately.

   A B C D E F G

   Not selecting special
   rewards for students
   who act appropriately.

5. Attributing the
   causes of most
   discipline problems
   to situations that
   arise outside the
   school.

   A B C D E F G

   Attributing the causes
   of most discipline
   problems to situations
   that occur within the
   school.

6. Expecting parents
   to play the major
   role in correcting
   their child's
   inappropriate
   behavior in school.

   A B C D E F G

   Expecting teachers and
   administrators to play
   the major role in
   correcting any child's
   inappropriate behavior.

7. Discouraging joint
   school-community
   participation in
   discussing the
   broad aspects of
   the discipline
   process.

   A B C D E F G

   Encouraging joint
   school-community
   participation in
   discussing the broad
   aspects of the discipline
   processes.

8. Developing
   students who do
   not need constant
   approval and
   recognition from
   others.

   A B C D E F G

   Developing students
   who need constant
   approval and
   recognition from
   others.

9. Discouraging students from taking personal responsibility for their own decisions in schools.

A B C D E F G

Encouraging students to take personal responsibility for their own decisions in schools.

10. Not providing appropriate punishments and penalties to students who violate school rules.

A B C D E F G

Providing appropriate punishments and penalties to students who violate school rules.

11. Not providing rewards to students as a result of their appropriate behavior.

A B C D E F G

Providing rewards to students as a result of their appropriate behavior.

12. Blaming the school environment for many of the discipline problems in the school.

A B C D E F G

Blaming the community for many of the discipline problems in the school.

13. Expecting the major influence for improving discipline problems to come from the home.

A B C D E F G

Expecting the major influence for improving discipline problems to come from the school.

14. Utilizing the data from student disciplinary records as a means of trying to solve discipline problems.

A B C D E F G

Not utilizing the data from student disciplinary records as a means of trying to solve discipline problems.

15. Developing students who usually need to put

A B C D E F G

Developing students who usually do not need to put their own their own welfare ahead of others.

welfare ahead of others.

16. Providing additional personal responsibilities to students who act appropriately.

A B C D E F G

Not providing additional personal responsibilities to students who act appropriately.

17. Not penalizing students for serious offenses.

A B C D E F G

Penalizing students for serious offenses.

18. Rewarding students at appropriate times for their correct social behavior.

A B C D E F G

Not rewarding students at appropriate times for their correct social behavior.

19. Suggesting that the causes of most discipline problems originate within the school.

A B C D E F G

Suggesting that the causes of most discipline problems originate outside the school.

20. Expecting school personnel to have the major responsibility for improving school discipline.

A B C D E F G

Expecting the major responsibility for improving school discipline to be that of the community.

21. Sharing the broad problems of school discipline with the community.

A B C D E F G

Not sharing the broad problems of school discipline with the community.

22. Developing students who need to dominate and control others.

A B C D E F G

Developing students who do not need to dominate and control others.

23. Developing students who take personal responsibility for satisfying their

A B C D E F G

Developing students who do not take personal responsibility for satisfying their needs without needs without burdening others.

burdening others.

24. Teaching students that penalties seldom follow intentional inappropriate student behavior.

A B C D E F G

Teaching students that penalties usually follow intentional inappropriate student behavior.

25. Reacting to the appropriate actions of students with rewards.

A B C D E F G

Not reacting to the appropriate actions of students with rewards.

26. Attributing the cause of most discipline problems to forces outside the school.

A B C D E F G

Attributing the causes of most discipline problems to sources within the school environment itself.

27. Placing the responsibility for correcting inappropriate behavior in schools on the home and community.

A B C D E F G

Placing the responsibility for correcting inappropriate behavior in schools on the school personnel.

28. Including the collection and use of incident reports in solving discipline problems.

A B C D E F G

Not including the collection and use of discipline reports in solving discipline problems.

Instructions for Completing the Discipline Organization Effectiveness Inventory II

If you completed Inventory I, use the same school population for responding to Inventory II. If not, you are asked to select a particular school population (building or district) with which you are especially familiar in terms of discipline practices. Respond to each set of items according to the specific directions given below.

1. On a blank sheet of paper, write DOEI II at the top and then list numbers 1 through 28 down the left-hand margin.

2. On your numbered sheet, you will record your response to each of the 28 items on the inventory by writing one of the letters A, B, C, D, E, F, or G after each number, 1–28. *Do not respond on the inventory itself.*

3. Letters A, B, C, D, E, F, and G represent seven possible responses to complete the following statement:

   I believe the discipline processes in my school should:

   A–Be very much like the item on the left

   B– Be more like the item on the left than the one on the right

   C–Be a little more like the item on the left than the one on the right

   D–Be a balance between the items

   E– Be a little more like the item on the right than the one on the left

   F– Be more like the item on the right than the one on the left

   G–Be very much like the item on the right

4. An example of the 28 items in the left and right columns of Inventory II is shown by the following:

Not penalize students who constantly misbehave.	A Ⓑ C D E F G	Penalize students who constantly misbehave.

   The selection or response "B" means that the respondent believes that students who constantly misbehave should seldom be penalized.

5. In each instance, select the letter that most closely represents your *expectations* for the discipline processes in your selected school. That is, your responses should reflect your personal preferences for ways of handling school discipline. There are no right or wrong answers.

   A–Very much like left

   B–More like left than right

   C–Little more like left than right

   D–Balance between left and right

E– Little more like right than left
F– More like right than left
G–Very much like right

I believe the discipline processes in_____school should:

1. Develop students who do not rely on their own judgment in making decisions.

   A B C D E F G

   Develop students who rely on their own judgment in making decisions.

2. Create students who do not trust their own feelings in making decisions.

   A B C D E F G

   Create students who have learned to trust their own feelings in making decisions.

3. Penalize students who constantly misbehave.

   A B C D E F G

   Not penalizing students who constantly misbehave.

4. Select a special reward for students who act appropriately.

   A B C D E F G

   Not select special rewards for students who act appropriately.

5. Attribute the causes of most discipline problems to situations which arise outside the school.

   A B C D E F G

   Attribute the causes of most discipline problems to situations which occur within the school.

6. Expect parents to play the major role in correcting their child's inappropriate behavior in school.

   A B C D E F G

   Expect teachers and administrators to play the major role in correcting any child's inappropriate behavior.

7. Discourage joint school-community participation in discussing the broad aspects of

   A B C D E F G

   Encourage joint school-community participation in discussing the broad aspects of the discipline the discipline process.

processes.

8. Develop students who do not need constant approval and recognition from others.

A B C D E F G

Develop students who need constant approval and recognition from others.

9. Discourage students from taking personal responsibility for their own decisions in schools.

A B C D E F G

Encourage students to take personal responsibility for their own decisions in schools.

10. Not provide appropriate punishments and penalties to students who violate school rules.

A B C D E F G

Providing appropriate punishments and penalties to students who violate school rules.

11. Not provide rewards to students as a result of their appropriate behavior.

A B C D E F G

Provide rewards to students as a result of their appropriate behavior.

12. Blame the school environment for many of the discipline problems in the school.

A B C D E F G

Blame the community for many of the discipline problems in the school.

13. Expect the major influence for improving discipline problems to come from the home.

A B C D E F G

Expect the major force and influence for improving discipline problems to come from the school.

14. Utilize the data from student disciplinary

A B C D E F G

Not utilize data from student disciplinary records as a means of

records as a means
of trying to solve
discipline
problems.

trying to solve
discipline problems.

15. Develop students
    who usually need
    to put their own
    welfare ahead of
    others.

A B C D E F G

Develop students who
usually do not need to
put their own welfare
ahead of others.

16. Provide additional
    personal
    responsibilities to
    students who act
    appropriately.

A B C D E F G

Not provide additional
personal responsibilities
to students who act
appropriately.

17. Not penalize
    students for serious
    offenses.

A B C D E F G

Penalize students for
serious offenses.

18. Reward students at
    appropriate times
    for their correct
    social behavior.

A B C D E F G

Not reward students at
appropriate times for
their correct social
behavior.

19. Suggest that the
    causes of most
    discipline problems
    originate within
    the school.

A B C D E F G

Suggest that the causes
of most discipline
problems originate
outside the school.

20. Expect school
    personnel to have
    the major
    responsibility for
    improving school
    discipline.

A B C D E F G

Expect the major
responsibility for
improving school
discipline to be that of
the community.

21. Share the broad
    problems of school
    discipline with the
    community.

A B C D E F G

Not sharing the broad
problems of school
discipline with the
community.

22. Develop students
    who need to

A B C D E F G

Develop students
who do not need to

dominate and control others.		dominate and control others.
23. Develop students who take personal responsibility for satisfying their needs without burdening others.	A B C D E F G	Develop students who do not take personal responsibility for satisfying their needs without burdening others.
24. Teach students that penalties seldom follow intentional inappropriate student behavior.	A B C D E F G	Teach students that penalties usually follow intentional inappropriate student behavior.
25. React to the appropriate actions of students with rewards.	A B C D E F G	Not react to the appropriate actions of students with rewards.
26. Attribute the cause of most discipline problems to forces outside the school.	A B C D E F G	Attribute the causes of most discipline problems to sources within the school environment itself.
27. Place the responsibility for correcting inappropriate behavior in schools on the home and community.	A B C D E F G	Place the responsibility for correcting inappropriate behavior in schools on the school personnel.
28. Include the collection and use of incident reports in solving discipline problems.	A B C D E F G	Not include the collection and use of discipline reports in solving discipline problems.

APPENDIX B

Development of the
DOEI Forms I and II

The DOEI Forms I and II were developed during the past six years. More than 3,000 educators from a dozen states have participated in research studies designed to assist in the development of this instrument. The instrument has sufficient levels of both reliability and validity for use in measuring discipline effectiveness. Reliability checks have shown test-retest scores of .797 to .956. Panels of experts examined the test items and definitions during the development of the instruments. Their suggestions were incorporated into the instrument. Five factor analyses of data obtained from approximately 1,800 of the respondents were conducted during the past six years. Clusters of test items were adjusted as were definitions to reflect the findings from these factor analyses. Research data is still being collected to further check its appropriateness, validity, and dependability.

The most recent study of the test items is reported in a research project completed by Carnes (Leslie Carnes, "Discipline Problems in Secondary Schools as Viewed by Teachers and Students," Ph.D. dissertation, George Peabody College for Teachers, 1979). The DOEI instrument published here contains improvements in several test items based on the findings in Carnes's study. Revisions of the instrument as it continues to be researched are available through the authors or the pubisher. A recent study by Morton indicates that a strong relationship exists between the gap scores of six of the seven DOEI profiles and the scores on the Organizational

Climate Indicator. Poor school climates are associated with large gap scores on the DOEI profiles (Linda Jane Morton, "A Study of the Relationship Between Organizational Climate and Teacher Perceptions of Discipline Effectiveness," Ph.D. dissertation, George Peabody College of Vanderbilt University, 1981).

Barrick's study also relates to the DOEI (Dorothy Ann Strange Barrick, "A Study of the Relationship Between Teacher-pupil Control Ideology and Discipline Effectiveness," Ph.D. dissertation, George Peabody College of Vanderbilt University, 1981).

Researchers are encouraged to assist in refining this instrument and others in the book that are in earlier stages of development.

APPENDIX C

Scoring Instructions for the Discipline Organization Effectiveness Inventory

Scoring the Discipline Organization Effectiveness

Beliefs that groups and individuals have about the disciplinary conditions that *should* exist are called disciplinary expectations. A person's values, priorities, needs and attitudes provide the basis for the expectations of what discipline should be in a school.

Beliefs that groups and individuals have about the disciplinary conditions that *do* exist are called disciplinary perceptions. Emphasis should be placed on the word *belief*, because occasionally the conditions in schools are not the way they are believed to be.

The degree to which an individual or group believes the *disciplinary expectations* and *disciplinary perceptions* are congruent is called the current level of Discipline Organization Effectiveness (DOEI).

231

The DOEI I and II are designed to identify disciplinary expectations and perceptions. The instructions for the scoring of these instruments and the steps for constructing the Discipline Organization Effectiveness Profile are given in the following sections.

Scoring the Inventories

For DOEI I:

1. Transfer each letter from your response sheet to the attached scoring chart. Be sure to place each corresponding letter in the blank box nearest the number for each of the inventory items. For example: A respondent selected the letter G for question 21. The transfer of this letter to the chart is as follows:

21	G	

2. Fill in the blank space immediately to the right of each letter on the scoring chart with a number using the following conversion formulas:

   a. If there is no asterisk to the right of the item

A = 1		E = 5
B = 2	D = 4	F = 6
C = 3		G = 7

   b. If there is an asterisk to the right of the item

A = 7		E = 3
B = 6	D = 4	F = 2
C = 5		G = 1

   Example:

2	G	7

3. Add the numerical responses for each index and place each sum in the appropriate blank space on the "total" line.

4. Divide the total numerical score of each index by 4 and place the resulting mean in the blank space of the "mean ranking" line (carry to two decimal places).

5. Calculate the range for each index by writing the lowest and the highest response numbers in the blank space opposite "range."

Example of Scoring

Letter Responses and Numerical Equivalents	Approval Process		
	21	G	7
	23*	B	6
	25	D	4
	32*	B	6
Total			23
Divided by			4
Mean Ranking			5.75
Range	4 to 7		

For DOEI II:

Follow the same scoring procedures for DOEI II as outlined above for DOEI I.

Interpretation

In order to interpret the DOEI scores, the mean rankings for each index on the DOEI I and II should be placed on the Discipline Organization Program Effectiveness Profile. Transfer the mean scores from Inventory I and II to each of the appropriate profile indexes as follows.

1. Locate the mean score along the bottom line of each profile that corresponds with each mean score on the scoring chart.

   Example: Approval Process Index *DOEI I* is 4.0. Locate the point along the line on the profile that corresponds to the mean score of 4.0.

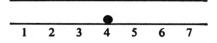

2. Mark a P (for perception) under the mean score point on the line and draw a vertical line to the top of the profile.

Example:

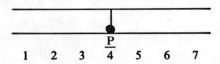

3. Repeat step one above for the mean scores on the DOEI II.

Example: Approval Process Index *DOEI II* is 6.0. Locate the
point along the line on the profile which corresponds
to the mean score of 6.0.

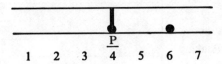

4. Mark an E (for expectation) under the point and draw the vertical
line to the top of the profile.

Example:

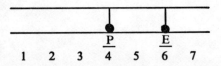

5. Shade in the area between the perception and expectation lines
representing the mean scores.

Example:

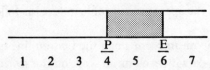

Any profile that indicates a difference in mean rankings greater than
1.5 should be examined carefully. Differences of 2.5 or greater are areas
that may need immediate attention. Discussions with the survey participants should lead to further understanding of these differences.

PROFILES

Letter Responses and Numerical Equivalents	Humanistic Philosophy	Reformation Process	Penal Process	Approval Process	Source Orientation	Discipline Responsibility Orientation	Problem Solving Orientation
	1	2	3*	4*	5	6	7
	8*	9	10	11	12*	13	14*
	15	16*	17	18*	19*	20*	21*
	22	23*	24	25*	26	27	28*
Total							
Divided by	4	4	4	4	4	4	4
Mean Ranking							
Range							

SCORING CHART FOR DISCIPLINE ORGANIZATION EFFECTIVENESS INVENTORIES I OR II

APPENDIX D

Discipline Position
Effectiveness

SURVEY FORMS I AND II

Discipline Position Effectiveness Survey Form 1

Circle the letter that best represents your desired expectation.

A. Very much like the item on the left
B. Like the item on the left
C. Balance between the item on the left and the item on the right
D. Like the item on the right
E. Very much like the item on the right

I expect a person in this position to be:

1. Secure	A B C D E	Insecure
2. Firm	A B C D E	Flexible
3. Objective	A B C D E	Sensitive

237

4. Aware of important information	A B C D E	Unaware of important information
5. Closed to suggestions	A B C D E	Open to suggestions
6. Bold, innovative	A B C D E	Cautious, careful
7. Withdrawn	A B C D E	Assertive
8. Pessimistic	A B C D E	Optimistic
9. Unaware of needs of others	A B C D E	Sensitive to needs of others
10. Lenient	A B C D E	Demanding
11. Warm, caring	A B C D E	Impersonal, distant
12. Suspicious of others	A B C D E	Trusting of others
13. Inconsistent	A B C D E	Consistent
14. Work-oriented	A B C D E	People-oriented
15. Systematic	A B C D E	Spontaneous

Circle the letter that best represents your desired expectation.

A. Very much like the item on the left
B. Like the item on the left
C. Balance between the item on the left and the item on the right
D. Like the item on the right
E. Very much like the item on the right

I expect a person in this position to:

1. Cover up own errors	A B C D E	Admit own mistakes
2. Closely supervise others	A B C D E	Allow others freedom
3. Listen to others	A B C D E	Ignore others
4. Put things off	A B C D E	Follow through
5. Organize, plan ahead	A B C D E	React to things as they happen

6. Treat others fairly	A B C D E	Give some special privileges
7. Share information	A B C D E	Keep others "in the dark"
8. Discourage people	A B C D E	Encourage and support people
9. Make people responsible for their own behaviors	A B C D E	Assume responsibility for the behavior of others
10. Make decisions alone	A B C D E	Share decisions with others
11. Provide recognition to others for accomplishments	A B C D E	Ignore the accomplishments of others
12. Punish people for mistakes they make	A B C D E	Ignore mistakes or help people learn from them
13. Avoid, ignore problems	A B C D E	Identify, solve problems
14. Act promptly	A B C D E	Hesitate and delay action

The questions in Survey Form 1 have dealt with what a person in this position should be or do. Write below at least four outcomes related to discipline that should be achieved by a person in this position. These can be outcomes related to discipline that should be achieved directly by a person in this position or by others who are influenced by the work of this person.

The important outcomes related to discipline that should be achieved by a person in this position are:

1.

2.

3.

4.

5.

6.

Discipline Position Effectiveness Survey Form 2

Circle the letter that is most closely associated with your perception of this person.

A. Very much like the item on the left
B. Like the item on the left
C. Balance between the item on the left and the item on the right
D. Like the item on the right
E. Very much like the item on the right

The person is:

1.	Secure	A B C D E	Insecure
2.	Firm	A B C D E	Flexible
3.	Objective	A B C D E	Sensitive
4.	Aware of important information	A B C D E	Unaware of important information
5.	Closed to suggestions	A B C D E	Open to suggestions
6.	Bold, innovative	A B C D E	Cautious, careful
7.	Withdrawn	A B C D E	Assertive
8.	Pessimistic	A B C D E	Optimistic
9.	Unaware of needs of others	A B C D E	Sensitive to needs of others
10.	Lenient	A B C D E	Demanding

11. Warm, caring	A B C D E	Impersonal, distant
12. Suspicious of others	A B C D E	Trusting of others
13. Inconsistent	A B C D E	Consistent
14. Work-oriented	A B C D E	People-oriented
15. Systematic	A B C D E	Spontaneous

Circle the letter that is most closely associated with your perception of this person.

   A. Very much like the item on the left
   B. Like the item on the left
   C. Balance between the item on the left and the item on the right
   D. Like the item on the right
   E. Very much like the item on the right

The person does:

1. Cover up own errors	A B C D E	Admit own mistakes
2. Closely supervise others	A B C D E	Allow others freedom
3. Listen to others	A B C D E	Ignore others
4. Put things off	A B C D E	Follow through
5. Organize, plan ahead	A B C D E	React to things as they happen
6. Treat others fairly	A B C D E	Give some special privileges
7. Share information	A B C D E	Keep others "in the dark"
8. Discourage people	A B C D E	Encourage and support people
9. Make people responsible for their own behaviors	A B C D E	Assume responsibility for the behavior of others

10. Make decisions alone	A B C D E	Share decisions with others
11. Provide recognition to others for accomplishments	A B C D E	Ignore the accomplishments of others
12. Punish people for mistakes they make	A B C D E	Ignore mistakes or help people learn from them
13. Avoid, ignore problems	A B C D E	Identify, solve problems
14. Act promptly	A B C D E	Hesitate and delay action

The outcomes related to discipline that should be achieved by the participant are listed below. These were compiled from the responses on the Form 1 survey. Determine the extent to which you *expect* each discipline-related outcome to be accomplished by someone in this position and the extent to which you believe the person *actually* achieves each outcome. Write the appropriate number in each blank, according to the following definitions:

(1) Never   (2) Seldom   (3) Sometimes   (4) Usually   (5) Always

Example:

I *expect* this outcome to be achieved by someone in this position.

This outcome *actually* is achieved by the person.

	Expect	Actual
Isolate students for serious inappropriate behavior.	5	4

This response would indicate that in every instance of inappropriate behavior you expect the student will be isolated by the person in the position, but that the person does do usually rather than always.

APPENDIX E

Discipline Unit Effectiveness

SURVEY FORMS I AND II

Circle the letter that best represents your expectations for a particular group of people.

- A. Very much like the item on the left
- B. Like the item on the left
- C. Balance between the item on the left and the item on the right
- D. Like the item on the right
- E. Very much like the item on the right

I expect people in this group to be:

1. Supportive of members	A B C D E	Lacking in support for their members
2. Open	A B C D E	Closed
3. Interested only in members of the group	A B C D E	Interested in others

4.	Independent	A B C D E	Dependent
5.	Firm	A B C D E	Flexible
6.	Planned	A B C D E	Spontaneous
7.	Concerned	A B C D E	Unconcerned
8.	Negative	A B C D E	Positive
9.	Nonintellectual	A B C D E	Intellectual
10.	Power-oriented	A B C D E	Unconcerned with power
11.	Emotional	A B C D E	Objective
12.	Willing to assume responsibility for the group's actions	A B C D E	Wanting to avoid being responsible for the group's actions
13.	Initiating	A B C D E	Passive
14.	High in morale	A B C D E	Low in morale

Circle the letter that best represents your expectations for a particular group of people.

    A. Very much like the item on the left

    B. Like the item on the left

    C. Balance between the item on the left and the item on the right

    D. Like the item on the right

    E. Very much like the item on the right

I expect people in this group to be:

15.	Unproductive	A B C D E	Productive
16.	Change-oriented	A B C D E	Status-quo–oriented

Circle the letter that best represents your expectations for a particular group of people.

    A. Very much like the item on the left

    B. Like the item on the left

    C. Balance between the item on the left and the item on the right

    D. Like the item on the right

    E. Very much like the item on the right

I expect people in this group to:

1. Help other groups   A B C D E   Hinder others
2. Make all decisions   A B C D E   Share decisions with
    by themselves   other groups
3. Closely observe the   A B C D E   Allow other groups
    activities of others   freedom to choose
4. Reject authority   A B C D E   Follow orders
5. Communicate with   A B C D E   Fail to communicate
    other groups   with other groups
6. Plan their activities   A B C D E   Lack a coordinated
                                                     effort
7. Recognize the   A B C D E   Ignore the
    accomplishments   accomplishments
    of their groups   of their groups
8. Work slowly   A B C D E   Work rapidly
9. Avoid conflict with   A B C D E   Challenge the activities
    other groups   of other groups
10. Create alternatives   A B C D E   Set responses to
                                                     problems
11. Set reasonable   A B C D E   Set unreachable or easy
    goals   goals

Circle the letter that best represents your expectations for a particular group of people.

A. Very much like the item on the left
B. Like the item on the left
C. Balance between the item on the left and the item on the right
D. Like the item on the right
E. Very much like the item on the right

I expect people in this group to:

12. Be prepared   A B C D E   Be unprepared
13. Evaluate own   A B C D E   Ignore evaluation
14. Avoid leading   A B C D E   Provide leadership

The questions on the Survey Form I have dealt with what people in this group should be or do. Write below at least four outcomes related to discipline that should be achieved by people in this group. These can be outcomes related to discipline that should be achieved directly by the members of the group or by others who are strongly influenced by the members of the group.

The important outcomes related to discipline that should be achieved by a people in this group are:

1.

2.

3.

4.

Circle the letter that best represents your perceptions of a particular group of people.

A. Very much like the item on the left
B. Like the item on the left
C. Balance between the item on the left and the item on the right
D. Like the item on the right
E. Very much like the item on the right

The group is:

1. Supportive of members	A B C D E	Lacking in support for its members
2. Open	A B C D E	Closed
3. Interested only in members of the group	A B C D E	Interested in others

4. Independent	A B C D E	Dependent
5. Firm	A B C D E	Flexible
6. Planned	A B C D E	Spontaneous
7. Concerned	A B C D E	Unconcerned
8. Negative	A B C D E	Positive
9. Nonintellectual	A B C D E	Intellectual
10. Power-oriented	A B C D E	Unconcerned with power
11. Emotional	A B C D E	Objective
12. Able to assume responsibility for its actions	A B C D E	Able to avoid being responsible for its actions
13. Initiating	A B C D E	Passive
14. High in morale	A B C D E	Low in morale

Circle the letter that best represents your perceptions of a particular group of people.

A. Very much like the item on the left
B. Like the item on the left
C. Balance between the item on the left and the item on the right
D. Like the item on the right
E. Very much like the item on the right

The group is:

| 15. Unproductive | A B C D E | Productive |
| 16. Change-oriented | A B C D E | Status-quo–oriented |

Circle the letter that best represents your perceptions of a particular group of people.

A. Very much like the item on the left
B. Like the item on the left
C. Balance between the item on the left and the item on the right
D. Like the item on the right
E. Very much like the item on the right

The group does:

1. Help other groups	A B C D E	Hinder others
2. Make all decisions by themselves	A B C D E	Share decisions with other groups
3. Closely observe the activities of others	A B C D E	Allow other groups freedom to choose
4. Reject authority	A B C D E	Follow orders
5. Communicate with other groups	A B C D E	Fail to communicate with other groups
6. Plan their activities	A B C D E	Lack a coordinated effort
7. Recognize the accomplishments of their members	A B C D E	Ignore the accomplishments of their members
8. Work slowly	A B C D E	Work rapidly
9. Avoid conflict with other groups	A B C D E	Challenge the activities of other groups
10. Create alternatives	A B C D E	Set responses to problems
11. Set reasonable goals	A B C D E	Set unreachable or easy goals

Circle the letter that best represents your perceptions of a particular group of people.

A. Very much like the item on the left
B. Like the item on the left
C. Balance between the item on the left and the item on the right
D. Like the item on the right
E. Very much like the item on the right

The group does:

12. Prepare	A B C D E	Remain unprepared
13. Evaluate themselves	A B C D E	Ignore evaluation
14. Avoid leading	A B C D E	Provide leadership

The outcomes related to discipline that should be achieved by the group are listed below. These were compiled from the responses on the Form 1 survey. Determine the extent to which you *expect* each discipline-related outcome to be accomplished by people in this group and the extent to which you believe the people *actually* achieve outcome. Write the appropriate number in each blank, according to the following definitions:

(1) Never (2) Seldom (3) Sometimes (4) Usually (5) Always

Example:

I *expect* this outcome to be achieved by people in this group.

This outcome *actually* is achieved by the group.

	Expect	*Actual*
The boys' restroom in the vocational educational wing should be free from students who are smoking.	5	4

This response would indicate that you expect students to avoid smoking in the boys' restroom at all times, but that the restroom is usually free from students smoking rather than being always free from such activity.

APPENDIX F

Creation and Use of a Discipline Data System

The process of effective problem solving in school discipline requires an openness toward the collection and use of data. Many schools lack a systematic approach to collecting information about discipline. An established discipline data system can aid the faculty in analyzing past responses to incidents of inappropriate behavior and in determining the range of appropriate responses for a student's offense. The development and use of the discipline data system are described in this appendix.

Faculty should work to agree on the seriousness of specific offenses and corrective measures. The importance of reaching such agreements on offenses and corrective measures is related to the necessity of establishing consistency in discipline. The first step in arriving at agreement among faculty members is to collect data on how educators believe offenses and corrective measures should be and are perceived by the faculty in their school. This includes the involvement of faculty and/or students in completing a set of instruments that rate student offenses and corrective measures.

A simple procedure for collecting data is through an individual rating and reconciliation process. A suggested process follows: The entire faculty is divided into groups of six to eight people. Individuals in each small group complete two ratings of typical student offenses on a predetermined list of offenses. Rating Form I (Figure F.1) and Rating Form II (Figure F.2) are used for this purpose. Figure F.1 shows a Rating Form used for determining how seriously offenses currently *are* viewed. The rating of offenses can be established through the use of Rating Form II shown in Figure F.2, which provides ratings of how each of the offenses *should* be viewed. Rating Forms III (Figure F.3) and IV (Figure F.4) show the corrective measure rating forms. Figure F.3 shows a form used for determining how corrective measures are viewed in terms of the severity of the corrective measure. Figure F.4 shows the rating of how corrective measures should be viewed.

Rating Form *I*

Classify each student offense as it is *currently* viewed by the members of your local school organization. Place one of the four rating numbers next to each student offense.

RATINGS

1–Extremely Serious Offense

2–Serious Offense

3–Moderately Serious Offense

4–Not Serious

_____ Making undue classroom noise

_____ Using profanity

_____ Tardy to class

_____ Major destruction of school property

_____ Rape

_____ Drug possession

_____ Defiance of teacher or other school official

_____ Lying to teacher

_____ Smoking on school property

_____ Refusing to do an assignment

_____ Truancy

_____ Assaulting a teacher

_____ Fighting with another student

_____ Extortion

_____ Kicking the chair of another student

_____ Indecent exposure

_____ Stealing from students

_____ Homosexual acts

_____ Unexcused absence from class

_____ Talking without permission

_____ Classroom harassment activities

_____ Stealing from teachers

_____ Major destruction of student property

_____ Possession of weapons

_____ Drug use

_____ Cheating

_____ Gum chewing

_____ Minor destruction of school property

_____ Writing obscene notes

_____ Sexual activity in hall

_____ Bullying other students

_____ Whispering in class

_____ Leaving school grounds without permission

_____ Throwing eraser in classroom

_____ Lying to another student

_____ Passing notes in class

_____ Using obscene gestures in hall

_____ Wearing clothes with obscene pictures

FIGURE F.1.   *Personal Rating of Offenses*

Rating Form II

Classify each student offense as it *should* be viewed by the members of your local school organization. Place one of the four rating numbers next to each student offense.

RATINGS

1–Extremely Serious Offense
2–Serious Offense
3–Moderately Serious Offense
4–Not Serious

_____ Making undue classroom noise
_____ Using profanity
_____ Tardy to class
_____ Major destruction of school property
_____ Rape
_____ Drug possession
_____ Defiance of teacher or other school official
_____ Lying to teacher
_____ Smoking on school property
_____ Refusing to do an assignment
_____ Truancy
_____ Assaulting a teacher
_____ Fighting with another student
_____ Extortion
_____ Kicking the chair of another student
_____ Indecent exposure
_____ Stealing from students
_____ Homosexual acts
_____ Unexcused absence from class
_____ Talking without permission
_____ Classroom harassment activities
_____ Stealing from teachers
_____ Major destruction of student property
_____ Possession of weapons
_____ Drug use
_____ Cheating
_____ Gum chewing
_____ Minor destruction of school property

_____   Writing obscene notes

_____   Sexual activity in hall

_____   Bullying other students

_____   Whispering in class

_____   Leaving school grounds without permission

_____   Throwing eraser in classroom

_____   Lying to another student

_____   Passing notes in class

_____   Using obscene gestures in hall

_____   Wearing clothes with obscene pictures

FIGURE F.2.   *Desired Rating of Offenses*

Rating Form III

Classify each corrective measure as it is *currently* viewed by the members of your local school organization. Place one of the four rating numbers next to each corrective measure.

RATINGS

1–Most Severe Corrective Measure

2–Severe Corrective Measure

3–Moderately Severe Corrective Measure

4–Least Severe Corrective Measure

_____   Student pays for damage to property

_____   Student repairs or maintains school property

_____   Teacher counsels student after class

_____   Suspend student from school

_____   Give additional classwork assignments

_____   Call police

_____   Shout at student

_____   Isolate student from group

_____   Withdraw a classroom privilege

_____   Detain student after school

_____ Hold parent conference with teacher

_____ Teacher sends letter to parents

_____ Expel student

_____ Student attends group counseling sessions

_____ Ignore student's behavior

_____ Have student make a public apology to class

_____ Refer student to Juvenile Court

_____ Send student to the principal

_____ Take away recess or free time

_____ Assign repeated writing of sentences

_____ Change student's seat in classroom

_____ Suspend student from class but let him or her remain in school

_____ Hold parent conference with teacher and principal

_____ Principal sends letter to parents

_____ Have student stand in hall during class time

_____ Request help from counseling service

_____ Belittle student in private

_____ Belittle student in front of class

_____ Give verbal reprimand in private

_____ Give verbal reprimand in front of class

_____ Lower student's grade

_____ Slap

_____ Paddle

_____ Penalize entire class for actions of a few

_____ Have student(s) write essays on an assigned topic

FIGURE F.3. *Personal Rating of Corrective Measures*

Rating Form IV

Classify each corrective measure as it *should* be viewed by the members of your local school organization. Place one of the four rating numbers next to each corrective measure.

RATINGS

1–Most Severe Corrective Measure

2–Severe Corrective Measure

3–Moderately Severe Corrective Measure

4–Least Severe Corrective Measure

_____   Student pays for damage to property

_____   Student repairs or maintains school property

_____   Teacher counsels student after class

_____   Suspend student from school

_____   Give additional classwork assignments

_____   Call police

_____   Shout at student

_____   Isolate student from group

_____   Withdraw a classroom privilege

_____   Detain student after school

_____   Hold parent conference with teacher

_____   Teacher sends letter to parents

_____   Expel student

_____   Student attends group counseling sessions

_____   Ignore student's behavior

_____   Have student make a public apology to class

_____   Refer student to Juvenile Court

_____   Send student to the principal

_____   Take away recess or free time

_____   Assign repeated writing of sentences

_____   Change student's seat in classroom

_____   Suspend student from class but let him or her remain in school

_____   Hold parent conference with teacher and principal

_____   Principal sends letter to parents

_____   Have student stand in hall during class time

_____   Request help from counseling service

_____   Belittle student in private

_____ Belittle student in front of class

_____ Give verbal reprimand in private

_____ Give verbal reprimand in front of class

_____ Lower student's grade

_____ Slap

_____ Paddle

_____ Penalize entire class for actions of a few

_____ Have student(s) write essays on an assigned topic

FIGURE F.4.   *Desired Rating of Corrective Measures*

After completing the four rating forms, the small groups should place each of the offenses and corrective measures in categories. For example, all of the offenses that were identified with a 1 on Form I should be clustered together on another sheet of paper; those offenses labeled 2 on Form I should be grouped together, and so on. This process of grouping items with the same ratings should be used for each of the four forms. At completion, there will be four sets of groupings, one set for each of the four rating forms.

Each small group then should rank each of the offenses and corrective measures within each of the four categories. For example, if rape, drug abuse, and extortion from Form I are in a common category, the group should decide which of these is the most serious offense, next most serious, and so on. The small groups should vote to arrive at a ranking only as a last resort.

Each of the sets of rankings for forms I through IV can be put on a master chart or overhead transparency for display. When the small groups assemble in one large group and each small group's results are displayed, differences in ratings and rankings between small groups are distinguishable. Significant differences between the ranking of offenses and corrective measures between groups may be evident; if so, discussion of these differences should occur. Through the method of problem solving just described, a substantial beginning can be made in resolving some of the differences that exist between individuals and factions within a school.

Teacher input on how student offenses and corrective measures should be viewed provides the basis for a systematic approach to the application of methods to change student behavior. For example, the principal or the faculty may examine the data from the ratings and rankings closely and assign offenses to four "classes." The classes may or may not be the same as the categories used to group items which had the same ratings. These classes, for example, may be labeled and constituted as follows:

Class 4:
Legal Offenses

Rape
Assaulting a teacher
Drug use
Drug possession
Possession of weapons
Extortion

Class 3:
Major Misconduct

Homosexual Acts
Major destruction of school property
Indecent exposure
Defiance of teacher or other school official
Stealing from teachers
Major destruction of student property
Stealing from students
Fighting with another student

Class 2:
Consequential Acts

Leaving school grounds
  without permission
Classroom harassment
  activities
Truancy
Bullying other students
Minor destruction of school
  property
Cheating
Using profanity
Unexcused absence from
  class
Lying to teacher
Lying to another student

Class 1:
Minor Violations

Wearing clothes with obscene pictures
Using obscene gestures
Writing obscene notes
Refusing to do an assignment
Petting
Smoking on school property
Making undue classroom noise
Kicking the chair of another student
Throwing eraser in classroom
Talking without permission
Whispering in class
Passing notes in class
Gum chewing

Similarly, the rankings of the severity of the corrective measures may be categorized into four "zones." These zones may be delineated as follows:

Zone 4:
Legal Corrective Measures

Refer to Juvenile Court
Expel

Zone 3:
Major Corrective Measures

Paddle
Slap

Zone 4 (continued):
Suspend from school
Call police

Zone 3 (continued):
Pay for damage to student property
Student repairs or maintains property
Send to principal
Suspend student from class but let him or her remain in school
Hold parent conference with principal and teacher
Request help from counseling services

Zone 2:
Consequential Corrective Measures

Isolation from group
Counseling of student by teacher after class
Withdrawal of a classroom privilege
Parent conference with teacher
Attendance at group counseling sessions
Public apology to class
Verbal reprimand in front of class

Zone 1:
Minor Corrective Measures

Penalize entire class for actions of a few
Give additional classwork assignments
Shout at student
Belittle student in front of class
Have student write essays on an assigned topic
Have student stand in hall during class time
Detain student after school
Send letter to parents
Ignore behavior
Take away student's recess or free time
Assign repetitive writing of sentences
Change student's seat within classroom
Belittle student in private
Give verbal reprimand in private

Classifying how various offenses and corrective measures should be regarded establishes a range of appropriate measures for particular offenses. The above classes and zones can be used as guides in determining the severity of corrective measures to be applied to various kinds of discipline offenses. For example, if a student is caught with a weapon in his or her possession—a legal offense—it would be appropriate to review the "Zone 4" corrective measures.

Finding the appropriate type of corrective measure for a student who has recently committed four offenses is more difficult. For example, suppose the student commits three offenses considered to be minor violations during the week of April 10th. Then, during the week of April 17th, the student is involved in a more serious offense, one considered to be a consequential act. To determine the appropriate corrective measure for the most recent offense, the student's previous offenses must be considered.

A model has been established to aid educators in judging the zone from which to select the appropriate severity of corrective measures. Figure F.5 shows this model—the Corrective Measure Indicator. By categorizing offenses and listing the dates and frequencies of those offenses, it is possible to determine the appropriate zone and range of corrective measures for specific offenses.

This model can be replicated by any school. The numbers across the top of the model represent the frequency with which an offense has occurred in a particular class. Four zones of corrective measures are denoted along the bottom of the model. The dates that offenses have occurred can be located on the horizontal dotted lines extending from each offense class. Figure F.6 shows the April dates on which the offenses occurred. The dates 4/10, 4/11, and 4/12 show when the minor violations occurred. The date 4/17 shows the consequential offenses. From which zone should the corrective measure be selected in considering the more serious consequential offense that occurred April 17?

The diagonal lines in the model each lead to an arbitrary zone value associated with each offense. For example, the zone value associated with the first minor violation offense on April 10th is 1. The zone value for the third minor violation offense is 3. The zone value for the one consequential act is 4. By combining the zone values associated with recent offenses in each zone, one may derive a total zone value. For example, the most recent offense of the minor violations is associated with a zone value of 3. The most recent offense of the consequential acts is associated with a zone value of 4. When these two zone values are added together, the total zone value is 7. The new zone value of 7 is located in Zone III corrective measures. It is probable that the appropriate level of corrective measure is associated with Zone III. The sum of the minor violations and consequential acts is equivalent to the severity of one or more major consequential offenses.

The assignment of zone values and the number of incidents of inappropriate behavior that reference each zone may vary from one school to the next. Discussions of these variables need to be initiated among school personnel and parents in arriving at the appropriate Corrective Measure Indicator model for a particular school. One related question that needs to be answered is how much time should elapse before a past offense is no longer taken into account when selecting a corrective measure. Information

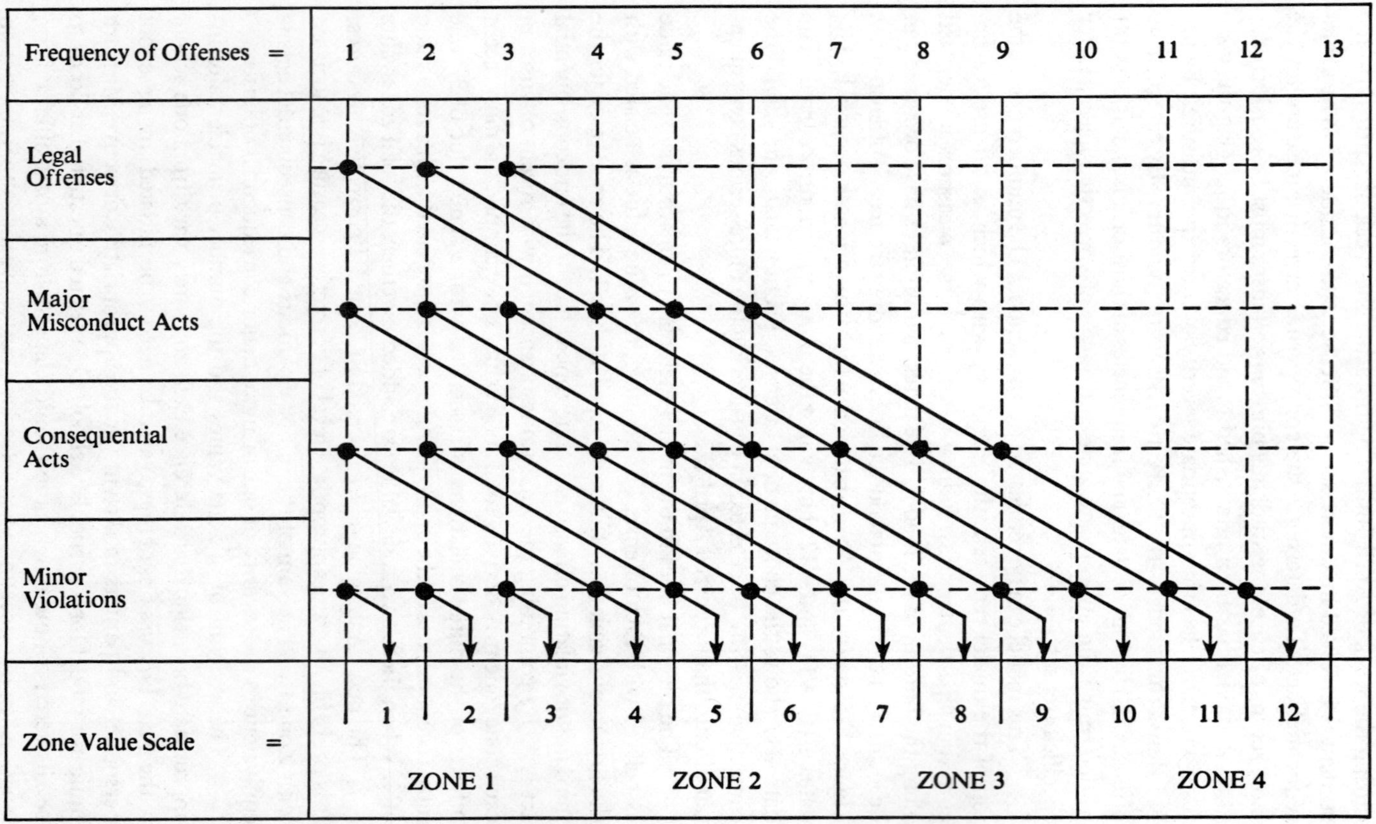

FIGURE F.5 *Corrective Measure Indicator*

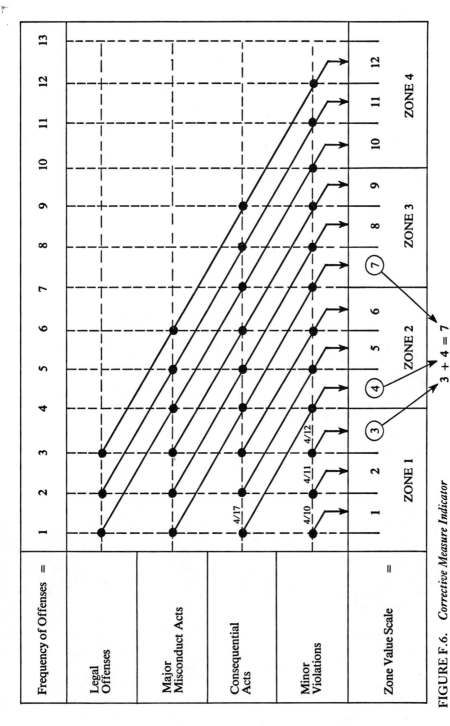

FIGURE F.6. *Corrective Measure Indicator*

about corrective measures and offenses may be displayed in a variety of formats, including variations of the Corrective Measure Indicator.

This indicator can be used to aid faculty members in understanding the basic conceptual relationships between the number and seriousness of offenses, and the severity of the corrective measures. Some administrators and teachers construct the Corrective Measure Indicator as a check on their own response to a wide variety of offenses involving students.

Index

Administration. *See* Organization;
    Principal; School
Approval. *See* Discipline process,
    approval; Leadership assets,
    approval
Assessment. *See* Measurement
Authority, obedience to, 13–14,
    38–43

Baker v. *Owens*, 214
Becomers, 107, 108, 126–129
    teachers as, 146
Behavior
    brinksmanship, 98
    change, 59–62. *See also*
        Discipline process,
        reformational; Leadership
        assets, reformational
    contract, 61, 69–74
    patterns, 49, 97–102
    and students' needs, 102–110
    problems of. *See* Discipline
        problems
    reinforcement of, 85–88. *See
        also* Discipline process,
        approval; Leadership
        process, approval
    of teachers, 143–151
Buckley Amendment, 205

Cheser, D. B., 150
Climate, organizational, 14–15,
    43–57
Committees, effectiveness of. *See*
    Unit effectiveness

Data support system, 47–57
Decision making, 47, 159
Deibert, A. N., 60, 67, 80, 85–86,
    90
Developers, 107–108, 135–137
    teachers as, 147–148
Discipline
    aims of, 13–14, 37–43
    custodial, 13–14, 38–43
    definition of, 4
    humanistic, 13–14, 38–43
    information. *See* Data support
        system; Information
    organizational effectiveness. *See*
        Organization
    position effectiveness. *See*
        Position
    problems
        causes of, 43–46
        profiles of, 22, 23
        solving of, 22, 47. *See also*
            Data support system
    process, 14. *See also* Leadership
        assets
        approval, 14, 21–22, 77, 83–91
        penal, 14, 21, 77–83
        reformational, 14, 20–21,
            59–74
    school responsibility for, 22–23,
        46–47
    situational factors in, 41–42
    unit effectiveness. *See* Unit
        effectiveness
Discipline Organization
    Effectiveness Inventories,
    18–23
Discipline Position Effectiveness
    Survey, 25–30

Discipline Unit Effectiveness
     Survey, 30–33
Douglass, H., 155
Doyle, W., 149
Due process
  procedural, 209–215
  substantive, 200–209

Effectiveness. *See also*
     Organization effectiveness;
     Position effectiveness; Unit
     effectiveness
  continuum, 5
  definition of, 4–5
Etzioni, A., 156, 158

Faculty. *See* School; Teachers;
     Unit effectiveness
First Amendment, 200
Fourteenth Amendment, 200
Frymier, J., 99–100

Glasser, W., 61, 78
Goss v. *Lopez*, 210
Gouldner, A., 160
Group
  activities, outcomes, and
     characteristics, 10–13. *See
     also* Unit effectiveness
  norms, and reformational assets,
     169–171
Guidance department,
     effectiveness of. *See* Unit
     effectiveness

Harmon, A. J., 60, 67, 80, 85–86,
     90
Home, of discipline problem
     student, 44–45
Huckaby, W. O., 24–25
Humanism, 13–14, 20, 40–43

Information
  behavior, 49
  discipline, 48

policies for use of, 51
system. *See* Data support
     system
Inventories, 18–23. *See also*
     Measurement

Kluckhohn, F. R., 184, 185
Kohlberg, L., 64–65
Kounin, J. S., 149
Kroeber, C. T., 100

Leaders, 107, 108, 131–134
  teachers as, 147
Leadership, 156–159. *See also*
     Position effectiveness;
     Principal
  assets. *See also* Discipline
     process
     approval, 156, 158–159,
        164–168, 184–188
     penal, 156, 158, 159–164,
        184–188
     reformational, 156, 158–159,
        169–176, 184–188
  errors in, 194–196
  and power, 157–158
  student, 175–181
Leadership corps, student,
     177–181
Licata, J. W., 98
Limit testing, 82–83
Loyalists, 108, 138–140
  teachers as, 148

Madsen, C. H., Jr., 60–61, 85
Madsen, C. K., 60–61, 85
Martin, M., 101, 102
Measurement
  inventories, 18–23
  of organizational effectiveness,
     17–23
  of position effectiveness, 23–30
  surveys, 25–33
  of unit effectiveness, 30–33
Milgram, S., 39–40
Myers-Briggs indicator, 99

Nyquist, E. B., 37–38

Offer, D., 100
Offer, J. B., 100
Onlookers, 104–105, 114–116
  teachers as, 144
Operators, 109, 140–143
  teachers as, 148
Organization. *See also* School
  climate of. *See* Climate
  discipline aims of, 13–14, 37–43
  discipline processes of. *See*
      Discipline process
  effectiveness, 6
    components of, 7, 13–15
    measurement of, 17–23
    profiles of, 19–23
  formal and informal, 156–157

Parents, effectiveness of. *See*
    Position effectiveness
Penalties, effects of, 80–81, 159.
    See also Discipline process,
    penal; leadership assets,
    penal)
Pennsylvania Dept. of Ed.,
    guidelines and data
    collection, 50, 52–56
Perfectionists, 105, 120–123
  teachers as, 145
Performers, 108, 129–131
  teachers as, 146–147
Piaget, J., 64
Police, in schools, 204–205
Position. *See also* Leadership;
    Principal
  effectiveness, 5
    components of, 6, 7–10
    measurement of, 23–30
    profiles of, 25–30
  power, 158
Power, definitions of, 157–158
Principal, 155–159. *See also*
    Leadership
  behavior, outcomes, and
    characteristics of, 7–10

effectiveness of, 188–194. *See
    also* Position effectiveness
  interpersonal relationships,
      161–163, 166–168
  perceptions and expectations of,
      188–194
  personal assets
    approval, 166–168
    penal, 162–164
    reformational, 169, 172–175
  positional assets
    approval, 165–166, 168
    penal, 159–162, 164
    reformational, 169, 171–172,
      174–175
  power of, 158
  value orientation of, 184–188
Problem solving. *See* Decision
    making; Discipline
    problems
Process. *See* Discipline process
Profiles
  organization effectiveness,
      19–23
  position effectiveness, 25–30
  unit effectiveness, 30–33
Punishment. *See also* Discipline
    process, penal; Leadership
    assets, penal
  corporal, 213–214

Redd, W., 78, 81, 90
Reform. *See* Discipline process,
    reformational; Leadership
    assets, reformational
Reinforcement, 84–88. *See also*
    Discipline process,
    approval; Leadership assets,
    approval
Rewards, use of, 85–86, 165–166,
    168. *See also* Reinforcement
Rules, establishment of, 159–160

School. *See also* Organization
  as cause of discipline problems,
      45–46
  responsibility of, 22–23, 46–47

School board, effectiveness of. *See* Unit effectiveness
Search and seizure, 204
Seekers, 105, 123–126
  teachers as, 146
Situation factors, in discipline, 41–42
Sleater, W. 78, 81, 90
Strodtbeck, F. L., 184, 185
Student conduct, laws on, 199–200. *See also* Due process
Student council, 176–177
Student demonstrations, 202
Student elections, 180–181
Student newspapers, 202
Student records, 205–208
Student rights, 199–200
  procedural, 209–215
  substantive, 200–209
Students
  aggressiveness and TV viewing, 44
  behavior of. *See* Behavior
  commitment to a plan, 69–74
  desire to improve, 65–69
  growth patterns of, 100
  leadership development of, 175–181
  married and/or pregnant, 205
  mental and moral development of, 64–65
  needs of, 97–110

personal appearance of, 208–209
recognition of the problem, 62–65
self-direction of, 38, 40–41. *See also* Humanism
Surveys, 25–33. *See also* Measurement

Tanner, L. N., 40, 41, 70
Teachers
  behavior of, 143–151
  effectiveness of. *See* Position effectiveness
  relationships with principal, 161–163, 166–168
Television, and behavior, 44

Unit effectiveness, 6
  components of, 6–7, 10–13
  measurement of, 30–33
  profiles of, 30–33
Untouchables, 105, 117–120
  teachers as, 144–145

Value orientation, 184–188

Willower, D. J., 13, 38, 40, 150
Wood v. *Strickland*, 210

DATE DUE